D1615179

Redefining Public Sector Unionism

As the largest and most influential trade union in the public sector, which is itself increasingly becoming the main base of British unionism, UNISON may be seen to be holding the key to the future success or failure of UK unions. Its creation was a sign of progress in a period of union despondency and decline. Its size and strength promised greater unity and effectiveness in the defence of its members' interests. Its radical governance proposals gave formal dominance to women, the largest membership category, and promised effective representation to a myriad other groups. Its rules and structures stressed union responsibility for the protection and improvement of public services as well as of public service employment, and promised new relationships with members, citizens and government.

This volume brings together a selection of contributions from expert academics and leading figures of the union itself, wherein the achievements and failures of UNISON since its creation in 1993, and the challenges it will face in the future, are scrutinised. In so doing, this work highlights the ways in which British public sector unionism in general, and trade unionism more widely, may develop, and will help deepen our understanding of the nature of modern trade unionism in the twenty-first century.

Michael Terry is Professor of Industrial Relations at the Industrial Relations Research Unit, Warwick University.

Routledge Research in Employment Relations

Redefining Public Sector Unionism

UNISON and the future of trade unions

Edited by
Michael Terry

London and New York

First published 2000
by Routledge
11 New Fetter Lane, London EC4P 4EE

Simultaneously published in the USA and Canada
by Routledge
29 West 35th Street, New York, NY 10001

Routledge is an imprint of the Taylor & Francis Group

Typeset in Baskerville by
BOOK NOW Ltd, London
Printed and bound in Great Britain by
St Edmundsbury Press, Bury St Edmunds, Suffolk

British Library Cataloguing in Publication Data
A catalogue record for this book is available from the British Library

Library of Congress Cataloging-in-Publication Data
A catalog record for this book has been requested

ISBN 0 415 23020 9

Contents

Figures and tables

Contributors

Rodney Bickerstaffe is General Secretary of UNISON, and prior to that of NUPE.

Mick Carpenter originally trained as a general nurse and is now Reader in Social Policy at the University of Warwick. He was the official historian of COHSE and was subsequently one of the three academic advisers to the UNISON negotiations. His major works are *Working for Health* (1998) and *Normality is Hard Work: Trade Unions and the Politics of Community Care* (1994).

Tim Claydon is Principal Lecturer in Industrial Relations in the Department of Human Resource Management at De Montfort University and a Visiting Lecturer at the College of Europe in Bruges. He has published work on industrial relations history, trade union de-recognition, union-management 'partnerships', and on patterns of organisational change. He is currently investigating, with Trevor Colling, change within local trade union structures, and 'high-velocity' organisational change.

Trevor Colling is Senior Research Fellow in the Department of Human Resource Management at De Montfort University and Associate Fellow of the Industrial Relations Research Unit, University of Warwick. He has published research on public sector employee relations, outsourcing and the employment relationship, and gender equality in the workplace. He is working with Tim Claydon and on an ESRC-funded project examining employee relations in American multinationals.

Michael Dempsey was until recently Assistant General Secretary (Strategic Services) at UNISON. He is now a Visiting Fellow at the Centre for Strategic Trade Union Management, Cranfield School of Management, and Associate Lecturer at the Open University Business School.

Bob Fryer is Assistant Vice-Chancellor, University of Southampton and Director of University of Southampton New College, where he has worked since 1998. Prior to going to Southampton, Bob Fryer was for 15 years the Principal of the Northern College for Residential Adult Education, South Yorkshire. He is currently also Chair of the government's National Advisory

Committee for Continuing Education and Lifelong Learning and is an Executive Director of the University for Industry. He has published in the fields of employment, redundancy, trade union organisation, adult education and lifelong learning. He was chief academic adviser to COHSE, NUPE and NALGO in the discussions to form UNISON, from 1988–94.

Mike Ironside is Lecturer in Industrial Relations at the Centre for Industrial Relations, Keele University. Co-author of *Industrial Relations in Schools* with Roger Seifert, and currently working with Roger on the final volume of the history of NALGO.

Maggie Jones is Director of Policy and Public Affairs at UNISON.

Allan Kerr is a National Officer for UNISON.

Anne McBride is a Research Fellow at the Industrial Relations Research Unit at Warwick University. Her detailed investigation of the representation of women in UNISON *Making a Difference? Gender Democracy in Trade Unions* will be published by Ashgate in 2000.

John Monks is General Secretary of the Trades Union Congress.

Peter Morris was formerly UNISON's Director of Policy and Research and represented European public service unions on the European TUC Social Policy and Employment Committees. He is now training as a barrister at the Inns of Court School of Law.

Anne Munro is a Senior Lecturer in Sociology at University College Northampton and a member of the Centre for Research in Employment, Work and Training. She is the author of *Women, Work and Trade Unions* (Mansell, 1999).

Helen Rainbird is Professor of Industrial Relations at University College Northampton and an Associate Fellow at the Industrial Relations Research Unit at the University of Warwick. She is the author of *Training Matters: Union Perspectives on Industrial Restructuring and Training* (Blackwell, 1990) and has researched and published widely on trade unions and training.

Tom Sawyer was Deputy General Secretary of NUPE and became the first holder of the same post in UNISON. He is a former Chairman and General Secretary of the Labour Party and is now a working peer.

Roger Seifert is Professor of Industrial Relations at Keele University. He is the author of *Industrial Relations in the NHS*, and with Mike Ironside, *Industrial Relations in Schools*.

Jim Sutherland was UNISON's first Director of Education & Training following a decade as NUPE's National Education Officer. Now retired he continues to be involved in lifelong learning initiatives, teaches at Warwick University and is an Associate Research Fellow at University College Northampton.

Michael Terry is Professor of Industrial Relations at the Industrial Relations Research Unit, Warwick University Business School. He was one of the academic advisers to the UNISON merger and has published widely on trade union affairs.

Carole Thornley is a Lecturer in Industrial Relations at Keele University. Author of academic and practitioner publications on health service pay and low pay: her research reports for UNISON have been used in evidence to the Nurses' Pay Review Body in each of the past five years.

Jeremy Waddington is a Senior Lecturer at the Industrial Relations Research Unit, University of Warwick and a Project Co-ordinator for the European Trade Union Institute, Brussels.

Margaret Wheeler is Director of Organisation and Staff Development at UNISON. She established the first Trade Union Organisation Development Unit and was project leader for UNISON's Strategic Review of services to members.

Editor's preface

This book has grown out of a conference held in May 1998 at the University of Warwick and co-sponsored by UNISON and the Industrial Relations Research Unit in Warwick Business School. Designed to commemorate the fifth anniversary of the formal creation of UNISON, the UK's largest trade union, and one of the largest public service unions in the world, the conference brought senior UNISON officials and lay representatives together with academics working in the area of public service trade unionism to reflect on the union's achievements and challenges.

Those who brought UNISON into being were guided by a sense of shared purpose to create not merely a large and well-resourced, powerful, trade union, but a union whose objectives and actions would redefine public service trade unionism for the twenty-first century. Rather than playing safe and relying on compromise and 'fudge' UNISON's architects took deliberate but calculated risks in designing a union whose approaches to governance, management and purpose would break new ground. Confronting problems of change and adaptation in the post-war concept of the Welfare State common to many countries but expressed in a particularly dramatic form in the UK, the UNISON experience contains lessons and implications for trade unions and their members in this country and internationally. Trade union leaders and members, here and overseas, are interested in what is happening to UNISON and whether its ambitions and aspirations are being met.

The conference and this book are the outcomes of many people's research into and reflections on those questions. Containing contributions in roughly equal numbers from UNISON members and academic researchers the book provides a diversity of insights into the union, reflecting different preoccupations, relationships to the union and analytical approaches. The book's commonalities are shared interests in UNISON's achievements and the challenges it faces, and these are discussed in many different voices. There is no claim to analytical or conceptual integration or homogeneity; the book's strengths lie in its diversity. The conference was designed to interest and engage trade union activists as well as academic researchers and the hope for the book is that it will do the same and more, providing food for thought also for managers and politicians concerned with public service provision in this country and overseas.

The book is largely based on papers presented at the conference. Two additional papers were commissioned; those by Carole Thornley and her colleagues from Keele University and by Trevor Colling and Tim Claydon at De Montfort University. Some of the contributions are in the form of a chapter and a comment (Morris and Thornley, Munro and Rainbird, and Sutherland) reflecting the conference's basic design. The contributions by Waddington and Kerr, in the same form in the conference, have here been combined. John Monks' contribution, initially a response to Bob Fryer's presentation, has been presented as a 'concluding comment' since it neatly highlights many of the wider issues for the trade union movement. Structurally the book is divided into two halves, with the contributions in Part I dealing primarily with UNISON's structures and governance, and Part II with its substantive objectives. This is as crude a structuring as it is a sociological distinction, but it is the best I could come up with. The chapter by Waddington and Kerr has been put at the end perhaps as a reminder that, in the case of the UK in particular, the best structures and policies are pointless if they do not attract and retain workers into trade unions; this is the ultimate yardstick of their effectiveness.

I am deeply grateful to all the authors for their hard work in preparing the papers and revising them for publication, and to Lesley Williams, then Administrative Officer of the Industrial Relations Research Unit, for organising the conference. Those who helped bring UNISON into being number in the hundreds, if not the thousands, and I thank them all for giving us such a challenging subject for analysis and understanding; I am delighted that a significant number of those who worked so hard on the project have contributed to this book.

One of those is Rodney Bickerstaffe, general secretary of NUPE at the time of the merger and UNISON's second general secretary. His huge contribution was matched by those of his colleagues, Alan Jinkinson of NALGO and UNISON's first general secretary, and Hector MacKenzie general secretary of COHSE. This book is dedicated through them to UNISON's members past, present and future.

Michael Terry

1 Introduction

UNISON and public service trade unionism

Michael Terry

Arguably the year 1987 marked the post-war nadir for Britain's trade unions. Their numbers and public prestige had been in steady decline for 8 years, the shock of the defeat 2 years earlier of the National Union of Mineworkers, totem of British trade union power, was still keenly felt, and Margaret Thatcher's Conservatives had been re-elected for their third successive term. Trade union despondency, sliding into fear of complete obliteration, was both tangible and understandable.

One clear organisational response was the flurry of union merger activity around that time. Willman (1996: 332) notes that 40 per cent of all unions had been involved in merger discussions (not all successful) in the period 1986–9. Undy identifies four major public sector mergers achieved out of initiatives around that date, starting with UNISON in 1993, and points to the remarkable fact that 'one result has been to concentrate some 30 per cent of the Trades Union Congress' (TUC's) total membership into just four newly-amalgamated public service sector unions by 1998' (Undy, 1999: 447).

The impulse to create a large public service trade union, initially through the merger of the National and Local Government Officers' Association (NALGO) and the National Union of Public Employees (NUPE), formally mooted at NALGO's 1998 conference, was seen by its promoters as a specific response to the external political threat (Undy, 1999: 450). Superficially at least the attractions of merger in such situations are obvious: increased size and resources and the greater unity offered are comforting, even though there may be an unhappy realisation that no *net* growth is likely and that 'unity', although a fine word for conference platforms, is often harder to achieve than its rhetorical use may suggest.[1] More generally it can be argued that experience of mergers tends to show that their apparent benefits are more elusive than might at first appear. First, they rarely produce the straightforward 'economies of scale' either in financial terms or in the rationalisation of management and bureaucratic structures that are sometimes claimed for them. Second, far from overcoming problems of sectionalism and lack of unity, they can exacerbate them, by entrenching previous mistrust and self-interest into the organisational fabric of the new trade union (Carter, 1991; Terry, 1996). Third, by providing a great deal of internal activity – there is an enormous amount of work for union officials in a merger – they can create the *illusion* of dynamic and progressive change and in so doing deflect attention and resources away from more pressing but more intractable problems. Merger alone, therefore, may provide no more than temporary relief, the sort a sick person gets from turning over in bed.

This book, and the conference in May 1998 on whose proceedings it is based, were designed to explore in detail whether anything more substantial than such 'temporary relief' has been achieved as a consequence of the enormous time and energy that went into creating the UK's largest trade union between 1988 and now. UNISON (the name stands for a great deal but it is not an acronym) was brought into being on 1 July 1993 on the announcement that members of the three unions[2] involved had voted in favour of merger. Since then it has been more studied and dissected than any other trade union; a tribute both to its generous openness to research and its belief in the value of such work and to its great significance for the future of trade unionism in this country. Its creation raised many hopes and some fears, but no one concerned with the subject is not interested in UNISON's progress and future.

The processes involved in the creation and development of UNISON are complex and multi-layered, but at this distance three appear to stand out. First, it was specifically a merger of public service sector trade unions. This gave it a particular character and significance, not least because public service unionism now has to be seen as the bedrock of trade unionism in this country after nearly two decades of decline in its industrial heartlands. Second, it was a merger of unions with different membership profiles, governance models, and political affiliations. Third, it was a merger that promised not simply consolidation but radical developments with regard both to union governance and to union agenda and activity. These dimensions of the merger form the basis of this introduction.

A public service union merger

In the voluminous literature on British trade unions there is virtually no treatment of public service unions as a distinct set of institutions.[3] In effect, they are treated as centralised, bureaucratic, traditionally rather right-wing versions of private sector unions. During the 1970s considerable importance was attached to the growing militancy of public service trade unions and to the rapid expansion of decentralised shop steward systems within them. Both were often cited as evidence that they were becoming more like private sector unions and hence, in some sense, 'real' trade unions. This tendency to see public and private sector unions as essentially similar social organisations may derive from the particular legal and institutional features of UK industrial relations which, unlike many other European countries, make no distinction between public and private, from the attention paid to the manufacturing sector as the focal point of industrial relations, especially after the publication of the Donovan Report in 1967, and perhaps also from Marxist analyses of the capitalist state that characterised employment relationships within the state sector as essentially similar to those found in the capitalist enterprise. Without directly engaging with these debates, however, a quite different view can be advanced concerning the *distinctiveness* of public sector, and in particular public service, trade unionism. This may be seen to derive from three related factors. First, and most obviously, such unions must engage with, and seek to influence, an essentially *political* process. This is so obvious as barely to need stating (although it rarely is), but it has profound implications for the organisation and structure of trade unions, their tactics, and the nature of the sanctions and pressure they can bring to bear. Second, public sector trade unions are, or at least were until recently, the closest we have in this country to single-industry trade unions. Unions in local government, the health service, the Post Office, and so on, had membership tightly limited to one or at most very few sectors. This gave them both an organisational preoccupation with, and detailed knowledge of, a particular sector (often also a single employer) in a way that could not be true of the big private sector trade unions. While it is obvious that, for example, the Transport and General Workers' Union understands and is concerned with the future of the motor vehicle industry, it cannot devote its entire organisational attention to this subject in the way that, for example, COHSE could to the health service. One consequence was a union engagement with the general and specific details of sectoral policy that provided a basis for engagement with employers and government on a range of issues significantly wider than that associated with the usual pay and conditions agenda of collective bargaining. Third, and more speculatively, it can be suggested that there are differences in the nature of the employment relationship between public and private sectors and that these may be summed up in the important but ill-defined notion of *public service ethos*. At its most simple this notion suggests that the existence of differences between public and private sectors in employees orientations to work and in the 'psychological contract'. In particular the concept suggests differences between public and private sector employment relationships reflecting differences between working to produce a free public good as opposed to a private commodity exchanged for cash. It is not necessary to infer from this, as some have done, a harmonistic view of the employment relationship (see Price, 1983: 158). The conflictual history of public service industrial relations over the last three decades is enough to scotch that idea. Rather we can suggest the need for analysis of public sector trade unions to be sensitive to distinctiveness in the ways members perceive their interests in work and hence in the demands they make on the representative of those interests, their union. This Introduction, and many of the contributions to this book, reflect analytical and policy interest in exploring such distinctiveness.

To argue this is not to suggest that the UNISON experience has no wider implications. First, the issues confronting UNISON are similar to those affecting many unions; the responses, if distinctive, are nevertheless relevant in other contexts. Second, more starkly, a plausible case can be made that the very future of trade unionism in the UK depends on stabilising and building on its public service base in the first instance. It would take a brave person to argue that the decline in private sector union numbers can be quickly arrested, notwithstanding the marginally more supportive political and legislative environment furnished by New Labour. Increasingly the public services sustain British unionism. A recent calculation suggests that around half of all trade union members work in the public services, although these account for only 19 per cent of total UK employment (Mathieson and Corby, 1999). Eight of the seventeen unions with more than 100,000 members were predominantly public service unions in 1996. While union membership and density in the private manufacturing sector plumetted after 1979, in the public services the picture, although serious, was less dramatic. Mathieson and Corby (1999: 208) claim that in the decade from 1979 public service union density remained roughly stable at around 80 per cent, but since then it has dropped to around 55 per cent in 1996, with notable falls in central government and in the health service.[4] Public service employees are now at the heart of British unionism, although it could be argued that this has occurred 'by default', as a consequence of their having fared less badly than their private sector counterparts.

The implications for the future of trade unionism in Britain (and in several other countries where similar patterns may be observed (see Bach *et al.*, 1999)) are mixed. Insofar as the crisis of trade unionism is first and foremost a private sector phenomenon it might seem logical to seek possible ways out by looking at strategies within that sector, as in Hyman's influential work examining unions' alternative strategies in this country and elsewhere (Hyman, 1996). It is of course true that even if every public service worker were unionised that would still leave a vast majority of British employees outside trade unions. However, a plausible case can be made for seeing the future of public service unionism as crucial to the survival of the wider union movement. First, there is still a managerial and employee culture in much of the public service sector more accepting and supportive of trade unionism than found in much of the private sector, especially the expanding private services. Second, the public sector trade unions may provide a more fertile test bed for innovation than the private. A combination of greater security and a more closely-focused set of preoccupations may facilitate new thinking. It is the public sector trade unions' potential for innovation that may constitute their most significant contribution.

Governance and management of the union

The merger brought together unions with very different traditions and philosophies of governance and democracy and these differences and their resolution dominated the merger talks (Terry, 1996). While all reflected the general tendency of national public service unions to have relatively strong central leaderships and powerful national executives, reflecting the exigencies of centralised bargaining and the need to influence political decision, they did so in markedly different ways. The rival perceptions of NALGO as 'member-led' and of NUPE as 'officer-led' (see Undy *et al.*, 1981; Fryer, this volume), while undoubtedly simplified caricatures, contained elements of a real contrast and of strongly-held differences among union activists concerning the best way to run a union. However, the merger negotiations made clear that the political context within which all were constrained meant that these were differences of degree only. NALGO stressed the importance of branch organisation and (limited) autonomy while keenly aware of the need to maintain credible central structures for policy co-ordination and to engage with government agencies, while the other two laid more emphasis on the latter, while conceding the inevitability of union decentralisation to reflect and match the decentralisation of employers' structures. What was being sought, although the phrase was not used, was a union of 'controlled decentralisation', to rebalance the articulation between branch and centre to reflect new needs and pressures (see Park, 1999 for a full discussion of this notion).

Important though this balance is to union governance, and much though it influenced the merger debates, it is perhaps not the innovation for which UNISON will be most remembered. Two others emerge: 'proportionality' and 'fair representation', the philosophies and mechanisms designed to create first a union whose governance structures reflect its numerical dominance by women, and second a union which tries to ensure that the voices of all groups are recognised and heard, have already been widely commented upon and analysed. They indicate a union in explicit search of internal governance policies that match its long-standing external policy commitment to equal opportunities and minority rights. While they in turn raise new challenges (see McBride's chapter in this volume), testifying to the dynamic exploration that is the constant feature of union democracy, they have been widely applauded for their boldness and novelty.

The second innovation has hitherto remained less public. It is an oddity that despite numerous studies of union governance over several decades, little attention has been paid to the processes of *union management*.[5] Instead most work has focused on the role and interactions of national executive committees, of decentralised structures of shop stewards and branches, and on a small set of union employed officials, usually those with collective bargaining responsibility, headed by the general secretary. The significant hinterland of union employees responsible for such matters as the management of finance, training, research, publicity and a myriad of other routine responsibilities has remained un-scrutinised, except insofar as it may be included within the portfolio term 'bureaucracy', deployed more often to denote polemical criticism than analysis. If any inference could be drawn from much academic analysis it is that the work of such people (managers) should flow unambiguously from policy set through approved democratic mechanisms (good) but that in practice they are more likely to be dancing to the tune of the general secretary (bad). Both comments are rooted in such naïve and simplified views of the government and management of complex organisations as to be laughable if they were transferred to other organisational contexts, such as the relationship between government and Civil Service.

The academic neglect of the study of trade unions' own 'civil service' is mirrored in unions' own uncertainties in thinking about how they should be managed. Many trade unionists feel uncomfortable in confronting the notion that their own organisations require management if they are to function effectively. In part no doubt this reflects unions' role as the critics or opponents of management, leading many to see 'management' in essentially negative terms. More fundamentally there is a view that management, with its emphasis on expertise and 'effective' decision-taking, threatens the democratic basis of decision-taking and policy formulation. Unions' longstanding preference for recruiting staff on the basis of their familiarity with and commitment to trade unions, rather than for their technical expertise (see Kelly and Heery, 1994: 53–60) reflects this view. This is changing in response to demands for more specialist technical staff to handle such areas as finance and computing, and to the need to engage with equality issues. But even this development is limited, as unions continue to see activity as shop steward or branch officer as the normal 'apprenticeship' for union employment, and provide limited opportunities for training and career development. The significance of these issues is neatly illustrated by Kelly and Heery's finding that union officers appointed from outside the union, who have not gone through the traditional apprenticeship, are more likely that those appointed from the inside to pursue novel, radical policies, reflecting 'the unease of more traditional officers with a new union agenda' (Kelly and Heery, 1994: 91).

While several unions have made serious efforts to improve the quality of their management processes UNISON, if only by virtue of its greater size and resources, has perhaps been able to go further than many. The chapters in this book by Dempsey and Wheeler, both senior officers of the union, and by Colling and Claydon, indicate the strategic importance attached to organisational development, and the ways in which the union has sought to embed the processes involved within the union's central policy objectives (those which in other organisations might be called its 'mission statement'). While the language of professional management practice, of managing cultural change, and of organisational development is unfamiliar, perhaps uncomfortable, in analyses of union governance, public sector unions of the size and complexity of UNISON cannot but confront the issues involved. It can be argued, as do Kelly and Heery (1994: 204) that the external challenges to trade unions require a co-ordinated response and that this 'entails a degree of centralization of power within individual unions if resources are to be conserved, mobilized and targeted on priority issues'. To do this requires not that processes of internal management be ignored or marginalised, but that they be integrated into the democratic structures and activities of trade unions. UNISON's initiatives in these areas provide important ideas as to how this might be done.

Union purpose and the centrality of politics

From the start of the merger discussions it was clear that the creation of a new union was to be more than the fusion of membership and governance structures. The need to reconstruct a sense of purpose and 'mission' appropriate to a public service union for the twenty-first century was strongly felt. The campaigns against privatisation and competitive tendering had revealed membership and public preparedness both to resist job (and service) reductions and to argue for the retention of public provision in defence of the basic tenets of welfare state provision of health and other services. But the same campaigns also exposed how distant public service trade unions had become from policy-making within these great social services except insofar as it impinged upon members' terms and conditions of employment. Forty years of taking the welfare state and the political arguments underpinning it for granted had tempted public sector unions into believing it was no longer necessary to devote resources to reinforcing and restating the case for state provision of public services. Privately, many union members were prepared to concede that there was some substance to the public and political accusation that public service provision had become ossified, distant from and unresponsive to the general public, and managed in a way that appeared to privilege the convenience of providers over the needs of users.

While much of the responsibility for this lay elsewhere than with the unions, they, as active and influential agents within the public services, could not entirely be blameless. In the 1970s a decade or more of incomes policy restrictions on earnings had served to focus attention on pay, collective bargaining structures, and the tactics associated with centralised pay bargaining in a tough climate. Unions' and members' continuing interest in the nature of service provision occasionally surfaced, as in the 'pay beds' disputes of the late 1970s, providing evidence of the persistence of the public service ethos, but such episodes were rare. Increasingly, public service unions' engagement with the politics of public services came to be seen as equated with action to weaken government policies restricting income growth.

The Conservative governments of the 1980s changed the environment for public service trade unions in two dramatic ways. They rejected the political and economic consensus of the post-war Welfare State, alleging the inherent inefficiency of public service, and championing private against public, individual as against collective provision of health, education and other services. While fundamentally changing the political terrain on which public service unions had to work, and in doing so virtually eliminating the unions' scope for influencing policy regarding service provision, the government was at the same time determined to confront and curb union rights and power, in particular with regard to the public sector and was apparently able to increase its electoral support in doing so.

The partner unions' eventual responses to these twin challenges reflected their different political traditions and affiliations. NALGO, radicalised by the experiences of the 1970s, not affiliated to the Labour Party, and with a stable membership, developed a strong campaigning profile against government policy, and became one of the most powerful voices within the TUC for an oppositional stance on public sector policy and trade union legislation. NUPE and COHSE, affiliated to the Labour Party, their members falling and, NUPE in particular, under constant pressure from Compulsory Competitive Tendering and other privatisation initiatives, increasingly came to see the electoral defeat of the

Conservative government as their central political objective. Within that perspective unions accepted the need for caution in respect of any action seen as prejudicing electoral support for Labour, and insofar as that included strike action this marked another distinction between NALGO on the one hand and NUPE and COHSE on the other both during and, in some ways since, the merger.

In a purely technical sense any potential conflict between the two political traditions has been resolved by the creation of the two separate political funds, an innovation whose intention and operation are analysed in Jones' chapter in this volume. While this constitutes a considerable innovation in itself, providing a degree of choice to members not available in any other trade union in respect of the funding of political activity, it does not, as Jones makes clear, resolve all tensions concerning either the governance and operation of such funds, or the nature of the relationship established with the Labour Party through affiliation. This latter, as Sawyer's chapter vividly illustrates, is going through a profound change, especially in respect of its traditional key function, vital to public sector trade unions, as a channel for influencing policy in government. New Labour's or, more precisely, Tony Blair's clear antipathy to the unions' long-established practice of influencing policy by the passing of conference resolutions (their own or the Labour Party's) poses a real dilemma. The present government's preferred alternative, based around informal discussions and flexibility of response creates real problems of apparent lack of transparency in policy-making, at the same time as it gives potentially great influence to those senior trade union officials involved in such processes. While the 'behind-the-scenes' influence of the general secretaries of the big unions during the 1960s and 1970s was undeniable, the bargaining position was such that it was widely appreciated within trade unions as an efficient way of achieving declared union policy objectives. Now, given the decline of unions' bargaining power (formal and informal) in dealings with both Labour Party and government, it may appear to at least some activists that the potential gains no longer justify the risks associated with the process. This may seem more problematic within some union traditions than others – within UNISON it is probable that the old NALGO tradition is more offended than those of NUPE and COHSE – but it clearly represents a significant challenge to accepted norms of action.

At the same time it is clear that public service trade unions in particular cannot hope to achieve many of their stated policy objectives without recourse to effective political influence; withdrawal from the political sphere is not an option (for a full discussion see Park, 1999). Whether in respect of issues related to members' conditions of employment, such as low pay, or to social policy provision in the areas of services provided by UNISON members, access to political influence is crucial, as shown in the chapters by Morris and by Thornley (on low pay) and by Carpenter (on social policy). For as long as public service unions' objectives include a desire to shape public policy in anything more than the essentially negative sense of seeking to defeat government initiatives such as incomes policy or privatisation, channels for the exercise of influence have to be maintained. Following the dismantling of the formal structures of union engagement with government policy-making in the 1980s and the recent election of a Labour government that shows no strong interest in a return to 'tripartism', even large public service unions such as UNISON have to work within a political environment significantly different from their ideal. The analysis of trade unions as 'secondary organisations' constrained to operate on terrain and within parameters laid down by other powerful actors applies as much to public service unions operating within the political sphere as to private sector unions within the industrial and commercial.

Although a simplification, there is a significant element of truth in the assertion that until very recently public service trade unions' dominant strategy for achieving a model of public services, and of a conducive employment environment within them, was the election of a Labour government that shared their philosophy, and which in various ways they could influence. The government elected in 1997 does not deliver this objective along traditional dimensions. Public service unions wishing to influence public policy have to find new approaches and these may lack the transparency and public democratic mandate of established methods. The new emphasis on expertise and informality throws into sharp relief once again the importance of structures that integrate rather than separate local and national levels, lay representatives and 'bureaucrats'.

Even these days, however, political influence does not derive simply from expertise. Public service unions' continuing need for such influence to achieve their objectives, whether relating to pay, social policy or anything else requires 'clout' as well. In the 1980s Batstone and his colleagues argued that the political influence enjoyed by public sector trade unions derived from: 'political arithmetic' (their ability to influence the voting decisions of many thousands of citizens); the political embarrassment and potential loss of electoral support caused by disruption to essential public services; and the central position of union leaders in key political networks (1984: 200). Sixteen years later it is clear that those sources of influence have either been sharply attenuated or eliminated by the political upheavals of the Thatcher years and the reconfiguration of 'New' Labour. It is a central argument of this analysis, reflected in others in this volume, that despite privatisation and the deployment of market-derived disciplines in the public service sector, political decision making remains critical. Unions in this sector cannot achieve their broad objectives by 'going private' themselves and replacing political influence with economic pressure on employers. Even if employers were to be discomfited, they rarely have the discretion (or the resources) to respond without political approval.

The reconfiguration of the welfare state, and of the conventional alignments of party politics in the UK confront UNISON with perhaps its biggest challenges. It must meet both if it is to continue to *successfully* represent the interests of its members. In this as in many other things it may be setting the trend for other unions in the UK and in many other countries where similar changes are in train, albeit in more measured ways. Public service unions the world over will be looking to see how UNISON copes with these issues; this book provides some first insights.

Notes

1   Indeed, in the case of NALGO and NUPE, the original merger partners in the
    eventual creation of UNISON, the entrenched *lack* of unity, bordering on occasional
    overt hostility, was a recognised factor (Undy, 1999: 453). At an early stage in the
    merger when things were not going well Bob Fryer, one of the academic advisers
    to the UNISON merger, once brought a roar of sympathetic laughter from a hitherto
    suspicious audience of NALGO and NUPE officials by pointing out that 'NUPE
    and NALGO have a great deal in common. You poach each other's members, you
    cross each other's picket lines . . .'. From that point on the meeting went much
    better.
2   COHSE (the Confederation of Health Service Employees) had joined the merger
    talks in 1989.
3   Exceptions include an essay by Fryer (1989) and the biographies of public
    sector unions, but even the latter make few attempts to analyse public/private
    distinctions.
4   In the partner unions of UNISON the picture is mixed. NUPE lost members heavily
    from the early 1980s and COHSE also declined, but NALGO actually grew slightly
    between 1980 and 1993 (Park, 1999: 4).
5   Two recent exceptions are the work of Undy *et al.* (1996) and of Kelly and Heery
    (1994).

References

Bach, S., Bordogna, L., della Rocca, G. and Winchester, D. (1999) *Public Service Employ-
    ment Relations in Europe: Transformation, Modernization or Inertia?*, London: Routledge.
Batstone, E., Ferner, A. and Terry, M. (1984) *Consent and Efficiency: Labour Relations and
    Management Strategy in the State Enterprise*, Oxford: Blackwell.
Carter, B. (1991) 'Politics and process in the making of Manufacturing, Science and
    Finance (MSF)', *Capital and Class*, 45: 35–71.
Fyer, R. (1989) 'Public service trade unionism in the twentieth century' in R. Mailly, S. J.
    Dimmock and A. S. Sethi (eds), *Industrial Relations in the Public Services*, London:
    Routledge.
Kelly, J. and Heery, E. (1994) *Working for the Union: British Trade Union Officers*, Cambrige:
    Cambridge University Press.
Hyman, R. (1996) 'Changing union identities in Europe' in P. Leisink, J. Van Leemput
    and J. Vilrokx (eds), *The Challenges to Trade Unionism Europe: Innovation or Adaptation*,
    Cheltenham: Edward Elgar.
Mathieson, H. and Corby, S. (1999) 'Trade unions: the challenge of individualism?' in
    S. Corby and G. White (eds) *Employee Relations in the Public Services: Themes and Issues*,
    London: Routledge.
Park, T-J. (1999) 'In and beyond the workplace: the search for articulated trade
    unionism in UNISON', unpublished PhD thesis, University of Warwick.
Price, R. (1983) 'White-Collar Unions: growth, character and attitudes in the 1970s' in
    R. Hyman and R. Price (eds) *The New Working Class? White-collar Workers and their
    Organizations*, London: Macmillan.
Terry, M. (1996) 'Negotiating the Government of UNISON', *British Journal of Industrial
    Relations*, 34, 1: 87–110.
Undy, R. (1999) 'Negotiating amalgamations; territorial and political considerations
    and administrative reforms in public-sector service unions in the UK', *British Journal
    of Industrial Relations*, 37, 3: 445–64.

Undy, R., Ellis, V., McCarthy, W. E. J., and Halmos, A. M. (1981) *Change in Trade Unions*, London: Hutchinson.

Undy, R., Morris, H., Smith, P. and Martin, R. (1996) *Managing the Unions*, Oxford: Clarendon Press.

Willman, P. (1996) 'Merger propensity and merger outcomes among British unions, 1985–1995', *Industrial Relations Journal*, 27(4): 331–8.

Part I
UNISON

Structures and processes

2 The creation of UNISON

Rodney Bickerstaffe

I have to make clear right at the outset that I am proud of the fact that UNISON has got to where it is today, and I am proud and pleased that the fifth anniversary of the creation of UNISON has been commemorated by a major conference at Warwick University's Industrial Relations Research Unit and by the publication of this important book. The creation of UNISON marks a significant achievement in the development of public sector trade unionism and the book and conference are indications of how that is already contributing towards our understanding of trade unionism into the next century. Only a few years ago I don't think that most of us would have guessed or hoped that we would have got as far as we have. People – perhaps too many people – still tell me that there is a long way to go and of course that is absolutely true. Any process of merger, and it is a process, not something that happened in July 1993 and that was the end of it, a developing thing that will go on, certainly over the next 4 or 5 years. The opportunity to stand back after 5 years that is provided by the contributions to this book, gives us a chance to study, to puzzle and to learn from the monumentous events that have taken place so far and to reflect on the very steep learning curve on which we all still find ourselves.

I want also to pay tribute to all those people, some of whom participated in the conference and have contributed to this book, and to many others who were involved in setting up and arguing for and determining the shape of the new union in 1993. I have to say that there were a lot of casualties; a lot of casualties before the merger and there have been a lot of casualties since. In trying to describe the process in a simple way, I have used before the image of 'tectonic plates' of movement in the organisations that came together to form UNISON, and since then, that have actually 'trapped' people together. There were people who had blossoming careers as employees or as elected members in the old partner unions. Some of them willingly gave way in order to help create the new union. Some fought and battled against it and either fell before 1 July 1993 or have gone away or gone into hiding, gone into whatever corner to lick their wounds because it was not what they wanted or because the new union has not already achieved what people expected or hoped. But part of the same 'tectonic movement' created among those who were committed to the idea, the vision and the drive, and the thrust towards 1 July 1993 that were magnificent. There were obviously backwoodsmen and -women who did not share in it but the real drive and commitment to get the project up and running, and the dream of the new union, were very, very powerful. And although we all constantly told one another, 'You know, it is going to be difficult, it is not going to be easy', in truth, we were driven forward in unity by the concept and the idea.

I have always strongly believed in the concept of industrial unionism and despite all changes, the mergers and amalgamations of recent years we are not much closer to my concept of industrial unionism in this country. We may never get there. In this context it is worth pointing out that a colleague union in Germany, the Gewerkschaft Öffentliche Dienste, Transport und Verkehr (ÖTV), that could be seen as the 'UNISON of Germany' is looking to merge with a number of other unions to form a union of 3.7 million which will straddle private and public sectors. For Germany at least that might indicate that the traditional concept of industrial unionism is obviously breaking up. Now, nothing stays together forever but I still think that there's more to be done in the direction of industrial unionism, as I understand it.

UNISON as a union for the public services

UNISON has been a huge step for me and for all of those of us who believed that NALGO on its own, COHSE on its own, NUPE on its own, were not what public service workers wanted and that we could do better than those three unions although we loved them dearly. In moving onto the new union, we were, making progress in three directions. First, it has been good for trade unionism, although I am aware that not all my colleagues will agree with this. Second, it has been crucial for the development and standing of public service trade unionism. Third, and this is perhaps less obvious but equally important, it has been good for public services themselves. During the late 1980s and into the 1990s, when we were developing this new union, the theme, the climate, the government push, were certainly against trade unionism *per se,* but at the same time also strongly hostile to the public sector and public services. And what we were doing was underscoring, bolstering the concept of public service and we were proudly saying: 'This is what we're about. We believe in it.' From the outset of the merger talks our clear decision that the new union would have at its heart an explicit statement of aims and values meant that wherever we talked, we talked about public services, not just about the new union. We talked about the jobs that our members did and the need for them for any modern society. So, in that high Tory period, with the attack on the public services, here was a body that was standing up proudly and saying: 'Well, whatever you're saying, we believe that there is a better path, a different path. It is not an old path, either. It is a new, very modern one. It was, in fact, a shot in the arm, in my view, for public service identity, for public service philosophy, or, to use that very over-worked expression, 'public service ethos.' And I am proud that, just by bringing the union together, we did give it that underscoring. And now there are more than 1.3 million of us who share that commitment to public services through their trade union.

It is that commitment that explains why we always wanted UNISON to be a campaigning union, not simply a union preoccupied with recruiting members and then not doing much more than providing individual services. We were determined to build on the campaigning skills that we had developed in NALGO, NUPE and COHSE, on the membership support and enthusiasm for our campaigns, and on the public sympathy and approval they created. We wanted to campaign on all the issues that are now familiar and important to us and which we are proud to support: the statutory national minimum wage; against the Private Finance Initiative; against Compulsory Competitive Tendering; and for quality in public services. Campaigning on all these issues means that we are not only concerned with the future of our union. We are closely tied up in and passionate about something wider, and our campaigning is not exclusively about UNISON members. It is about a much broader front and a broader agenda that was spelled out in detail in the final report made to our three conferences that endorsed the creation of UNISON (COHSE, NALGO, NUPE, 1992), and now it is effectively in the rulebook. Our desire to create an outward-looking, *generous* trade union now lies at its heart. I have never accepted for a moment the idea that unions are self-centred organisations, concerned only for themselves and their members' sectional interests. It is a widespread view that we had to confront during the 1960s and 1970s, and unfortunately during the 1980s and possibly – who knows – to the end of the 1990s as well. But it is a mistaken view and it is up to us through all our actions to prove that. We are not only about ourselves. We are about the excluded; we are about the poor, the damaged, the dispossessed and the dying. Our people are about that and our union is about it as well. We are a voice, a powerful voice, not just for our own members but for something much broader. By the very nature of our work as public servants we are directly in touch with public policy and will help to redefine many of the concepts and many of the practicalities and problems of public policy. That is not to say that as individual unions we did not have an effective voice in these matters in the past. But I believe that as UNISON we are going to make a much bigger difference, partly because of the new Labour government but primarily because of the very fact that we are UNISON and we are together.

We are a modern organisation. We are risk-takers, not conservative, backward-looking organisations. Just getting the union together was a huge risk, a huge leap of faith which succeeded because many people were prepared to make a generous contribution towards a vision, towards a idea, an ideal, that was untested and whose achievement was not guaranteed. The status quo would have been a lot easier and more comfortable and it has to be said that there were some, both within and more especially outside, the three partner unions who worked and prayed for it not to work. Of course we insist on our continuing right and duty as unions to protect conditions, to protect wages, to protect our ideas. But we insist only on our right to protect, not to defend mindlessly. And when people say to me that it is only through change that you can really be prepared for the future, we agree with that also and what we try to do is a bit of both. We have tried to protect our members and we have tried to work forward and look forward as well. We're certainly looking forward now. I have always wanted UNISON to be a trade union centre of public service excellence. The idea that trade unions are antediluvian, that they are always putting the brakes on progress, that they are not appropriate to the times in which we live now, has always upset me and it still does. Because it is demonstrably wrong.

Of course the greatest contribution we can make to public service excellence comes from our one million and more members who know about all the jobs and all the problems but are never, ever asked their views. We have often properly criticised management for that failure, but we have to say that we have not always made use of all that expertise ourselves. We have 1.3 million members, who cover all aspects of public service work, but only very rarely are individual members asked their views, nor is the union, on their behalf. From now one we need to see ourselves and be seen as a *repository* of all that information, all that knowledge, all those skills. And I would like, in the future, no academic, no person from the media, no politician would think of commenting on any of the key social policy areas without asking the view of UNISON and its members. We can be the channel, the funnel, for all that. And I think that we're making steps in that direction. On issues such as truancy, whistle-blowing and corruption our views are being sought. On devolution, and in particular on Northern Ireland, UNISON, on both sides of the border, has made a massive contribution, which will be acknowledged, by ministers and Secretaries of State. Already we are making a difference, so this is not just a wish-list idea, and we have got to try and build on in the future. Over time we can develop a situation where the union and our members can change policy.

UNISON and the future of trade unions

What kind of union does UNISON want to be? As I have argued above, its central identity is as a union for the public services. But that does not say much about what it will be like to be a trade union member within UNISON. Here I want to stress our attempt right from the word go, to be women-friendly, to be user-friendly, to be family-friendly, to be *different*; not just a servicing organisation but one that has a gentler side, a *family*-feel about it. Against that many argued that it could never happen because we were going to be too big, bureaucratic and anonymous. But those of us who were active in supporting the concept of the new union argued that it was not fundamentally a question of size but of political will. It is a question of whether or not all of us actually try and do the job of working as active trade unionists, part of which involves reaching out to people rather than just being bureaucratic. And I think that we are slowly but surely achieving that. That is not to say, of course that there are no tensions within the union. Some of them are proper, some of them are based in misunderstandings, either deliberate or unintentional and these need sorting out, sooner rather than later. Because there are plenty of possibilities that the union might break up, even now. Even if it exists, it could be broken within itself. We have not finished resolving some of the tensions and there is much more work to be done in that area. But at the same time we want to develop and utilise positive tensions because it is not a bad thing for tensions to exist between national and regional levels, between branch and regional, between lay and full-time, between north and south even. They can lead to important debates about democracy and governance, inclusion and exclusion, centralisation and decentralisation; about the identity of the union.

I want to touch on the matter of democracy, an issue which is routinely debated at all levels of the union, and not least at conference. Some may say that the debates are politically inspired or even party-politically inspired, but the truth is that there will be a continuing and proper debate about who's running the union and in what way. I believe that the democracy of the union is second to none. The structures, the committees, the ways through for individual members and for activists are myriad. Not so many that people cannot eventually see how it all fits together, but there are all sorts of ways into the union and through the union and I believe that we are building and developing those without the need for any further strategy to deal with it. In particular, on this issue, I do not welcome outside attention and outside pressures and all of us, as activists on behalf of this union, need to stand up and say: 'We are an independent trade union, we are not in the pockets of any government, we are not in the pockets of any party. We are certainly not in the pockets of any unrepresentative groups on right or left and we are an independent organisation.' And we need to stress that.

Of course this close to the merger it is easy to criticise us for being too top-heavy and bureaucratic at the centre. This is of course a major problem of a newly-merged organisation. We had three of everything. But we had to deal with that gently and sensibly, because the union clearly takes pride in the way it treats its employees. We had to get through that process without people creating too many waves. There was a great deal of generosity from the start, as a number of people at all levels, lay and full-time, stood back to help the organisation's birth and to move it on and that is going to continue in the future. We got a strategic review that we had round our neck from a conference decision but in fact has not been an awful thing. We needed a look, a studied look, and the strategic review and the follow-on functional reviews of national level and regional level are going to show us the way forward. As a result we are slowly but surely reducing our top-heaviness. We have a clear policy obligation, widely approved throughout UNISON, to move away from national and central to devolved throughout the union and that is what we are doing and will continue to do.

On the subject of devolution, I ought to mention Scotland, Wales and Northern Ireland and their important moves towards decentralisation and local governance. We don't know how that is going to affect our new union (or the TUC, for that matter). The development in Scotland, in particular, we ought to watch and study closely. I would not like to see the development of different union structures as exist now between Canada and the USA. I acknowledge the different countries and I believe that we need now to be thinking about how we should respond if in the future there are calls for an independent Scottish public service union. Maybe it will never happen, but we cannot take this for granted.

Still thinking regionally, but at a different level, we could become the public service arm of European trade unionism for the future. At that level as well we do not know where things are going but we have to look at new approaches. We have reached an agreement with the Finnish nursing union They so that when their members are in the UK, they will be deemed to be UNISON members, for all intents and purposes, and vice versa. Now, that sort of exercise is going to develop across Europe and one doesn't have to be too much of a crystal ball watcher to understand that developments in Europe may mean that there will be European development in public service unionism as elsewhere. Perhaps not a pan-European single trade union but there could be confederations and federations down the line, and those are ideas worthy of serious thought. Our role within Europe is constantly developing and improving. Our involvement in the European Public Service Committee has helped us progress and develop ideas far more effectively than we previously could as individual unions. We now have a major international role as one of the biggest players on the public service international scene. Internationally, UNISON has got an excellent name – in South Africa, and in Cuba certainly, and in all the places that you would imagine – and we can and will be even better involved internationally in the future. Not just for trips here and there but for real help with education and training; a transfer of much of our knowledge and expertise, and of money and resources, to a lot of developing trade unions across the world.

What about here in the UK, though? I actually believe that we cannot stop where we are. I think the future will not be UNISON. I think the future will be something else more than that and, anyway, the name and the individuals involved, in a sense, do not really matter. It is the collective will and the collective efforts and the collective outcomes that are important. I hope that there will be a teaching arm of this new organisation in due course. I hope that there will be a civil service arm. We need to start talking within the union to recognise that a public service union is not only about the seven services we cover at the moment. Regional development and devolution will force us to consider that cusp between the civil service and the local authority and health members that we have. Now, this is not a crude effort at a takeover. It is nothing like that, but my vision has always been that we need to move further forward and even these ideas of progress and development require discussion and analysis. I know plenty of people are saying that we ought to slow down and check where we are and consolidate our position Certainly we do not intend to jeopardise what we have achieved by moving on too fast. But as UNISON does settle down we need to be actively thinking about the future. There is active discussion as to whether we are moving towards a situation where we may only have six or seven unions in the UK. I am not concerned about the number of unions as such but I am constantly interested in the future of trade unionism in the public service area and for me, UNISON should not be the last word. We should already be thinking about how to go forward from where we are now.

Of course we also need to consider our role within the TUC. I believe it is an effective role. We have always believed in a TUC although recently there has been an increasing questioning of its role in a future where we may have only five or six huge unions like UNISON. My view is that of course it remains necessary, perhaps even more necessary, if only to handle disputes and arguments between the affiliated unions – and perhaps their leaders.

Finally, what will the individual members want by the year 2010? I believe they will want what we are giving now and that's value for money. At the moment we have an income of about £104 million per annum and an expenditure of £104 million and a penny! The strategic review and the follow-on from that, combined perhaps with more rigorous management should get us in a better position in the future. The financial side is not unimportant. You cannot talk about a merger and the development of the union without talking about finances. Increasingly we need to take clear long-term decisions about financial allocation, based in our strategy of delivering increased benefits to union members. That is not just – or even largely – about what are described as individual services to members. Value for money for the members included continuing and strengthening our public campaigning, because that is what they want us to do. But at the same time members want more information more quickly, and their want their difficulties sorted out rapidly and with authority by the union. That is why we are going down the road of UNISON*direct*, because that is going to be the way of the future. The IT developments matter. It is reaching out to the future – the Internet, the intranet – we are into it all and we have to be, despite the cost, and despite other worries that it may generate, because our members and activists need, and expect, that quick and efficient access to the information they need. UNISON*direct* provides, for example, individual members with direct access to a call centre where they get directed towards answers and towards solutions to their problems. Members will no longer be prepared to go through a maze of different channels and be pushed from here to there to answer a query. They know what the new technologies can do and will want the union to be involved in developing its use for trade unions and members. Of course it costs a lot and has already generated controversy – is it about help in the structure and organisation of the union or does it risk bypassing the structure and organisation of the union and thus weakening them? This is all open for discussion but our profound hope is that UNISON*direct* and all the new technologies will help the development of the collective organisation, and it will if we are determined to use it that way. These are important debates but what is more important is the fact that we are taking the risk. We are having a go. We are reaching out to the future. We're not afraid to look at ourselves and allow other people to look at us.

The key to it all is to develop an attractive union that will provide members with what they want and will help us to go out and recruit and organise those hundreds of thousands of public service workers who are in no union at all. At the start of the merger talks we told ourselves that once we were 'the' public service union, people would flock to our banner. Well, we have recruited hundreds, thousands of new members into UNISON but we could and should be recruiting a hell of a lot more. And in particular we must urgently discuss how we appeal to young people. We are an ageing organisation, as indeed most trade unions are. The average age of our members is 45 or 46 years. That cannot be the way of the future or we simply die.

In five years we have made enormous progress in staking out the culture and identity of UNISON. We are moving away from the language and assumptions of the old partner unions into something new. This was difficult but vital. For months, at the start of the new union, I had to go around apologising for saying 'NUPE'. And people say, 'caught you!' And it was great to be able to catch people in NALGO and people in COHSE. This was a reflection of the transition. People had absorbed and used the traditions of those three great trade unions and they were still in all our minds. They were difficult things to leave behind. I was at the last conferences of all three unions at some point and we all loved those unions. The youngest one, I think, was 75 years old and all had huge and honourable traditions and a huge sense of history behind them. Now we have got to build our own history in UNISON. We are recruiting people now who have never been in COHSE, never been in NUPE, never been in NALGO. They are the people of the future. And the more of those that we get in, the more it will be the time for the rest of us, perhaps, to stand by. I said before, it is not a name that matters, nor is it about the individuals involved. It is about that collective will and the power towards the future. I think UNISON has got those and I hope that the conference and the book and the progress they mark and reflect on will make a further important contribution to push us forward into the 21st century.

Reference

COHSE, NALGO, NUPE (1992) 'Towards a new union'. Report of a special conference.

3　The making of UNISON

A framework to review key events, processes and issues

Bob Fryer

The making of mergers

Organisational mergers are messy, complex, social processes. They involve the dynamic and unique interplay of personalities, structures, resources and philosophies. As mergers are secured and implemented, they turn upon particular intersections of histories, biographies, politics and power struggles. So, mergers offer exquisite opportunities to those interested in the political manoeuvres and stratagems deployed to secure organisational advantage, whether they engage as either protagonists or merely as observers. If the making of UNISON is anything to go by, they also involve episodes of high drama, confusion, tedium, farce, mourning, good humour and amusement. Thus, organisational mergers are equally the occasions of hope, despair, exhilaration and foreboding. They constitute a very special terrain for the forging of new friendships, alliances and suspicions that will extend well into the life of the merged body, across and beyond the boundaries of the once-separate organisations.

Above all, mergers afford opportunities for the main players in the process to 'imagine the future', in terms of what they believe would constitute ideal, preferred or, at the very least, achievable organisational arrangements for the new body. In this sense, mergers give those principally involved a rare chance to design entirely new structures for the proposed organisation, laying out for debate its intended values, goals and priorities together with its main suggested structures. If this cannot ever be done entirely from scratch, as appears to be more possible when organisations are initially 'founded', at least it can be according to a more or less clearly articulated set of objectives. Even then, of course, such organisational designs have to be shaped within known and accepted constraints, always taking account of acknowledged divisions of opinion.

This last point is particularly relevant in mergers between trade unions, with their characteristic preoccupation with formal constitutional and representative matters. One of their principal organisational features is collective decision making and they explicitly espouse the legitimacy of differing viewpoints amongst their number, each claiming validation on the back of the principle of 'democracy'. As self-governing, membership organisations, trade unions' representatives and their governing bodies also pay particular attention to questions of purpose, method and organisation. Given these aspects of trade unions, not surprisingly they vary greatly in the detailed ways they deal with such issues as objectives, authority, finance, relationships and powers. There are many choices to make for those in a position to influence a union's proposed shape, as in the making of a 'new' union through merger.

As historical example after example demonstrates in abundance, there is certainly no 'one best way' of organising British unions, with what the Webbs called their 'kaleidoscopic constitutions' (Webb and Webb, 1975: 28). There are no ready-made blueprints to hand; rather the choices exercised by the partners at merger, although inevitably shaped somewhat by their respective pasts, usually reflect their various allegiances to different 'models' of union democracy and organisation (Held, 1987). Hence, debating and determining the proposed direction and shape of any proposed trade union merger is virtually certain to open up conflicting views of the desirable ways of working and doing business in the future, as much within the ranks of each of the intending partner unions as between them.

Aims and methods

For the researcher, the negotiations, debates, compromises and statements made, and the drafting of documents undertaken, in preparation for merger all provide valuable evidence to chart the differing strategies and tactics of the various would-be partners. They also provide insights into the key players' respective values, priorities and what might be termed their 'organisational rhetorics'. That is the main focus of this chapter. In addition, taking stock of a trade union merger 5 years on, as in the case of UNISON, constitutes an opportunity to reconstruct elements of the merger process itself, map progress since and assess both its successes and its failures, as perceived by the different protagonists involved.[1]

Hence, the aims of this chapter are threefold. First, it examines how the particular shape and structure adopted for UNISON were influenced by the approaches taken by those charged by each of the eventual partner unions to negotiate the 'deal' to establish the new union. Secondly, it aims to contribute to the development of an analytic framework for studying and comparing different types of union mergers under different conditions. Thirdly, and important for both of the other objectives, the chapter represents a brief essay in method and interpretation in the study of trade union organisation, by shedding light on one aspect of the process of trade union mergers (Undy *et al.*, 1981: Waddington 1995, 1997).

The chief method adopted in this chapter is to draw upon participant observation and the notes, papers and data collected as a consequence of my own direct involvement in the merger discussions as an 'academic adviser' between 1988 and 1994.[2] I also make some use of materials collected during previous work with all three unions, especially with the National Union of Public Employees (NUPE) during the mid-1970s when I assisted with and studied the reorganisation of that union in one of the first 'action research' projects of its kind undertaken in this country (Fryer *et al.*, 1974). To that extent, both of these first sources of information have the advantage (and limitations) of having been collected at the time of the activities or issues reported. They are not based principally upon memory, hindsight or reconstruction. Finally, I use some other published data and studies of the three partner unions, of British unions more generally, and of the wider social context in which they have recently operated.

Who would have thought it?

The very creation of UNISON out of the three constituent unions, the Confederation of Health Service Employees (COHSE), the National Association of Local Government Officers (NALGO) and NUPE, over the period 1988–93, was itself a remarkable achievement. At first blush, there were no utterly compelling reasons why this particular trade union merger should have occurred at all, or at the particular time that it did. There was no evidence of the prior or widespread acceptance of a convincing case for the merger in any of the three eventual partners. Nor, objectively, could obviously overwhelming arguments be advanced for the creation of this particular 'new' union. Indeed, significant external commentators frequently made the point to me, both in private, confidential discussions and in public comment, that the proposed merger was most unlikely to come about and, even less likely, to become a success in the terms of those most keen to see it happen.

NALGO was a very large, financially sound union, one of the few significant TUC affiliates to have continued to grow in the 'scoundrel times' of Thatcher's anti-union 1980s, continuing the substantial expansion already enjoyed over the previous five decades (Willman *et al.*, 1993*)*. In its chief organising domains of local government, gas and electricity NALGO was the undisputed principal union for the representation of 'white-collar', non-manual staff. Its members and their jobs had, up to then at least, been left relatively unscathed by the impact of compulsory competitive tendering and privatisation of the public services, certainly by comparison with the manual unions, especially NUPE. In addition, and to its clear advantage, NALGO's principal focus for recruitment appeared to be in line with the observable drift of occupational and labour market change, towards more white-collar and less manual employment, both in the economy at large and within the public services more narrowly.

Throughout the 1970s and 1980s, NALGO had raised its public profile considerably, as its membership rose to over three-quarters of a million. This included rapidly extending its network of workplace stewards, developing novel, and often highly contentious, internal systems for organising 'under-represented' union members through 'self-organisation'. Over these two decades, the union had also become increasingly involved in industrial disputes. Moreover, standing officially outside of the Labour Party, the union was able to forge its own 'independent' political perspective, often to the 'left' of Labour party trade union affiliates (Kelly, 1998: 52–4). NALGO was thus also somewhat removed from the growing pressures for reform and modernisation, which were already afoot in the Labour Party and its trade union affiliates, when the merger discussions began in the late 1980s (Minkin, 1991).

In NUPE's case, things were rather different. Along with NALGO, the union had enjoyed unrivalled 'home-grown' growth from the mid-1930s until the advent of the first Thatcher government in 1979, becoming one of the half dozen largest affiliates to either the TUC or Labour Party. During the 1970s NUPE had also firmly established its role and reputation in the world of modern British trade unions. It had become the champion of the low-paid and, at that time, virtually a lone voice in favour of a statutory minimum wage (Fisher and Dix, 1974). NUPE had been a stout and militant defender of public services, even against the policies of a Labour government and in the face of hostility from other major unions (Fryer, 1979). It proudly claimed to be the organiser of more women trade unionists and more part-time workers than any other British union. With a long-established commitment to 'industrial unionism', NUPE was once characterised as a 'popular bossdom' (Turner, 1962). In the 1970s and early 1980s the union had self-consciously sought radically to reform its internal organisation in order to widen membership participation. The union had decided to reflect more accurately the composition of its members (especially women), to advance its policy programme more effectively and to demonstrate its commitment to membership mobilisation (Fryer and Williams, 1993).

The mid-1980s had been less propitious times for NUPE. Successive restrictions on public expenditure, contracting out and compulsory competitive tendering, private sector growth in residential homes and secular change in the composition of the labour market combined with a virulent climate of anti-unionism had all taken their collective and cumulative toll upon the union's membership and finances. Yet, despite all of this and despite the union's long-standing rulebook (and some would say purely rhetorical) commitment to 'industrial unionism', it was still possible to ask why the union should seek to merge now with NALGO and COHSE. For many members in NUPE (and often the sentiments were vigorously reciprocated) NALGO represented part of the problem faced by the union, not the solution.

Rightly or wrongly, many in NUPE saw NALGO members (or at least some of them) as their 'bosses'.[3] Senior management, organised by NALGO, constituted the channels through which cuts in manual staffs were imposed, drawing up and implementing plans for contracting out services and introducing the dreaded compulsory competitive tendering.[4] Even NALGO's own industrial disputes, which might otherwise have been opportunities for expressing solidarity between the two unions, occasionally hit NUPE members and their wages hard, especially when payroll staff were involved or the strike was prosecuted with vigorous picketing. In addition, there were plenty of examples of the two unions' members crossing the other's picket lines. Finally, one of NUPE's most senior officers (and one who was decisively to lead the eventual merger negotiations for the union), the Deputy General Secretary Tom Sawyer, was now himself a leading advocate of Labour Party change and 'modernisation', an apparent far cry from NALGO's public stance. How were the respective unions' members going to be convinced that they should get into bed with such seemingly different and often bitterly opposed prospective bedfellows?

There was no immediately obvious stronger case for this particular merger where COHSE was concerned. Its rivalry with NUPE was legendary and long-standing, including at senior officer level. Its particular claim, vital in its recruitment battles with the Royal College of Nursing (RCN), was to be a specialist health service and health care union, not a general public service union. Its main need, as far as both leaders and activists were concerned, was to shore up and advance its claims against rival membership organisations in health, especially the RCN and some of the professional bodies. Earlier merger overtures from NUPE had been politely but firmly rejected and, when COHSE was briefly excluded from the TUC in the early 1970s, there had been fierce rivalry between them (Carpenter, 1988). Thereafter COHSE's membership growth of 139 per cent had been spectacular.

Even in the protracted NHS dispute as recently as 1982, when inter-union solidarity against the Thatcher government united their cause, COHSE and NUPE had conducted relatively independent campaigns, occasionally resulting in friction and difficulty. At the time, the two unions' leaders were regarded as representing very different sorts of organisations by senior government figures.[5] When the other two unions' national conferences were endorsing the first enabling resolutions in 1988 to start discussions, COHSE's conference resolved at first to keep out. COHSE's General Secretary at this time had been a junior officer in South Yorkshire when NUPE's General Secretary had also been a junior officer in the same area in his own organisation. This had been a time, well remembered by them both, when relations locally between the two unions had been very difficult. Even COHSE's resolution to join the talks, a year after the other two unions had opened discussions, was cautious, expressed in the form of a 'twin-track' approach, which could, theoretically, lead eventually either to involvement in some sort of a new union or to continued independence.

So, if this union merger was going to be achieved, it would clearly require much hard work and a considerable amount of clever footwork by those favouring it. In practice, the eventual establishment of UNISON demonstrates clearly that the accomplishment of merger between the three partner unions required the sophisticated construction and mobilisation of all sorts of aspirations, stories, interpretations and vocabularies (Mills, 1963). These were advanced both at the time of the making of the merger itself and long thereafter, to ensure that it 'made sense', so to speak. In that respect, the merger was not, and could not have been, entirely 'completed' at the point of formal amalgamation, on Vesting Day in July 1993.

Of course, there is nothing especially unusual in that. All organisations are always to some extent continuously engaged in 'making' and 'remaking' and, in that sense, are never 'completed'. Mergers are simply a formal, legitimate and focused instance of this general feature of organisational life. Many of those supporting the merger to form UNISON went out of their way to emphasise that it would take time to build an entirely new organisational identity and 'culture', as they described it. They were much less likely to acknowledge that this might never be fully achieved, nor to accept that continuing loyalties to one or other of the previously independent partners to the merger (and its myths) might be long-lived. In UNISON, as in other mergers, such divisions would be typically massaged by folk memories, nostalgias and grieving, but might also be based on the 'official' accounts of the respective unions' pasts, all of which served as rallying points of resistance to the new union.

Organisational analysis

There is not very much by way of a well-established, specific framework of concepts and theory in the published literature on trade unions, especially that based upon previous studies of union mergers, to help us understand the making of UNISON. This is partly because we lack so few detailed contemporary accounts of the inner life of trade unions and their processes (including union mergers).[6] Even the best historical records of unions' early formation are often based largely upon a few surviving documents and some scattered biographical and autobiographical reflections.[7] But the absence of established conceptual frameworks arises also from the reluctance of many industrial relations scholars, in Britain at least, to delve into the murky waters of theoretical analysis. The otherwise valuable accounts of aggregated patterns of trade union merger activity are, of necessity, couched in terms of high level generalisations, which lose their analytical purchase when applied to the natural history of one particular merger.

By contrast, there is an almost terrifyingly extensive literature on organisations, of almost every kind.[8] It ranges from detailed case studies of companies, public sector bodies, hospitals, schools, military and naval organisations, political parties, faith communities and voluntary groups to comprehensive surveys of the field, although little of it so far has been explicitly focussed on trade unions as organisations.[9] The published analysis includes wide-ranging theorisation about organisations as such, 'cook book' recipes to guide organisational design and secure strategic change and studies of organisational conflict, division and struggle. In many respects, the study of organisation also lies at the centre of attempts to construct sociological accounts of the development of modern societies and, in one way or another, usually represent a continuing debate with the work of Max Weber.

Most usefully for this account of the making of UNISON, previous work in this field includes critical scrutiny of the role of organisation as a constituent feature of human beings' attempts 'to shape their cooperative activities' (Albrow, 1997). Albrow's explicitly sociological perspective underlines the point that organisations are essentially human and emergent constructs in which the values, goals, assumptions, intentions, and 'working theories' of the actors involved combine to produce outcomes which are both planned and unplanned. This insight is essential to understanding the formation of UNISON and to mapping the approach taken by different parties to the negotiations at various points in the process. In addition, it remains a useful way of understanding many of the continuing concerns and disappointments of some of the key *dramatis personae*.

In the case of UNISON, the cast of 'actors' was (and is) vast and changing. Crucially for this chapter it includes those representatives who were most centrally involved in hammering out the deal for merger between the once separate unions, COHSE, NALGO and NUPE, together with the assorted advisers, consultants and specialists appointed to help them up to Vesting Day. It also includes the views, aspirations and expectations of those to whom the very nature of trade unionism also gives a legitimate voice – elected representatives at various levels, collectivities such as conferences, committees and branches and members at large. Not that this means that every voice counts (or counted) equally in the merger. As C. Wright Mills memorably remarked, in a devastating but simple critique of the political disingenuousness of Parsonian grand theory, in all institutions 'the expectations of some men seem just a little more urgent than those of anyone else!' (Mills, 1959: 29–30). One of the tasks of a sociological analysis of the making of UNISON is precisely to unravel whose aspirations and expectations prevailed and whose were deflected, ignored or defeated.

'Form' and 'character' in trade union organisation

In addressing these issues, and seeking better to understand both the merger process and how UNISON came to be as it is, I make use of two key heuristic terms in this chapter. They are *union form* and *union character*. I make no claim for either their originality or their scientific precision or universal acceptance. Their only value is if they help interpretation and add to understanding. In developing these ideas, I am seeking to build, especially, on the richly textured, suggestive but nowadays somewhat neglected work of H. A. ('Bert') Turner. Both of the terms *form* and *character* are used by Turner (1962) in his discussion of the 'morphology' of trade unions and of trade union democracy. Although he makes frequent use of the two terms, Turner never defines them precisely, although their meaning for his purposes is pretty clear from their application. The term 'union character' has also been used before, notably by Blackburn (1967), but his usage embraces what I divide into the two elements of form and character and I am not following his approach here.

Reference to what I call the *form* of UNISON includes all those many explicitly 'rational' arrangements of structure – organisation, finance, rules, procedures, structures – which were established in the so-called 'partner' unions, or for the new union, or which were actually in evidence from Vesting Day onwards. It thus includes formal and empirical provision for union positions and roles, constitutional authorities, and, powers, staffing and managerial organisation. Questions of union form are often captured in writing and embedded in organisational systems, charts, regulations, job descriptions, codes and other typical technical features of bureaucracy. The term is also intended to include but go further than the notion of *union government* which once was a familiar, and useful, way of analysing some of these aspects of union life.[10] Union form is also intended to capture both formal and informal organisational arrangements, as well those which are sanctioned, approved or tolerated (though not necessarily officially) on the one hand and those practiced in the union without either approval or indulgence, on the other.

By the *character* of UNISON I mean that rich collection of aims, values, purposes, ways of working, relationships, moods, signs, symbols, rites, 'feel', orientations and identities which go to make up what has sometimes been referred to as the *ethos* of an organisation. A union's character is also recognisable from its reputation, style and the typical vocabularies and attitudes expressed by its leaders and members. The notion of organisational character thus deliberately acknowledges the affective and emotional dimensions of organisational life and its construction, which are utterly central to the understanding of trade unions' purposes and methods, with their inescapable preoccupations with matters of aims, values and ethics.

I should say at once that the distribution of those stressing one or other of these two approaches to making the new union did not always neatly coincide with union boundaries. Some protagonists moved from one side of this duality to the other, according to the issue in hand and the stage reached in the negotiations. Admittedly, some individuals identified themselves most frequently with a concern with the construction of a recognisably distinct character for UNISON whilst some, and the perspective they represented, felt far more at home with discussions about the new union's intended form.

There were six main ways in which UNISON's intended character was broached by those who saw this as critical, initially to win widespread support for the establishment of a new union through merger of the three separate partner unions. Later those who focused on the character of the new union did so with the intention of shaping its future style of work, priorities and pattern of relationships, both internal and external. They did so:

- Through the enunciation of a 'vision' for the new union and the core principles which should drive it and underpin its identity. This was done through the medium of the various joint reports to the partner unions' conferences, in speeches and in presentations and including the key projected roles of service groups and equal opportunities.
- Through the declaration of the key new tasks of new union, especially in the field of public policy, and in relation to the users of the services provided by its members.
- By attempting to incorporate and respect the union's two distinct political 'traditions' in an organisationally innovative and unique combination.
- Through the drafting of an agreed, and extensive, set of aims and values for UNISON, to be included in the union's Rulebook.
- By means of the levels, titles and functions of the senior officer positions and their national and regional responsibilities.
- Through a diffuse array of training programmes, project groups, change

management initiatives, commitment to strategic planning and review and the continuing construction and use of quite new vocabularies for a trade union setting.

At the time of the merger negotiations, those less convinced of either the objectives, vocabulary or likely effectiveness of this emphasis on matters of union character, were seen by the protagonists of the approach as rather dyed-in-the-wool, old-fashioned and even reactionary 'structuralists'. They were thought to show too much faith in the efficacy and representativeness of what their opponents regarded as relatively empty organisational arrangements, peopled by a narrow group of activists, with the time, opportunity and inclination to attend seemingly endless and uninspiring meetings. Those favouring an emphasis on form were also portrayed as being mainly interested in an old-style, and not entirely healthy, preoccupation with capturing office and securing positions in the new union.

Moreover, those giving more attention to matters of union form were suspected of using their declared preference for its alleged greater transparency and certainty as a stalking horse for their less openly preferred outcomes of the distribution of power in the new union. To some extent, and especially within the confined and intimate context of the detailed negotiations, these differences were handled through humour – jokes, 'piss taking' and friendly repartee. But behind the gentle fun there was also quite serious intent. Not to put too fine a point on it, many of the protagonists felt that they were engaged in an initial struggle for the very soul of the new union.

Those wanting to be sure of success, certainty or predictability for their particular proposals for a given power or right, or for a particular sort of representation in the new union, were far more inclined to resort to suggesting the adoption of specific elements of form. They centred attention on structures, rules, procedures and so on. This was especially true where their proposals for the new union were either contested by the other parties or where their 'success' in the negotiations needed to be signalled to a wider constituency of members whose continued support was deemed necessary.

However, there was one main reason why some of the key players in the merger discussions were more inclined to emphasise union form at the relative expense of union character, and increasingly did so as the UNISON merger discussions reached their peak. They always believed that the principal organisational dimensions of form could be more easily laid down, written and published in advance, as rules and procedures. Even if the contours of union character might seem to have more to do with the actual, lived processes and relationships of union life, they maintained that these were always likely to be much more difficult to prescribe in advance of the new union itself coming into existence. Thus, centering on the new union's form was not just a matter of ideological preference on their behalf (as their opponents often alleged), but also their inclination to what they saw as a purely 'practical' approach to the merger.

Establishing aspects of UNISON's character

Attempting to frame and express features of the new union's intended future character, and convey them clearly and convincingly to others in such a way as to win their support, was indeed a very tough task. Admittedly, it was a lot easier to do it in the early stages of the negotiations, when building support for the proposed merger was the top priority, than as things moved towards a final agreement, when more interest began to focus upon the precise details of the proposed merger. In all of these circumstances, those whose approach was concerned more with trying to set an appropriately 'new' mood, tone, style or ways of working for the new union found it much harder to carry their arguments much beyond either the statement and re-statement of general principles.

In the early stages of the discussions between the then prospective partners, especially in the vision and rhetoric of being determined to create a decidedly 'new' union, what was being envisaged and argued for centred mostly on its future character. All of the language and public declarations were couched in terms that this would be no 'mere amalgamation' of what already existed in the three unions separately, no matter how good. This new union would be recognisably 'new' in at least five senses. First, it would be new in being far more than the sum of its parts. Second, it would be new in its structures and organisation, building new forms of representation into the core of its arrangements and not just 'bolting them on'. Third, it would be new in its principal aims, values and purposes, taking the union into new realms of influence and new functions. Fourthly, as a new kind of merger, the new union would be a genuine partnership of equals, despite the very different sizes and resource bases of the three merging unions and the later arrival of COHSE in the talks. Finally, it would be new in its ways of working, bringing in approaches and styles typical of modern organisations and less redolent of an older trade union past.

Given the challenges of past relationships between the three intending partners and to established ways of working represented by this promise of newness and vision of a determinedly 'new' union, it was hardly surprising that much early energy was devoted to 'talking up' the new union's character. The early advocacy of the merger also centred upon identifying the common interests and shared objectives of the suggested partners, which, it was claimed, would be best served by joining together in a truly 'new' union. By contrast, opponents of the merger tried from the outset to shift the debate from questions of vision and values to practical matters of money, authority and the difficulty of securing the effective representation of quite divergent interests in the proposed merger. But, they did not prevail: quite simply, this was not the way to challenge the protagonists of a 'new' union at this stage in the making of UNISON.

Those leading the negotiations for NUPE were most likely to focus on elements of the new union's desired character. They gave most attention to matters of the vision for the new union, and the aims and values it should espouse. In this, they laid emphasis on the distinctive 'newness' as a trade union that the merged union should manifest, breaking with some of the conventional and, as they saw it, 'out-dated' approaches still abroad in British unions, with their conventional preoccupation with producer interests and 'bureaucratic' methods. UNISON, they declared, should be a 'modern' union, reaching out to the users of services, and should be far more than a mere merger of the 'old' unions, with their established traditions, structures and ways of working.

NUPE's negotiators also wanted to establish new kinds of relationship between the union's officials and its lay members, based on 'partnership', and to shift influence from the minority of union 'activists' to the membership at large. In this, there was much talk by those leading the negotiations for NUPE of the need to establish an entirely 'new culture' for UNISON, as a 'member-centred' trade union. It was NUPE's representatives, supported by COHSE, who also led the way, both in the run up to merger and thereafter, in giving emphasis to matters of organisational change, change management and the *joint* determination of future strategy by senior paid officials and national lay representatives. For those coming from NALGO, by contrast, a main element of the new union's character had to be its leadership and control by lay members at all levels. This clear conflict of perspectives ran right through the negotiations and debates prior to merger, and continued into the new union itself, as we shall see.

Focusing on elements of UNISON's form

At the same time, of course, NUPE's team did not entirely neglect questions of union form. They stoutly defended the idea of union affiliation to the Labour Party, and established it in UNISON in a way that protected the interests of affiliated members in the former NUPE and COHSE. The senior representatives of both unions had several good reasons for taking such a stance. Each union's Deputy General Secretary was already a member of the Labour Party's National Executive Committee and one of them, Tom Sawyer, was already established in the Party as one of its leading advocates of the modernisation which was eventually to culminate in the idea of 'New Labour'.

NUPE representatives were also aware that the future fortunes of both their members and the organisation itself were probably dependent on the election of a Labour government. Continued and supportive affiliation to the Labour Party would help secure a Labour committed to the introduction of a statutory national minimum wage, the scrapping of compulsory competitive tendering and the injection of additional resources into the public services. The COHSE representatives shared this view, and also looked to a Labour government to claw back the unfair advantage which the union's representatives felt the Thatcher governments had afforded its principal rival, the Royal College of Nurses. The two unions' negotiators were also keen to establish some kind of a 'Chinese wall' in the new union between their own 'loyal' Labour Party affiliated members and the rather more critical individual Party members in NALGO, some of whom they suspected as having more 'extreme' views and connections.

The negotiators from COHSE and NUPE also argued for 'flat structures' of union management, demarcating it clearly from the much-maligned hierarchies and bureaucracies said to be too characteristic of unreformed local government and other public services. NUPE's Deputy General Secretary had been one of the TUC's early delegates to a new kind of management training for senior trade unionists held at Cranfield University's School of Management. He was keen to introduce lessons from the programme into the new union's management arrangements. In the final stages of agreement, NUPE's team also secured arrangements in rule for separate representation for low-paid and female members on the new union's lay National Executive Council, Service Group Executives and Regional Committees.

Similarly, from the moment of their entry into the joint discussions, COHSE's representatives single-mindedly fastened hard onto the objective of establishing distinct and influential 'service groups' within the new union. As the smallest of the three partners, and with the vast majority of their members working in health, they were bent on securing the creation of a section specifically for members employed in that sector. They were keen to relate virtually every aspect of the proposed new union's structure to their preferred organisation on the basis of service groups. Unless they achieved this, it was hard to see how COHSE's leadership could hope to 'sell the deal' to the members and secure a majority in favour of the new union. To their credit, COHSE's negotiators largely succeeded in this endeavour, giving ex-COHSE members and officials the only chance they had of not been numerically overwhelmed by the much larger numbers coming into UNISON from the other two partner unions.

In similar vein, it was essential for NALGO's representatives, as they saw things, to focus on some key elements of UNISON's planned form. They set out to secure a continuing element of autonomy for the new union's branches, including in respect of branch finances and the right in rule to campaign against national union policy. They wanted too to retain direct branch representation at the new union's national conference, a powerful and 'lay-controlled' inter-mediate structure at regional level and political independence of any established political party. Again, in each of these respects, they eventually enjoyed a fair amount of success, including uniquely the establishment of two separate political funds for the new union. At one point in the negotiations NALGO's repre-sentatives had even argued for separate 'divisions' for the merging unions, partly to secure their goals, one of the clearest preoccupations with one version of union *form* manifested in the whole of the preparations to establish UNISON.

The interaction of character and form

As might be expected, aspects of the character and form interacted, sometimes as proposals moved from initial vision and values to practical application. Some-times they were complimentary, sometimes they stood in mutual contradiction. Some of the key initiatives in the making UNISON figured in the guise of both character and form, such as those concerned with equal opportunities. These matters were first broached as matters of character, figuring strongly in the projection of UNISON as a self-consciously 'new' union, with a powerful vision for the equitable representation of all types of members. This commitment eventually developed into a more specific focus on proposals for self-organisation, proportionality and fair representation in rule. Interestingly enough, the precise manner in which each of these separate dimensions of the new union's equality agenda was expressed differed not only as between matters of form and character, but they did so too at different levels of the organisation and member representation. Thus, generally, the detailed proposals for self-organisation never really manifested themselves as elaborated forms, possibly contributing to the continued ambivalence and struggles about them, begun especially in NALGO, and carried through into UNISON.

Similarly, below national level, the specific regulation of fair representation for lower-paid workers was not explicit, but covered rather by guidelines and Codes of Practice, whose methods of enforcement were either unclear or weak. When, after merger, the exact composition of UNISON's first representative bodies at regional level became known, there was dismay and outrage at the apparent under-representation of manual, lower-paid and ex-COHSE members. Yet, even where explicit rules were established to ensure such representation nationally, it was sometimes difficult to secure sufficient nominations to run a competitive ballot or, even on occasion, to fill the position.

Whilst it is really the union's character which breathes life into its form, it is not unusual, perhaps especially in the making of a new union, to attempt to express many aspects of character in the guise of form. This is perhaps especially true in trade unions, which (to date at least) have given high political salience to their rules and constitutions. Hence, as has rightly been observed, 'a union's internal character will be at least partially reflected in its constitutional development', but by no means entirely and rarely to everyone's satisfaction (Turner, 1962: 297).

In highly charged political situations, such as negotiations for merger, typified by change, uncertainty and insecurity, such seemingly hard, focused and more conventional proposals as those expressed through organisational form are also more likely to 'stick' than the apparently softer and more diffuse initiatives in respect of organisational character. Yet, much of the vision of the new union as a genuinely new form of organisation, representing a positive rupture with the past and differentiating it from other 'mere' trade union mergers, was couched in the distinctive language of the projected character of the proposed merger.

A resort to reliance on elements of organisational form usually occurred in the negotiations where the pursuit of so-called 'bottom lines' by one or other partner was in question. In as much as NALGO articulated many more routine bottom lines than the other two partners did, its representatives in the negotiations were also more inclined to seek satisfaction in the formal provision of rules, structures and procedures. By contrast, NUPE in particular were more likely to do so when they were trying to limit or restrict practices claimed by NALGO representatives to be part of that union's established and inviolate practices, as for example in the two matters of 'internal' campaigning and union discipline.

The striking paradox of this is that we all know from our own experience, even in trade unions, that an understanding of an organisation's form alone is an inadequate and incomplete guide to what the organisation in question is *really* like and how it *actually* goes about its business. That often has more to do with the subtle interplay of union form and character. What is more, you certainly cannot simply 'read off' one from the other. That always needs to be remembered when analysing a union's rules, constitution, procedures or organisational structure, whether formal or informal. As Turner has commented: 'two unions of essentially the same real governmental type may present very different characters to the outside world' (Turner, 1962: 291).

There was one interesting example of this interplay of character and form, where the latter was not the victor. This was the response to the emerging consensus between the negotiators leading for COHSE and NUPE that the new union needed to break out of the familiar trade union straightjacket of an excessive preoccupation with structures, committees, formal business and meetings. These were alleged to be barriers to widening genuine membership participation in the new union, especially from lower paid and part-time workers, and to the development of new, high quality membership services characteristic of a new contract with members. This argument led to a series of training initiatives on matters of organisational change for appointed staff and lay representatives and to a focus on 'strategic management'. It led, too, to the establishment of a network of senior officers, and later senior lay representatives from UNISON's regions concerned with these two elements of the new union's ways of working. For Vesting Day of the new union, approval was given to the creation of senior paid officer posts with specific responsibility for organisational development. There followed the adoption at national level of the practice of setting an reviewing organisational objectives and targets, on both the elected representative and paid official sides, seeking to work through task groups and project management – all reflecting a very different world to that usually encountered in trade unions (see the chapters by Dempsey and Wheeler in this volume).

Of course there were always dissenters and sceptics and their doubts have not entirely gone away. But as, first, the negotiations drew to a climax and then the new union was actually approved by the membership and implemented, they did not always line up according to union of origin. For example, there were minority voices raised from all three partners (though especially from one) that the developments reported above smacked too much of modernisation, of the reforming zeal of 'Kinnockite' Labour and a naive and dangerous acceptance of 'new realism' and managerialism. Perhaps not surprisingly, the whole role and function of change and strategic management in UNISON still excite minority murmurs of doubt, suspicion and hostility today, even at some senior levels in the union.

For some people this was (and is) almost a purely visceral response. They could not, and cannot, conceive of 'management' as being a merely neutral tool of organisation. In the British context at least, and especially in the services in which UNISON members work, especially the lower paid and those at or near the typically long hierarchies of status, power and money, the very term 'management' is for them heavily redolent of class, domination, exploitation and manipulation. This is exactly what those opposed to the adoption of a 'management culture' for UNISON believed trade unionism should be designed to challenge. In their view, the simple and uncritical adoption of the language, practice and assumptions of a 'managerialist' perspective constituted a contradiction of the defining features of union character they were seeking to preserve or build in UNISON. They wanted, they said, a union predicated on the principles and practice of 'democracy', not management.

Another significant example of the interplay of UNISON's character and form, once the new union had officially been established, was a key early symbolic rule change. This was the successful campaign to persuade the union's national conference delegates to shift the wording of the union's rules from describing UNISON as a 'member-centred' union to one declared to be 'member-led'. It is important to be clear that this was not simply the post-merger exertion of organisational domination by one of the constituent partners: to succeed the proposition needed to secure support from conference delegates drawn from each of the previously separate partners, and overwhelmingly did so. Without doubt, this was one of the key influential events in the short history of UNISON and is itself worthy of detailed discussion. This apparently simple, even innocuous and almost self-evident shift of vocabulary in a trade union, touched deep into the intended identity and character of UNISON. Incorporated into the new union's very form and rules, it added up to a notable change of philosophy and orientation. It was at once both deeply emblematic, yet strictly practical and fateful in its implications. Once achieved, the change in language provided the basis and legitimation for further developments, or attempted developments, in the union's form and character.

A similar struggle over the union's identity and ways of working also occurred early in the life of the new union, at its first national conference in 1994. This was over the manner in which the whole union might properly seek to influence the Labour Party and the respective roles and powers of UNISON's National Delegate Conference on the one hand and the institutions of the Affiliated Political Fund on the other. Again this dispute went to the heart of the new union's character and to the settlement embraced in the terms of the agreement to merge. On this occasion, the initial position was upheld, but the very debate was an early indication that the matter of political influence and mobilisation, especially in respect of the Labour Party and, possibly, a future Labour Government would continue to be on the agenda, or in my terms 'unresolved'. In successfully maintaining the Affiliated Political Fund's relative autonomy from the control of UNISON's main delegate conference in this instance, nobody believed that the relationship of character to form had been fixed for all time in the new union (see Jones, this volume).

'Culture' as a resource in the struggle over UNISON's character and form

Some analysts, drawing especially on the traditions of social anthropology, have sought to chacterise organisations by reference to their 'cultures'. There is a considerable and imaginative (if somewhat confused) modern literature on the subject, especially in the field of management studies.[11] I have deliberately not used that term myself as part of my own analysis of the making of UNISON for several reasons. First, despite the vast literature on the subject, there is no agreement on its meaning in the literature. Secondly, the notion of 'organisational culture' often includes elements of both form and character, as I am using the terms here. Finally, and most interesting, I do not deploy the notion of culture in examining the merger myself precisely because it was a term deployed by some of the key protagonists themselves in their attempts to secure their own objectives in the making of UNISON. Hence, references to the 'cultures' of one or other of the partner unions or for what was intended in UNISON become rich and suggestive sources of data, essentially as 'participants' theories'.

In other words, I want to suggest that, in analysing the making of UNISON, the idea of 'union culture' should itself be a *topic* of enquiry rather than a *tool of analysis*. More particularly, the notion was advanced in a number of ways by key figures at important moments in the merger process as part of their own interpretation of what was going on, or to influence events and shape developments. In these circumstances, it is valuable to see who exactly is making use of the notion, in exactly what meaning of the term, how and to what ends. For example, once an external management consultant had used the term 'culture' to describe the main characteristics of each of the three partners on the basis of her interviews, both the language and some of the depictions were seized on for their own purposes by various protagonists (Ouroussoff, 1993). They did so to aid their own attempts to shape a distinctive philosophy, style and ways of working for the new union. They also did so especially where this either confirmed their own interpretations or where it made otherwise difficult conversations rather easier to conduct. Before long, it was not at all unusual for one or other party to refer to their own union's 'culture' or to impute 'cultural' traits to one of the others.

In this way, the notion of union culture was pressed into service as a 'vocabulary of motives', deployed to explain and underpin a particular (and sometimes it has to be said rather stereotypical) analysis of the situation claimed to obtain in one or other of the three partner unions. At a later stage in the preparations for the new union, the notion of organisational culture, or more precisely a very particular analysis of the three partner unions' respective 'cultural webs', subsequently served to provide a focus for a programme of change management in the new union.[12] The idea of union culture was also used to 'mobilise bias' in the merger discussions to legitimate assumptions and attitudes. It became a useful concept to be deployed by those aiming at skewing the agenda of the merger discussions away from a preoccupation with organisational structures and form generally and more towards organisational values and union character.

For example, NALGO was quite seriously said by some people from the other two partner unions to operate and even 'feel' rather like a local authority. This was said to manifest itself in an easy familiarity with procedural formality and enabling those used to it to work comfortably in a world of detailed written papers. They argued that this also gave rise to a specific division of responsibilities between elected lay representatives and appointed officials mirroring the world of local government. Even NALGO's head office buildings were believed by some as likely to cast a local government-like shadow over the 'culture' of the new union. For some people, this was a good enough reason alone to propose an entirely new headquarters for the new union, as a contribution towards building a distinctly UNISON culture – a move which was thwarted even before it became a formal proposition.

Similarly, representatives in the negotiations from both COHSE and NUPE unselfconsciously talked of their respective unions as being rather like 'families'. This was often used as a sort of code for describing the flavour of easy and informal relationships, suffused with high levels of often unspoken trust and reciprocity, amongst officers and between full-time officials and lay members, as they themselves perceived and represented them. In particular, this was a way of signalling that they did not think of their unions as being stuffy, bureaucratic and hierarchical. Some representatives from NUPE referred to that union's 'oral tradition', reflecting the dominant class composition of its members. They were less used to conducting discussion through detailed and complex documents, but expected appointed full-time officers to give proper attention to such matters on their behalf and to discuss them and report back by word of mouth. In like fashion, key players in the former NALGO summarily characterised parts of their own union (and its senior committees and conferences) as being very 'clever'. Their professional skills and experience made them watchful on questions of written papers and procedures, insistent on the primary role of elected lay representatives and, if skillfully recruited as allies by the 'right' package, able to assure its delivery at the NALGO conference.

Of course, all such references to 'culture' and such self-images have their organisational uses. They are sometimes helpful as initial shorthands and can serve as high levels of generalisation or as quick ways of attempting sharply to differentiate one organisation or approach from another. However, their use always needs to be explored: mistaking such shorthands for serious interpretation is always dangerous. In the matter of trade union mergers and particularly in the case of the delicate making of UNISON, using such shorthands was risky, although sometimes quite deliberate, and always threatened to descend into oversimplification and stereotyping. The particular examples I have in mind particularly here is thinking of (or describing) NALGO as ineluctably more 'bureaucratic', 'middle class', or as largely a 'bosses union' or as intrinsically more 'democratic' and 'member-led' than its two partners. Stereotypes of NUPE presented it as essentially more 'centralised', 'authoritarian', (once) 'militant' or 'working class' than the other two. COHSE was similarly portrayed as purely a 'nurses' or 'bin-man's' union, run by 'gifted amateurs', with an interest only in those prospective parts of the new union which would be directly concerned with health matters.

Presentations or orchestrations of the supposed 'culture' of each of the partners, which were actually deployed by influential individuals or at critical stages in the making of UNISON, had fateful implications for elements and stages of the negotiations to establish the new union. For example, anxieties about possibly excessive committee structures in the new union led COHSE and NUPE representatives to press the case for the importance of aims and values in the new union and their inclusion in its rulebook. This was a subtle shift from future imputed (and feared) union character to a straight concern with one feature of the form of the new union, particularly its organisational structures and rules.

In similar fashion, NALGO's conception that its 'culture' was expressed particularly in the key roles played in the union by lay representation and national conference clearly informed that union's strategy and tactics throughout the making of UNISON. For example, It underpinned the union's more extensive use of internal consultation throughout than the other two partners, the holding of an 'extra' special conference with its own papers and agenda for NALGO alone in advance of considering the Final Report. It was a reason, too, for circulation of the incomplete draft UNISON rules to NALGO's 1992 Conference together with an Executive Council critique. Again, senior representatives from NALGO who subscribed to the view that NUPE was markedly officer-dominated and centralist were understandably alarmed at rumours that there was alleged to be a plan for senior officers from NUPE to take the lion's share of senior and strategic posts in the new union. This perception clearly coloured their response to proposals for both posts and their filling in the new union.

Some of these depictions of the partners' cultures by themselves, and of each other, were elicited through surveys of opinion and focus group discussions, both of which were used to inform elements of the merger negotiations. They were clear enough ways of gathering undiluted and genuinely held, if sometimes over-generalised and ideological, representations or images of the partners or of issues to resolve, especially from those with a particular and usually unrevealed axe to grind. That is perfectly acceptable, provided always that is how such uses of 'culture' are to be understood as figuring in the merger talks. Often they were not, but were simply taken at face value, as 'objective' descriptions of one or other of the partner unions. As I have argued, of course, they were no less influential upon proceedings for all that.

The point of these examples is to underline the argument that self-images, short-hand depictions, projections, simple characterisations and generalisations about 'union culture' have quite different uses for those organisational members deploying or responding to them as against those whose task is to understand their organisational use. Participants' theories and interpretations are an invaluable source of data and contribute to explaining behaviour, but they are deeply problematic if understood as 'authentic' portrayals of the world. Many of them, including powerful, if often diffuse, self-images of the partner unions, were elements of the patterns of myth and assumption promoted in the discussions, which also coloured proposals and responses to proposals. Some even constituted self-fulfilling prophecies. I have alluded to them here for two main reasons. First, they serve as clear examples of the influential role of discourse and rhetoric in organisational practice. Second, they were of particular salience in the merger discussions, particularly in underpinning each of the partners' views of the others and of the various proposals for UNISON's suggested form and character. Thus, they contributed to the shaping of the new union, as well as to some of those unresolved matters carried through into the on-going life of UNISON.

'Unresolved' issues

All complex organisations, including unions, necessarily entail elements of balance between conflicting perspectives or priorities and embrace continuing dimensions of contest, despite the attempts of senior figures, or observers, on occasion to present them as essentially unitary or unified and purely corporate bodies. Attempts to overlook or deny matters of organisational contest should always be seen for what they are, part of the inherent and constantly emergent struggle to establish dominant practices or discourses. Some of the unresolved matters in UNISON did not only become so because of the merger; they were already evident in one or more of the partners *prior* to the discussions between them. What the merger did was to make such matters more explicit or visible, or at least provided a new opportunity to address them.

In the making of the new union, there were eight principal matters of unresolved balance and contest, which were carried through into UNISON and which still figure to some extent today. In no particular order, they are as follows:

- What should be the appropriate balance of influence, resources, membership identity and emphasis as between general or 'whole union' (UNISON) matters on the one hand as against those concerned more particularly with the interests of particular services, industries or occupations on the other. This is best illustrated in the debate about the respective roles and significance of service groups as against regions and national bodies in the new union, such as the National Executive and National Delegate Conference. The issue only really loomed large once COHSE determinedly entered the talks with its own agenda, almost 8 months after NALGO and NUPE had begun their discussions, with an initial joint declaration of the main rationale for a prospective merger.
- How the balance of the union's resources, activities, power and accountability should be distributed between UNISON's 'centre' (often, but not always, meaning national level) and its constituent regions and branches as well as between staffing and other activities. This is well exemplified by the prolonged and difficult debates about the central collection of members' subscriptions and the amount of branch 'retention' and still figures as part of the union's recently concluded 5-year strategic review.
- What should constitute the proper relationship between (mostly) appointed full-time officials and elected lay representatives and members in the conduct of the union and which positions, including those occupied by paid officials, should be subject to periodic re-election. This matter has surfaced in many

different ways. It lies behind the shift from the originally agreed language of a 'member-centred' centred union to one declared to be 'member-led'. It figures in rules to regulate appointed officers' relationships with branches and other levels of lay representation and in the development of the role and functions of elected Regional Convenors. And it is central to the (so far unsuccessful) proposals to subject certain paid full-time official posts to election.

- How best the arrangements for 'self-organisation' amongst particular groups of so-called 'disadvantaged' members (the language came from NALGO) should be reconciled with more mainstream methods of membership representation and decision-making in the new union (including proportionality and fair representation) without weakening or distorting either. This tension long predates the formation of UNISON itself and lay at the heart of some difficult, and occasionally bitter, disputes within NALGO in the 1980s where these innovative elements of trade union organisational form had been pioneered. These arrangements also raised the role and focus of some paid officials, working with self-organised groups.

- What would and would not constitute legitimate forms of 'campaigning' at branch and other levels, and with what acceptable use of union resources or arenas, to shape or change UNISON policy. This has been tied up with a series of enquiries in the new union, especially at branch level and, in the minds of some protagonists goes to the heart of other matters of resource allocation and democratic rights and responsibility.

- How and through which authoritative mechanisms the new union should engage in and 'position' itself in politics. This includes how the union as a whole might legitimately seek to influence the Labour Party and the policies of a Labour Government, given the decision to create two distinct political funds in UNISON, one affiliated to the Labour Party and one not so affiliated. More broadly, what explicitly political activities might have legitimate recourse to UNISON resources and which might be deemed to be *ultra vires*?

- How to establish a proper balance between the 'traditional' union concerns of collective bargaining and the conventional approach to terms and conditions of employment and conventional politics on the one hand and the 'newer' agendas of trade unionism on the other. This latter perspective increasingly focuses on providing more individual member services, making explicit provision for matters concerning identity politics, giving greater emphasis to learning and even coming to terms with the agenda of post-modernism.

- How, or whether, it would prove possible to establish a single identity, ethos or 'culture' for UNISON, given the very wide disparity of incomes, backgrounds (including class), status, authority, occupations, industries, ways of working and outlooks of different groups of members of the new union. This diversity was bound to be overlaid by the traditions and identities of the three partner unions, for some time at least. So, would it be possible to establish a new and genuinely inclusive or pluralist culture for all members, or would a dominant mode emerge and if so, why and how?

There are no absolutely right or wrong answers to any of these matters. But the balance of either their resolution or their continuing aspect as matters of contest has had important consequences for how the union goes about its business. For example, the question of placing greater emphasis on service groups and sections, and the issue of identity politics, is seen to affect the levels of attachment to the union felt by certain groups of staff and members (or potential members). The method of collecting subscriptions and agreed level of branch retention matters for how the union's resources are deployed and which initiatives are pursued or abandoned. The issue of the possible development of a distinctive, recognisable and genuinely inclusive culture for UNISON affects the perception and image of UNISON in the wider world.

Matters such as these are rarely, if ever, finally settled in trade unions nor has their expression or the particular emphasis given to them in UNISON been utterly constant since first they arose in the joint negotiations and earlier, before UNISON came into being. To a degree, even regarding them as 'unresolved' is itself somewhat misleading: there is a very real sense in which these matters are *intrinsic* to UNISON, part of its very lifeblood. Even if such matters are resolved in one way or another, whether temporarily or for a longer period, other similarly vexed and complex questions are likely to arise in their place. That is the nature of organisation and especially of trade unionism.

Conclusion

In this chapter, I have attempted to show how an understanding of UNISON's making can be started, by employing a distinction between the form and character of the union, both as envisaged and in practice. In the early stages of the discussions between the then prospective partners, especially in the vision and rhetoric of being determined to create a decidedly 'new' union, what was being envisaged and argued for centred mostly on its future character. All of the language and public declarations were couched in terms that this would be no 'mere amalgamation' of what already existed in the three unions separately, no matter how good. This new union was intended to be recognisably 'new' in many senses, as we have seen, all of them captured in its new character. It would be new in being far more than the sum of its parts. It would also aim to be new in its structures and organisation, building forms of representation into the core of its arrangements and not just 'bolting them on'. It would be new in its principal aims, values and purposes, taking the union into new realms of influence and new functions. It would be new in being designed to express genuine partnership between the constituent unions and their members and not assuming domination by one of them. Finally, it would be new in its ways of working, bringing in approaches and styles typical of modern organisations and less redolent of an older trade union past.

Despite the early emphasis all round on these defining features of the proposed new union's character, it was perhaps inevitable that, once more detailed questions of power and resources were broached, questions of the union's form would soon arise. After all, this was more familiar territory for most of those involved in the negotiations. The strictly empirical world inhabited by seasoned trade unionists, such as most of those responsible for making UNISON, is composed of negotiated deals, industrial relations procedures, and debates around motions and amendments. It is typified by conflicts of interest and divisions of opinion that are usually pragmatically resolved by resort to constitutions, specified rights and duties and rule-governed structures. In this world, everyone is at ease with the greater formality and explicitness associated with organisational form, rather than the more elusive notion of character, except when it comes to the matter of conference speeches and oratorical mobilisations to action.

The lawyers advising the three intending partners and the public authorities, such as the Certification Officer, charged in statute with overseeing union mergers, were also more likely to prefer to see proposals expressed in terms of form rather than character in specific rules and regulations. Meeting their requirements was bound increasingly to shift the emphasis of discussions towards union form in the making of UNISON, at the expense of a fuller consideration of the new union's character. Those who continued to stress the importance of this latter feature of the proposed new union were thought by others to be rather unworldly, utopian even. Their critics accused them of seeming to want to secure the merger at almost any cost.

There is also a sense in which, *a fortiori*, negotiations which entailed giving up familiar, and cherished, organisational structures and rules were typically and somewhat unavoidably what Alan Fox dubbed 'low trust' situations, and focus disproportionately on matters of form.[13] Low trust is typified by the development of elaborate, non-discretionary systems of rules, procedures, checks, routinisation, imposed compliance and, crucial to the conduct of union mergers, bargaining – as Jeremy Waddington's historical analysis has correctly indicated. This was even more likely to be the case where there was a pre-history of conflict between elements of the intending merging parties, as there was in UNISON's case. It was also predictable where one party or other to the talks had a very specific set of goals it wished to secure (which there also was). It was also only to be expected where there was some anxiety that a key danger to avoid was the dominance of one party or element to the deal (which there also was).

On the other hand, organisational design in unions, as elsewhere, might be thought to be increasingly required to deal with matters of ambiguity, uncertainty and ever-shifting boundaries in the contemporary 'post-modern' world. It follows that the various dimensions of organisational character would be given proportionately more attention than traditional matters of form in the new union. In a striking and colourful image, Silvia Gherardi (1995) pictures a (female) a dragon symbolically tearing up a (male) organisation chart in her quest to uncover the dynamics of gender in organisations, often lying deep in what she calls their 'shadowlands'.

Emphasis upon choice, play, autonomy and flexibility might be all well and good for those trade union members whose work responsibilities increasingly manifest some or all of these features. Of course they would inclining one away from the necessarily more prescriptive world of organisational form, not just for employment issues but also for trade union purposes.[14] But where workers' jobs are still typified by routine, subordination and lack of choice (as is the case for large numbers of low-paid UNISON members), too much emphasis upon organisational character would (and, in practice, did) open the proponents of such an approach to a charge of misplaced romanticism. More seriously, such a focus appeared to its critics to leave the field clear for those UNISON members with more space and discretion to shape the union in their own interests. In other words, some sorts of members' needs might have been better protected by paying more attention to matters of union form, through the familiar mechanisms of written rules, constitutional rights and so on.

So, despite the various initiatives to capture the new union's ethos in advance, talk of matters to do with the its character in the merger discussions themselves was always bound to sound rather strange. It could all too easily appear somewhat vague or 'waffly', even exciting suspicion and being seen as potentially dangerous. Those pursuing this line were usually met by a combination of puzzlement, cynical amusement and benign tolerance. On occasion, their forays were also counteracted by the proposal of a specific rule or other provision. This was particularly the response where it was felt that behind an emphasis on the new union's character lurked a more sinister potential consequence, providing scope for either subtle manipulation or a decisive shift in the focus and direction of the new union, once it came into being. In tolerant mood, the response was to incline simply to indulgence, on the assumption that 'it wouldn't make much difference anyway'. But, when seen as potentially damaging or challenging, the response was to neutralise or reverse the drift to matters of character by resort to a focus on dimensions of the new union's proposed form. Nevertheless, in the end, not even this degree of single-mindedness could guarantee a once-and-for-all settlement of some of the most intractable issues in the making of UNISON. After all, that is precisely the continuing social, constitutional and emotional lifeblood of the organisation.

Notes

1 Throughout the paper I have chosen to use the term 'merger' to describe the joining together of previously separate trade unions, encompassing both amalgamations and transfers of engagement, each of which has a distinct legal (if not necessarily sociological) meaning within the British context. More importantly, in the case of UNISON's formation, for a long time the uses of both 'merger' and even 'amalgamation' were mostly eschewed, with references to the creation of a 'new union' being preferred. This was until the requirements of the legal processes regulating union mergers in Britain required the adoption of the term 'amalgamation'.

2 I was first approached to help with the planned discussions between NALGO and NUPE in late 1988. An immediate issue was my own greater familiarity with NUPE and personal friendship with some of that union's key figures likely to be involved in the discussions. Hence, it was agreed between myself and the two (then) Deputy General Secretaries of NALGO (Alan Jinkinson) and NUPE (Tom Sawyer) delegated to carry forward the negotiations that it would be helpful for a second

academic adviser to be brought in. In part, this was to counteract any fears or dangers of 'bias' towards one of the then two prospective partners. My own proposal of Mike Terry as a second adviser, who had previously undertaken successful studies of local union organisation in Local Government and was an established expert on union workplace organisation, was subsequently accepted by both unions. When COHSE joined the discussions in August 1990, one aspect of the terms of the union's engagement with the already established processes was that it should nominate its 'own' academic adviser, to assist with preparations for the negotiations and with the joint discussions themselves. COHSE's nomination of an adviser was Mick Carpenter, who had previously been an active member of COHSE, and had already produced an extremely well received history of that union. Mick also brought considerable expertise to the discussions in the field of social policy, particularly in areas of concern to the three unions and, hopefully, to the new union.

Throughout the merger discussions, the three of us acted as advisers and 'facilitators' to various aspects of the joint discussions. In addition, Mike Terry attended a number of NALGO's separate 'side' meetings and occasionally offered NALGO some independent advice and Mick Carpenter did the same for COHSE. Although I attended some such NUPE meetings, I also attended separate meetings with representatives of NALGO and, later, with COHSE. I saw my principal task as giving advice to all three partners and preparing papers for discussion between them, especially seeking to resolve points of difference and other knotty problems standing in the way of agreement. During the course of the discussions and into the first year of the new union, I wrote in excess of one hundred papers. Preparation for the merger was, in truth, a very *paper-driven* process, a feature which some observers have remarked may have favoured those more used to such a way of conducting trade union affairs. For 22 months up to mid-1994 (one year after Vesting Day), I was seconded to work half-time with the three partners and then UNISON, to help with implementing the agreed arrangements for the new union. The notes and papers I wrote and collected at this time are currently in my personal possession and are presently archived at University of Southampton New College. The four main joint reports to the unions' annual national conferences were all published in the unions in 1989, 1990, 1991 and 1992.

3 This was confirmed in early 'focus group' research undertaken on images of NALGO and NUPE held by members.

4 For case studies of the early effects of 'contracting out' upon trade unionism and industrial relations in local government, see Ascher (1987) and, in health, Milne (1987). Marsh (1992) has a useful, if somewhat over-sanguine review of the effects on trade unions of the various elements of privatisation.

5 Recalling the dispute in his later autobiography, the Conservative Health Minister at the time, Norman Fowler, wrote that an encounter with Rodney Bickerstaffe, the newly elected General Secretary of NUPE showed Alan Fisher's successor to be determined to win. 'I saw no prospect of any sensible compromise'. By contrast, direct secret talks with Albert Spanswick, COHSE's General Secretary were friendly and paved the way for a later pre-rehearsed exchange in negotiations. In the end, Fowler regretted, Spanswick was over-ruled by 'the hard men of his committee' (Fowler, 1991: 173–77).

6 This contrasts markedly with the pioneering work in the field by the Webbs (1920a, b), although even their hugely impressive work was based principally upon documents and interview, rather than prolonged observation and involvement. Three exceptions to this generalisation are the studies by Lipset, Trow and Coleman (1956), Moran (1974), Batstone, Boraston and Frenkel, (1977) and Beynon and Austrin (1994).

7 Amongst the best, and most relevant, in this regard, are Coates and Topham (1991), Lloyd (1990) and Beynon and Austrin (1994).

8 I hesitate to depend on just one or two references as overviews of this dauntingly vast field. However, those unfamiliar with it could do worse than begin with Morgan (1986).
9 The most notable exception here is the work of Edelstein and Warner (1975).
10 For example, see Goldstein (1952), Roberts (1956) and Hughes (1967).
11 Gareth Morgan defines organisational culture as 'the slogans, evocative language, symbols, stories, myths, ceremonials, rituals, and patterns of behaviour that decorate the surface of organizational life (and) merely gives clues to the existence of a much deeper and all-pervasive system of meaning' (Morgan, 1986: 133). See also Hofstede (1991), with its inspiring sub-title, 'software of the mind'.
12 I have in mind here the innovative work of the Cranfield School of Management in this field.
13 See the brilliant analysis in Fox (1974).
14 For a discussion of the possible implications of postmodernism for organisation, see Hassard and Parker (eds) (1993).

References

Ascher, K. (1987) *The Politics of Privatisation: Contracting Out Public Services*, London: Macmillan.

Albrow, M. (1997) *Do Organizations Have Feelings?*, London: Routledge.

Batstone, E., Boraston, I. and Frenkel, S. (1977) *Shop Stewards in Action*, Oxford: Blackwell.

Beynon, H. and Austrin, T. (1994), *Masters and Servants*, London: Rivers Oram.

Blackburn, R. (1967) *Union Character and Social Class*, London: Batsford.

Carpenter, M. (1988) *Working for Health: the History of COHSE*, London: Lawrence and Wishart.

Coates, K. and Topham, T. (1991) *The Making of the Labour Movement*, Oxford, Blackwell.

Edelstein, J. D. and Warner, M. (1975) *Comparative Union Democracy*, London: Allen and Unwin.

Fisher, A. and Dix, B. (1974) *Low Pay and How to End It*, London: Pitman.

Fowler, N. (1991) *Ministers Decide: A Personal Memoir of the Thatcher Years*, London: Chapman.

Fox, A. (1974) *Beyond Contract: Work, Power and Trust Relations*, London: Faber and Faber.

Fryer, R. W. (1979) 'British trade unions and the cuts', *Capital and Class*, 8.

Fryer, R. and Williams, S. (1993) *A Century of Service*, London: Lawrence and Wishart.

Fryer, R., Fairclough, A. and Manson, T. (1974) *Organisation and Change in the National Union of Public Employees*, London: NUPE.

Gherardi, S. (1995) *Gender, Symbolism and Organizational Cultures*, London: Sage.

Goldstein, J. (1952) *The Government of British Trade Unions*, London: Longmans.

Hassard, J. and Parker, M. (1993) *Post-Modernism and Organization*, London: Sage.

Held, D. (1987) *Models of Democracy*, Oxford: Polity.

Hofstede, G. (1991) *Cultures and Organizations: Software of the Mind*, London: McGraw Hill.

Hughes, J. (1967) *Trade Union Structure and Government*, London: HMSO.

Hyman, R. (1989) *The Political Economy of Industrial Relations*, London: Macmillan.

Kelly, J. (1998) *Rethinking Industrial Relations*, London: Routledge.

Lipset, S. M., Trow, M. and Coleman, J. (1956) *Union Democracy: the Internal Politics of the International Typographical Union*, Glencoe, Ill: Free Press.

Marsh, D. (1992) *The New Politics of British Trade Unionism*, London: Macmillan.

Mills, C. W. (1959) *The Sociological Imagination*, Oxford: Clarendon.

Mills, C. W. (1963) 'Situated actions and vocabularies of motive', in Horowitz, I. L. (ed.) *Power, Politics and People*, New York: Free Press.

Milne, R. (1987) 'Competitive tendering in the NHS', *Public Administration*, pp. 156–60.

Minkin, L. (1991) *The Contentious Alliance*, Edinburgh: Edinburgh University Press.

Moran, M. (1974) *The Union of Post Office Workers*, London: Macmillan.

Morgan, G. (1986) *Images of Organization*, London: Sage.

Ouroussof, A. (1993) 'UNISON: building a new culture', unpublished presentation to UNISON Senior Management team.

Roberts, B. C. (1956) *Trade Union Government and Administration in Great Britain*, London: Bell.

Turner, H. A. (1962) *Trade Union Growth, Structure and Policy: a Comparative Study of the Cotton Unions*, London: Allen and Unwin.

Undy, R., Ellis, V., McCarthy, W. E. J. and Halmos, A. (1981), *Change in Trade Unions*, London: Hutchinson.

Waddington, J. (1995) *The Politics of Bargaining: The Merger Process and British Trade Union Structural Development 1892–1987*, London: Mansell.

Waddington, J. (1997) 'External and internal influences on union mergers: a response to Roger Undy', *Historical Studies in Industrial Relations*, 3.

Webb, S. and Webb, B. (1920a) *Industrial Democracy*, London: Hutchinson.

Webb, S. and Webb, B. (1920b) *History of British Trade Unions*, London: Hutchinson.

Webb, S. and Webb, B. (1975) *A Constitution for the Socialist Commonwealth of Great Britain*, Cambridge: Cambridge University Press.

Willman, P., Morris, T. and Aston, B. (1993) *Union Business*, Cambridge: Cambridge University Press.

4   UNISON's management of the merger and beyond

Michael Dempsey

Management in a union

The argument of this chapter is that UNISON managed the merger process in ways that, flawed as they inevitably were, contained examples of good practice from which future union mergers can learn. An understanding of the challenging task of creating a new union with a new culture over a lengthy period helped to create an awareness within UNISON of the importance of good management during that difficult journey. UNISON's actions since Vesting Day have reinforced that awareness, with the result that it has developed a strong and substantially shared commitment to valuing good management as an important and significant factor in the achievement of its goals. This commitment may in turn have led to a quality of management higher than would have otherwise been the case although this assertion has not yet been empirically tested.

The importance of UNISON's actions is that the concept of management within a trade union has not, until recently, been a comfortable one. Those who work for unions have often been generically described as 'officers' or organisers. But as the performance of managerial tasks becomes more overt, so it is necessary to identify those who are performing those tasks and to endeavour to define their roles. It is not a task that has been recognised widely in the past. Indeed, NALGO's programme of management development courses for senior managers, started in the late 1980s, was probably unique in unions in the UK at the time. Senior union managers had always been required to practise management skills and this programme for the first time recognised that management was a defined role for which training was required.

The discomfort associated with the notion of management within trade unions is reflected in the 'deep ambivalence towards the concept of management itself' which Ouroussof (1993) found in the UNISON partner unions, and more generally by Orlans (1991: 11) who talked of the 'traditional ideological resistance amongst trade unions to the concept of "management".' Indeed, management has been a controversial and difficult concept not only in trade unions but in voluntary organisations generally. Paton and Hooker suggest that the problems are both linguistic and value-based, arguing that 'to use the language of management means buying into a tradition of thinking and practice that is at best inappropriate to the needs of voluntary organisations and at worst a real threat to some of their central values and greatest strengths' (1990: 8). Others, however, have pointed to the value of voluntary sector managers understanding, for example, the way people react with each other or with organisations. 'It may not feel good to be managed but it is still better to be organised than disorganised' (Handy 1988: 4).

In academic literature, a recognition of the existence of the defined role of union manager has been made by few. One substantive discussion of union managers as a category is by Dunlop (1990) who comments that union management has until recently been regarded as an oxymoron. He makes the point that his observations are confined to the United States and this is clear in the trade union model applied which involves extensive elections of senior managers, rare though not unknown in the UK. Nevertheless, the analysis is of interest. Dunlop compares the role of 'executives' in four fields – business, government, academia and unions – and suggests that there are six commonalities among these categories of manager: in environmental analysis; setting roles and priorities; selection and development of people; shaping the structure of the organisation; negotiating and consensus-building skills; and generating and introducing innovation. He goes on to identify six differences between the four fields which suggest that distinctive elements between management in the four fields are largely of degree rather than being fundamentally different. For example, there is a discussion of where managers in the four sectors fall on a continuum of efficiency and equity, the analysis of which suggests that union managers are in similar positions on the spectrum to academic and government managers.

Such a discussion echoes the notion of the conflict between administrative and representative rationality identified by Child *et al.* (1973). The former emphasises efficiency and outcomes; the latter, democratic checks and balances. Yet in managing a union, as Willman *et al.* (1993) point out, both of these rationalities have to co-exist and it could be argued that a key skill in managing a union is the management of that co-existence. In their study of the activities of union managers, Willman *et al.* examine the management roles of union finance officers. Three were identified, those of administrator, manager and expert. *Administrators* were concerned with day-to-day affairs and their function was distinct from, and subordinate to, policy making. *Managers* combined long-term planning and short term management and their role was comparable with the role of the Financial Controller in a business. *Experts* were primarily advisory, recognising that administrative decisions arose from policy making and contributing expertise on budgeting and financial planning.

One has a glimpse here of the real world of union management in which managers seek to balance the complex relationships between the component parts of an organisation which aspires to be at once collective, democratic and effective in delivering services. Within trade unions one of the most difficult and sensitive sets of relationships is that between union officers, in most unions the largest employed group, and central union management functions. Union officers have to balance a range of complex relationships, for example with individual members, branches, regional organisation, and employers and their representatives at several levels. The management of such union officers requires great sensitivity to these complex and contradictory forces. Kelly and Heery (1994) found that in most unions officers were in practice subject to dual systems of control, from lay representatives and superiors, but with comparatively light control from the latter, a finding that Brooke (1984) identifies as characteristic of many voluntary organizations. The majority of unions studied by Kelly and Heery argued that their officers had a great deal of autonomy from central, 'superior' management in their work although this autonomy was intruded upon in three sets of circumstances: the allocation of responsibilities; a crisis in the officer's work; and to further a national campaign or policy initiative. Officers themselves valued their autonomy and were highly focused on serving the members for which they were responsible, with limited sympathy for policy initiatives which blurred that focus. A majority regarded accountability to the members as more important than accountability to union management; arguably a false dichotomy but an important perspective for any union to understand.

These important studies demonstrate the importance of management issues for the study and practice of trade unions, and suggest that despite that they are often neglected or oversimplified. The remainder of this chapter will show how UNISON, through its experience of the merger process, came to accept the importance of confronting issues of management head-on and to see them as values central to the achievement of the union's objectives.

Managing the merger

UNISON is the result of the largest and most complex merger in British union history. There were enormous cultural, organisational and democratic differences between the three organisations which were reflected in and accounted for the many years' discussion and decision making. The richness of complexity, compared for example with mergers in other sectors, was enhanced by the democratic structures of the merging unions. The welding of the new organisation into a unified whole, therefore, was a daunting enterprise.

Managing a merger represents one of the most challenging tasks for any manager. Few are trained for it; few will experience it more than once in a lifetime. In the trade union movement it has until recently been comparatively rare for much resources to be devoted to management training at all. Yet mergers are significant life events for thousands of staff and millions of members. Hundreds of millions of pounds are involved. It is not unreasonable to expect unions to manage the merger process in ways which take account of experiences and practices in other organizational contexts. Nevertheless, as the account presented below makes clear, the importance of processes and structures of management was not grasped at the start of the process; rather it was learned and developed as the merger unfolded.

Stages in the merger process

The following analysis of the phases of the UNISON merger uses the framework adopted by Buono and Bowditch (1989) who suggest that the merger process can be broken down into seven stages as shown in Figure 4.1.

Pre-combination

The initial impetus for the creation of a new union came from conference decisions in NALGO and NUPE, with a similar decision by COHSE the following year. Cartwright and Cooper (1996: 115) propose a checklist to improve management of the pre-combination stage. This involves knowing your own

The Organisational Combination Process

Stage	Characteristics
Stage 1 Precombination	Degree of environmental uncertainty (technological, market, sociopolitical) may vary, but respective organisations are relatively stable and members are relatively satisfied with the status quo.
Stage 2 Combination planning	Environmental uncertainty increases which precipitates discussion concerning merger/takeover possibilities, fears that unless the union grows, it may fail; the union is still relatively stable and discussion is confined to top executive level.
Stage 3 Announced combination	Environmental uncertainty continues to increase, influencing decision, the union is still relatively stable and while members have mixed emotions concerning the merger, expectations are raised.
Stage 4 Initial combination process	Organisational instability increases and is characterised by structural ambiguity (high) and some cultural and role ambiguity (low), although members are generally co-operative at beginning, goodwill quickly erodes.
Stage 5 Formal physical–legal combination	Organisational instability increases as all these increase, more rigid organisations take on some more fluid characteristics for a period, conflict between stakeholders increases.
Stage 6 Combination aftermath	High instability, lack of co-operation and 'us–them' mentality exist, violated expectations lead to mutual hostilities structural ambiguity decreases, but cultural and role ambiguity remains high, dissenters leave the organisation.
Stage 7 Psychological combination	Organisational stability recurs as ambiguities are clarified, expectations are revised, renewed co-operation and tolerance, time-consuming process.

Figure 4.1 Phases in the merger process. Adapted from Buono and Bowditch (1989: 88)

culture, researching that of the prospective partner and arriving on day one with an agenda of people issues for discussion to test implicit or pre-formed ideas of culture. The objective is to be in a position to re-consider the whole idea if it appears that a successful marriage is not likely to result. In practice, from my own experience of events, nothing like this happened in the early stages. In NALGO at least there was very little attention paid to the prospect and consequences of merger. Early discussions involved small numbers of key people; staff were informed as and when it was considered important in individual cases. But many NALGO headquarters staff simply did not want to know details of the proposed merger and I was criticised for over-briefing on the issue in team briefing sessions. It is likely that this was a consequence of wish-fulfilment; staff in an organisation in which change was largely unwelcome just hoped the whole thing would go away.

Combination planning

In a union context this stage covers the lengthy period when negotiations take place, leading to decisions on how the merger is to be effected. Decisions by lay members are involved throughout the process; in the UNISON merger confer-ence decisions were made in four successive years (1989–92) by two of the partner unions with an additional special conference held by NALGO.

Buono and Bowditch (1989: 92) believe that early combination planning should focus on: determining the goals of the combination; selecting an appro-priate merger strategy;·determining appropriate merger criteria·devising a way to gain employee support; and commitment to make the transition work.

It is unlikely that any union merger processes have ever come close to these prescriptions and in a democratic organisation they are even more difficult to take on board. UNISON, however, did undertake a 'cultural survey' of the three partner unions (Ouroussof, 1993). This arose from the initial work undertaken by Adam Klein, a consultant whose brief was to produce management structures for the new union, who had proceeded on the classic basis that structure had to take into account culture. When his appointment was terminated, the Senior Management Team (the three general secretaries and other senior staff respon-sible for overseeing the merger) accepted this argument and took over direct management of the contract for the survey initiated by Klein. It was not, how-ever, obtained until after the decision to merge had been taken. The report itself is discussed below. At this stage, it should be noted that commissioning it was certainly a unique initiative amongst British unions and it was a decision which demonstrates the importance which, even at this stage, was attached to cultural integration.

Despite this initiative in practice very few positive decisions affecting the hundreds of people who were employed by the three merging unions were made before the ballot, although extensive staff protection measures had been put in place in 1992. In NALGO there had been demands by the staff unions that all structures should be determined before the ballot and this had resulted in the

Secretariat producing a series of position papers on how managers saw the new union looking; the other partners obviously had their own positions. The intention had been to have staffing structures in place before Vesting Day and the enforced change in consultant support seriously inhibited this objective.

Announced combination

Some research on mergers (Buono and Bowditch, 1989: 98; Cartwright and Cooper, 1996: 118) attaches great importance to the handling of what they see as a moment of shock or distress as people learn of impending dramatic change. It may be difficult to take full account of this in announcing the result of the ballot confirming that merger will take place. This is a highly political event. It comprises, as it did in UNISON, a press conference and a letter to staff; though, of course, in practice staff would have heard the result, probably on the grapevine, very quickly. There is no research on the effect of this although the management of change workshops, referred to below, did reveal many feelings of loss. Buono and Bowditch (1989: 197) note that virtually every case study of a merger reports communication shortcomings, at this moment above all. They suggest the need for a well-formulated and transparent communications strategy designed to reassure as well as inform.

Within unions, there is a widespread but incorrect tendency to make assumptions about staff commitment to changes that have been agreed through proper democratice procedures For example, a majority of non-organising staff may not have been directly involved in the negotiations or campaigning. Their joy at the announcement cannot be assumed and there are bound to be concerns about the future amongst all staff. This is demonstrated by Thorpe who (1991: 67) found that 35.7 per cent of staff in his survey of activists and staff in the North East District of NALGO were unsure of the benefits accruing from merger. Union managers need to realise that creating commitment amongst staff is a key responsibility since it cannot be taken for granted.

Communicating reassurance to staff about their future is important in this context. I have referred to the staff protection measures put in place in 1992. In practice there were stresses and strains about exactly who would be allowed to take early retirement and the delay in implementing voluntary severance caused a setback to cultural integration. The reason for the delay, however, was managerial in that management wanted only to release staff where economies of scale could be achieved. Structural decisions were required before this objective could be implemented.

Cartwright and Cooper also say (1996: 122) that employees in merger situations have a tendency to attend to information which reinforces their worst fears regardless of the validity of the source. Some of the astonishing rumours which circulated in UNISON support this view. Staff were perfectly prepared to believe that the Senior Management Team were all to be given limousines, and serious worry was caused by a counterfeit management report circulated which suggested that all those with less than 2 years' service would have their contracts terminated. Management acted on several fronts to assist and facilitate the announcement process. A staff newsletter was started, edited by a journalist, which conveyed hard news, features and contained a letters page in which staff could ask anonymous questions which were guaranteed a response from a member of the Senior Management Team, a practice similar to that used by the John Lewis Partnership and innovative within a union. Reactive communications followed particular events. Managers individually briefed their staff when they thought it appropriate as well as, in one or two cases, in a strategic, co-ordinated way. However, lack of staff resources led to communication becoming piecemeal and it was not possible to develop the required strategic communication policy. Certainly, UNISON's experience supports the importance of communicating strategically, openly and regularly. It is a lesson of which the Senior Management Team remains acutely aware.

Initial combination

Buono and Bowditch (1989: 96) characterise this period as being one of increasing instability in which goodwill can quickly dissipate as cultural and role uncertainty increases. People become aware of possible cultural conflict and go through a process of cultural learning that heightens their awareness of their own culture and highlights the differences between the organizations. Typically, organisations appoint joint committees to resolve differences and negotiate to establish policies and procedures. Rarely, they say, are there explicit attempts to deal with the cultural issues that underlie structural concerns.

It is a characteristic of trade unions that, given the low formal priority they traditionally attach to such matters, it will only be after a merger decision has been taken that managerial and human resources issues will be addressed in detail. This can lead, as it did in UNISON's case, to a perception amongst the staff that their concerns were a lot lower down the agenda than many other structural issues. Perceptions are important, even if ill-founded. UNISON, however, did undertake activities which in a union merger context were at the time probably innovative and reflected good management practice. First, counselling was available for staff through an Employee Assistance Programme, extended from one partner union to the whole. Buono and Bowditch suggest (1989: 208) that individual counselling may be required to help people 'get a grip' on what is happening in their lives. The take-up of this service was very high; analysed by reference to employee population , access for counselling increased by 81 per cent between 1993 and 1994 and by a further 25 per cent between 1994 and 1995.

Secondly, UNISON, which had established a 'Management of Change Taskforce' to try to develop an organisation development (OD) approach to change and eventually an OD Unit (see Wheeler, this volume), commenced a programme of management of change workshops throughout the country. These were run by Patricia Hodgins and followed the approach of focusing on how to cope with the stress and anxiety created by mergers by the use of a bereavement model of reaction to change (Buono and Bowditch, 1989: 115). (They are discussed in detail in a later section.) Typically, people realised that it was not disloyal or reprehensible to feel bad.

Thirdly, an explicit attempt was made to use management development as a tool in facilitating the better management of the process. Senior managers attended a compulsory programme at Cranfield School of Management which had at its core the identification of the dominant cultural paradigms of the partner organisations through analysing their 'cultural webs' (Johnson 1988: 84) followed by an assessment of what the future cultural web of UNISON would look like. (The idealised web is shown in Figure 4.2.) The commitment to the programme shows a high managerial awareness of the need to develop managerial skills and understanding even at that early stage, an awareness that had been developed and learned through the earlier merger stages. The following year, a second programme was run which, *inter alia*, revisited the cultural web and assessed how far it was in place (see below). The Senior Management Team itself attended facilitated strategy workshops to develop its own ability to manage the merger.

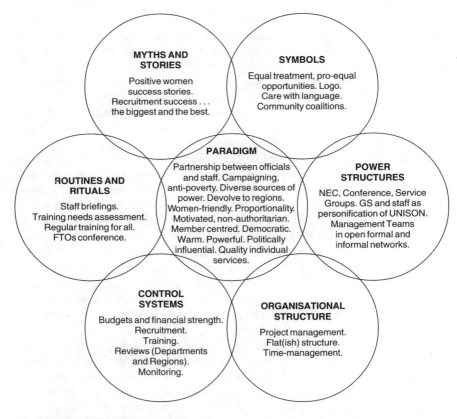

Figure 4.2 The UNISON 'cultural web'

Formal physical–legal combination

It is suggested above that cultures should be identified, surfaced and their implications confronted from a very early stage in the merger process. By the time physical combination is effected, it follows, the cultural implications of the merger should be being carefully and sensitively managed. Uncertainties and tensions can, Buono and Bowditch assert (1989: 98) create not only personal stress but organisational stress as well. 'Management must combine different organisational components that are only similar in terms of task objective or formal structure. Informal arrangements, prevalent management style and other cultural considerations are rarely, if ever, the same across organisations. As a result, significant tensions occur as these different cultures clash with each other.'

The specific cultural characteristics of the three merging unions were the subject of a detailed study by Alexandra Ouroussof who found (1993: 4) in particular that in NALGO there was institutional inertia, in which discussion of problems was valued as an end in itself. This led to a failure to develop a strong management ethos in that the committee system was used as an excuse to duck and ignore problems. In NUPE, by contrast, it was the ability to make a fast and effective decision that was valued for its own sake though the principles on which those decisions were based were often obscure. The consequence was that people were often left feeling resentful or manipulated. In COHSE there was great value placed on informality but without any clear notion of accountability.

Based on these findings, strategies for cultural integration were carefully formulated into a carefully worked-through approach to the management of the new union. It was a prime objective that no single organisation would be the dominant partner. Explicit attempts were made to make sure that UNISON did not resemble any of the three partners. New names for institutions were devised, more parsimonious committee systems were planned, project team working and matrix management were developed to create task orientation and to span boundaries. Staff communication was, at least in theory, given a high priority. Decisions were planned taking into account UNISON's 'aims and values', a statement enshrined in the new Rule Book. Integration of different stakeholder groups was monitored and was the subject of a study and report on 'Integration and Participation'. The objective was to prevent traditionally articulate white-collar activists, usually white and male, from dominating union structures and imposing their own cultural certainties, whilst alienating other important groups. There was and is a high awareness of the need to manage to achieve cultural integration. It is understood to be a long term project and it continues.

Combination aftermath

Buono and Bowditch say (1989: 99) that as a result of continuing instability there is a danger of 'merger standstill' or 'postmerger drift' whose severity and intensity depend on the nature of the combination and the quality of its management. The problem is typically manifest in decreased productivity and operating effectiveness. It is suggested that, even in a properly managed merger, it can take 18 months before productivity returns to pre-merger levels.

Certainly, there was an element of standstill following the voluntary severance exercise, but since then, at least at national level people have operated increasingly comfortably within the new structural boundaries. The trauma has certainly gone but there is anxiety in many places about the possible consequences of the functional reviews, to which I refer below. Where this has been managed well – as in the Education and Training Department where the Director 'sold' his vision of a new role for a strategic function in the vanguard of lifelong learning for members and staff alike – it has been possible to generate a more positive sense of antici-pation.

In terms of the development of cultural integration some barriers persist. First, unions representing staff in the three old organisations remained largely unmerged for some time which helped perpetuate and reinforce old cultures. On the other hand, as Buono and Bowditch point out (1989: 176), old networks can be seen as calls for help in stressful times 'when existing support systems have broken down and people are attempting to regain some control over their lives.' Supportive networks of old friends and colleagues may actually help people get through the process even though there is a danger that they may be implicitly waiting for the old culture to re-assert itself. Second, management styles them-selves continue to reflect the cultures of the organisations from which those managers came. A willingness to learn about management does not necessarily mean that people find it easy to change the behaviour of a lifetime. It is not therefore surprising that the issue of changing management styles features strongly in feedback from managers and staff. Third, the process of voluntary severance put back consensual cultural integration by some time as a result of the trauma caused. There remains a shared objective that the process should con-tinue and succeed; one innovation which makes a significant contribution to this is the proposed annual meeting of significant numbers of staff with the General Secretary and leading lay members to generate involvement in achieving UNISON's objectives, enthusiasm for the future and a sense of partnership between lay members, managers and staff.

Psychological combination

Buono and Bowditch suggest (1989: 101) that this level of 'true' integration may not be reached until there is a new 'enemy' which serves as a focal point for hostility and threat. Since UNISON was intended as a focal point for public service trades unionism, perhaps this is something which should give it comfort as it continues to manage its merger process. But there is a clear recognition that psychological merger will not arise by accident.

The development of management within UNISON

During and since its creation UNISON has worked to develop an understanding of the need for skilled and sensitive management. All three partner unions had management training programmes which were carried forward into UNISON by the use of trainers with whom each felt comfortable. But three initiatives unprecedented in trade unions, laid the basis for this work: strategy sessions for the Senior Management Team (SMT); management development work for senior managers organised through Cranfield School of Management; and a change management programme. These are discussed below.

The SMT organised regular strategy sessions facilitated by Professor Alan Mumford, designed to develop the SMT as a strategic management unit, with objectives and priorities consistent with those of UNISON as a whole. Approaches to leadership were addressed. Visiting lecturers were invited to give expert input on significant issues – usually managerial ones. Action was taken to brief other managers on the outcomes. An evaluation of the programme in 1995 revealed general satisfaction alongside a feeling that the strategic intent of the meetings had not been adequately reflected in the way the SMT did its business.

A second vital strand in managerial development was the programmes organised for UNISON senior managers at the Centre for Strategic Trade Union Management at Cranfield and the idealised cultural web produced there. Following Vesting Day as closely as they did, these programmes had particular importance. They tackled head on the perceptions of UNISON managers of the characteristics of the three partner unions and enabled those managers to work through them and develop an approach to managing in UNISON. This focus is apparent from a reading of the course programme. From the opening session, which proclaimed UNISON's commitment to developing its management skills, it sought to identify perceptions of good and bad management.

The feedback from this programme emphasised the participants' desire to make UNISON work and be successful. Two specific managerial questions were identified as of particular importance: first, the establishment of formal systems and structures including a budgetary regime which gave clear budgetary responsibility to managers; second, tackling specific people management issues, in particular target-setting, delegation, appraisal, motivation and discipline. The participants also challenged the Senior Management Team as to whether its members were undertaking their strategic leadership role and were readily accessible to assist managers with problems.

At the time of the second Cranfield activity in 1995 several concerns remained, exacerbated by the implementation, shortly before the second programme, of a large and speedily-executed exercise in voluntary severance, in which around 25 per cent of staff left the organisation. This had reduced morale and inhibited cultural integration as people saw their friends leaving and, in some cases, resented the fact that they had not been allowed to leave. 'Survivor syndrome' literature predicts reduced motivation and loyalty and increased insecurity and stress in such circumstances (see. e.g. Doherty *et al.*, 1996). It is very much to the credit of the UNISON managers who attended the second Cranfield programme that they found it possible to be as constructive and positive as they were. Once again, the cultural web was used as a way of examining the extent to which UNISON had developed since Vesting Day. Particular importance was attached to developing women managers, which had been a feature of the 1993 cultural web. Other key themes developed from the first programme were communication, performance, influencing skills and delegation. The last of these attracted particular interest as many managers recognised their deficiencies in this area and 'the passion in the discussion was certainly founded on their belief that *they* be allowed to manage.' (Lloyd and Brewster, 1995). Out of this activity seven 'critical success factors' were identified which were:

1   Improving (managerial) communications within the union;
2   Improving the motivation of all staff;
3   Improving administrative coherence;
4   Recognising the changing role of lay members;
5   Making a reality of equal treatment, particularly for women;
6   Developing the campaigning role, particularly within 'community coalitions';
7   Delivering quality individual services.

In April 1998 a further Cranfield programme was held, in which the focus was on what sort of organisation UNISON would be in 2002, taking into account all the initiatives for change which were in train and the feedback from managers and staff about managerial changes they wanted to see. Participants (from national headquarters) envisaged that they would be undertaking a much more strategic role, centred around accountability and performance management. One desirable consequence was seen to be the ability of regional managers in particular to perform a more external role, involving social partnership and members' lifelong learning. They foresaw also a more transparent relationship between head office and the regions with service level agreements defining that relationship in appropriate cases. They recognised that information and communications technology might mean the development of different forms of communication between levels but continued to value the personal interface between national and regional staff. They also believed that if UNISON*direct*, the multimedia call centre project (which *was* piloted from June 1998 and went live in 1999), was a success, major changes in role and structure would be required.

One of the many things that was notable about the Cranfield programmes, and may be seen us uncharacteristic of 'traditional' union approaches was the comfortable way in which participants shared a common *managerial* language in which to discuss these major strategic issues. Whilst recognising the distance they still had to travel and the extensive training needs identified, they also recognised how far they personally had travelled to be able to engage in such discourse.

The management of change workshops were not explicitly managerial in the same sense as the Cranfield courses because they were trying to help members of staff, not always in managerial roles, and also, in some cases, lay members, to cope with change. They are however of importance because of their sheer scale. Between June and December 1993, thirty-one seminars were held with more taking place in 1994. Five Regions had by December 1993 put all their staff through the programme, two were in the process of doing so and a further five had involved their Regional Management Teams and key administrative staff. Two national functions had also participated. These workshops looked at change at individual and organisational levels and encouraged teams to work together on some 'live' issue involving change management and identified both personal training needs (e.g. time management, confidence building and asser-tiveness) and organisational development needs (e.g. motivation, feedback, styles of management).

There was an understanding within UNISON that it was necessary to diffuse management development programmes throughout the organisation and ensure that the Cranfield programmes were not seen as elitist. Between 1995 and 1997 Patricia Hodgins directed a series of courses called *Management in UNISON* in which 101 national and regional managers, to the level of Senior Regional Officer, participated. The core elements were culture, change management, leadership style and skills, team roles and team management. The work on culture picked up the cultural web activities undertaken at Cranfield. The report on these courses identifies one other constant cultural theme; the need to replace a 'blame' culture with an 'enabling, encouraging, supportively challenging culture, modelled in behaviour and language from the top downwards' (Hodgins, 1998: 7). Once again, however, the strength of the vision of a union working well for members in a partnership between members and staff is only exceeded by the recognition of the managerial solutions required to achieve this. A similar recognition lies in the themes identified by participants in examples of good management which they have experienced and of their wish list of initiatives which would help them to become more effective managers. Patricia Hodgins concludes that 'managers in UNISON are committed to learning and developing the skills and qualities necessary to help them to manage and lead effectively. They want to be good managers' (Hodgins, 1998).

Organisational innovations

As a consequence of UNISON's increasing sensitivity to the need to implement strategies for the development of managerial skills and behaviours a number of initiatives have been launched. Three of particular significance are detailed below.

The Women's Development Project

Of particular importance is the first report of the Women's Development Project (UNISON, 1998). This project was established by the Senior Management Team in 1995 as part of its strategy of developing women staff. The report defines six key aims:

1 Bringing women together;
2 Developing all women;
3 Improving training and career development;

4   Making UNISON jobs better for women;
5   Making managers equality aware;
6   Building a 'women-friendly' UNISON.

The objectives involve the use of classic organisation development methodology based in part on the work of Cheung-Judge and Henley (1994) and Wheeler in this volume. The project involved networking meetings attended by a third of UNISON's women staff and a range of workshops held for the project team and at national and regional levels. A programme of personal development, the Springboard programme, was established for women in UNISON, feedback from which informed the Project Team. One hundred and nine UNISON managers attended equality awareness programmes in 1996/7 which resulted in a report from the consultants to the Senior Management Team which was taken on board by the Project.

The report examines the current organisational profile of UNISON, identifying the location of the 'glass ceiling'. It makes the case for developing women and sets out a statement for UNISON of achieving equality. It gives voice to the many women who participated in the project to date. Running through the feedback from women is a recognition (alongside a deep commitment to rewarding and helping members) of the importance of good management as a driver for equality and, correspondingly, of the damage that poor management can cause. And the Report makes a series of challenging recommendations, all of which require significant and explicit managerial actions to achieve. These include continuing women's networking, an enhanced Springboard programme, the institution of development reviewing (see below), programmes of secondments, job shadowing, study visits, job swaps and acting up along with job enrichment programmes, training and support for women managers, challenging the 'long hours culture' and a new approach to job design. The language and content of the recommendations are managerial; the objectives are squarely within the framework of UNISON's aims and values.

Managerial stress

A staff stress survey was carried out in 1996 (Oasys Management Consultancy, 1997). The fact that such a survey was undertaken is an indicator of the importance attached within UNISON to minimising the stress on UNISON staff, implicitly by the institution of managerial improvements. Indeed, the Senior Management Team accepted the conclusions of the report and committed itself to undertaking a new survey in 1999 to measure its performance. The survey was concerned with obtaining a wide variety of information about individuals in which work-related stress formed a significant focus. All but two of the seven most stressful situations identified by staff had implications for the way in which staff were managed. Of the seven situations in which staff enjoyed their work, it is significant that 'helping members' was the highest rated. But five of the remaining seven situations were the result of the style adopted in managing the staff: achieving goals; being thanked; being left to get on with their work; being given time to plan and prepare; and being in control. It will be noted how these circumstances mirror most of the managerial priorities of UNISON managers in 1993: setting targets, delegation, appraisal and motivation. Not surprisingly, the accepted recommendations were for managerial action in these areas.

Management job specification, training and development

There is little base data against which to match UNISON's performance in this area. The most recent work is that of Kelly and Heery (1994) who examine the work relations of full-time officers. They find that 69 per cent of unions issue their officers with job descriptions but that only 15 per cent made use of performance appraisal. Written job descriptions and appraisal were found primarily in unions with 'bureaucratic employment relations' (1994: 84) and such unions were more likely to train their officers. Appraisal was found exclusively amongst unions practising open recruitment, which were also exclusively white collar with narrow job territories in the public sector or privatised corporations. The study also found that although unions relied on lay apprenticeship to equip officers with expertise, it had become commonplace to supplement this with formal training (Kelly and Heery, 1994: 62). 39 per cent of unions had sent at least a quarter of their officers on training courses in the previous year and 48 per cent had sent more than half in the previous five years. However, the study found that few unions developed a strategic approach to training, specifying the objectives of training policy and providing release.

UNISON is the largest user of the services of the TUC's National Education Centre. Regional training programmes are substantial. By far the most extensive example is in the South East; in 1997, Regional Officers were trained in communication, time management, managing difficult situations, working together, handling disciplinary cases, appeals and grievances, negotiating skills and advocacy, and courses were also arranged on Gay and Lesbian Awareness and stress management. The Regional Officer Trainee Scheme, set up in 1997, delivers a wide range of training to the young trainees, many women and several from ethnic minorities, structured around the National Vocational Qualifications (NVQs) for trade union officers.

UNISON's policy is that all staff are issued with job descriptions. Although not a white-collar union, it has a system of open recruitment as part of a commitment to equality. Kelly and Heery (1994) found that 11.8 per cent of officers in the unions they studied were female; although 21 per cent of UNISON's Regional Officers are female, only one third of staff above senior administrative levels are women despite the fact that two-thirds of UNISON staff are women. The open recruitment policy requires that all managers involved receive prior training in selection interviewing in order to ensure that the policy actually delivers equal opportunities.

UNISON has had a training strategy since 1994, one which stated that: '[UNISON] recognises the vital role of managers in the process of identification of training needs, preparation of individuals for training experiences and monitoring the feedback following them. In this and other respects, the importance of management development to the success of this and all UNISON's strategies is clearly asserted.' In 1997, it commenced the implementation of a system of Development Reviewing for all staff. In the preface to the scheme guidelines, Rodney Bickerstaffe wrote

> Helping staff to develop their skills, knowledge and abilities to the full is a central part of the role of all UNISON managers. Development Reviewing provides an opportunity for managers to meet on a regular one-to-one basis with their staff to fulfil this responsibility . . . Linking individual develop-ment with the wider objectives of UNISON will help staff to deliver the best possible service to our members. It will also contribute to the gradual develop-ment of UNISON towards a more open, learning-orientated, organisation.
>
> (UNISON, 1997a: 2)

The scheme provides for regular meetings between staff and their line managers, identifying achievements, difficulties, satisfactions and frustrations. It looks forward to potential successes and difficulties and objectives and targets are agreed for the future. A personal development plan is also agreed, setting out development needs and methods of meeting them. The conclusion contribute to functional development plans which feed into the budgetary process.

The scheme is clearly linked to other developments in UNISON, such as women's development and the achievement of the Investors in People award, which UNISON is intending to seek, initially on a Regional basis. Such Develop-ment Reviewing is explicitly not an appraisal scheme. It is not linked to rewards or sanctions of any sort. It does, however meet the criteria identified in the stress survey report. It also depends for its success on a recognition by both manage-ment and staff of the importance of skilled and sensitive people management for the achievement of UNISON's goals.

The Strategic Review

The Strategic Review is dealt with in more detail in Margaret Wheeler's chapter but requires reference in any review of management in UNISON. There is a literature on strategic planning for trade unions (for example Weil 1994; PSI 1996) but the UNISON review followed a process dictated by a Conference resolution rather than any academic model. It followed the budget reduction exercises in 1994, after which Annual Delegate Conference in 1995 instructed steps to be taken to reorientate UNISON towards members and regions and to produce an organisation which was efficient and cost-effective. The Review was undertaken by a steering committee of lay members from the NEC, service groups, regions and self-organised groups and reported to Conference in 1997. The report (UNISON 1997b) proposed branch and regional development plans and regional branch support plans together with a five year financial plan to meet the resource needs of branches and regions.

It also proposed a challenging programme of change for managers, including a staffing plan which would reduce the numbers of senior managers, sought to redress the gender balance at regional officer and managerial level, and planned a movement of resources from the Centre to the regions. It also set up a series of functional reviews of all services to analyse those services and plan for a future in which decentralisation was an objective.

From the outset it was agreed that these functional reviews would be management-led. Consultant support was provided but working with managers and review team members in a mentoring and supporting role. The method-ology, though not that of business process re-engineering, uses the language and some of the concepts of that technique. The reviews were led by teams of senior staff from both national and regional level, working with managers to help them to analyse their 'business processes', cost their outputs and produce a 5-year functional plan.

The result of the process has been a new staff structure at national and regional level, approved by the NEC in December 1998. A smaller Senior Management Group will provide strategic management and clusters of smaller functions at national level will be managed by a tier of 'Level 1' managers, many of them women. The size of the Centre has been, and continues to be, reduced as part of the process. The process has been exciting, in terms of the contribution it will make to securing UNISON's future, but stressful and traumatic for many people. The sensitivity with which change is managed will be the key to its success.

This has been a managerial process. Virtually every manager within UNISON has been involved. Its explicitly managerial character and techniques, and the managerial activities of communicating and involving staff, would have been inconceivable in an organisation without a deep-rooted understanding of the importance of management and of the roles and responsibilities required of managers in order to achieve the union's goals.

Conclusion

This chapter has endeavoured to show that UNISON, through and beyond the merger process, has developed a shared value that good management is capable of making a substantial contribution to the achievement of its goals. If this is true, it demonstrates an important step in the development of trade unions.

In her report to UNISON in 1993, Alexandra Ouroussof concluded as follows:

> In my view, ineffective management, especially in relation to staff, should not only be seen in terms of its effects on performance but in terms of the harm it does to the Union. The fact that unions are inefficiently managed is highly visible in the public domain. It diminishes respect for the unions in the eyes of your members and of course it plays into the hands of your enemies. Developing policies that will overcome the deep-seated hostility to trade unions has always been one aspect of the role of trade unions. I suggest that a policy of good management be adopted not only for the sake of the people

employed in UNISON and for the sake of the members but also for the sake of trade unionism.

(Ouroussof, 1993: 7)

I believe that such a policy has been adopted. It will be for others to examine its utility and effect.

References

Brooke, M. Z. (1984) *Centralisation and Autonomy*, London: Holt, Reinhart and Winston.
Buono, A. F. and Bowditch, J. L. (1989) *The Human Side of Mergers and Acquisitions*, San Francisco: Jossey Bass.
Cartwright, S. and Cooper, C. L. (1996) *Managing Mergers, Acquisitions and Strategic Alliances*, Oxford: Butterworth-Heinemann.
Cheung-Judge, M. Y. and Henley, A. (1994) *Equality in Action: Introducing Equal Opportunities in Voluntary Organisations*, London: NCVO.
Child, J., Loveridge, R. and Warner, M. (1973) 'Towards an organizational study of trade unions', *Sociology*, 71: 1.
Doherty, N., Bank, J. and Vinnicombe, S. (1996) 'Managing survivors: the experience of survivors in British Telecom and the British financial sector', *Journal of Management Psychology*, 11: 7.
Dunlop, J. T. (1990) *The Management of Labor Unions*, Lexington, Mass.: Lexington Books.
Handy, C. (1988) *Understanding Voluntary Organization,* Harmondsworth: Penguin.
Hodgins, P. (1998) 'Management development in UNISON', unpublished report to UNISON Senior Management Team.
Johnson, G. (1988) 'Rethinking incrementalism', *Strategic Management Journal,* 9.
Kelly, J. and Heery, E. (1994) *Working for the Union: British Trade Union Officers*, Cambridge: Cambridge University Press.
Lloyd, J. and Brewster, C. (1995) 'Cranfield seminars for managing UNISON 1995', unpublished report to UNISON Senior Management Team.
Oasys Management Consultancy (1997) 'UNISON stress survey', unpublished report to UNISON Senior Management Team.
Orlans, V. (1991) 'Stress interventions with trade unions', *Personnel Review*, 20: 2.
Ouroussof, A. (1993) 'UNISON: building a new culture', unpublished presentation to UNISON Senior Management team.
Paton, R. and Hooker, C. (1990) *Developing Managers in Voluntary Organisations: a Handbook*, Milton Keynes: Open University Press.
Public Services International (1996) 'Charting a union's future', Ferney Voltaire Cedex: PSI.
Thorpe, M. (1991) *Trade Union Merger*, unpublished MA dissertation.
UNISON (1997a) *Development Reviewing Guidelines*, London: UNISON.
UNISON (1997b) 'Strategic review: making local organisation our priority', *NEC Report to Annual Delegate Conference*, London: UNISON.
UNISON (1998) 'Women, work and UNISON', *First Report of the Women's Development Project*, London: UNISON.
Weil, D. (1994) *Turning the Tide: Strategic Planning for Labor Unions*, New York: Lexington Books.
Willman, P., Morris, T. and Aston, B. (1993) *Union Business*, Cambridge: Cambridge University Press.

5 UNISON's approach to organisation development in a democratic organisation

Margaret Wheeler

This chapter charts the development of organisation development (O/D) in UNISON and looks at how support for a strategic 'O/D approach' to the union's work and future development is being built up among lay members, managers and staff. It also describes the work of the union's specialist O/D Unit as an internal 'consultancy' undertaking work and offering advice on strategic development, management of change, staff development and internal communications. Finally, it discusses two key O/D projects: the strategic review of the union's services to members; and the development of women staff.

The approach to organisation development in UNISON has been intuitive, and instinctive rather than a planned or 'textbook' development. The emphasis from the outset has been on building an O/D style and approach for UNISON that staff, activists and members feel comfortable with, understand and can relate to – on the importance of O/D being rooted in the business of the organisation and what it needs to achieve for its members and the services they work in. The development of O/D has been, and still is, a learning process

One of the starting points for O/D in UNISON was that its remit should extend to all aspects of the organisation: the culture, lay member and staffing structures, and the development of the organisation at national, regional and branch level. Significantly, the first discussion paper on the role of O/D in UNISON was drawn up for a lay member committee – the O/D panel of UNISON's Interim National Executive Council – recognising the importance in a democratic organisation of building support and champions of change in the lay member structure.

The 'learning while doing' philosophy that has informed UNISON's approach to O/D comes from Beckhard and Pritchard (1992):

> Probably the most important single process involved in effective change is the process of learning while doing . . . of managing the change effort through the normal operational 'hierarchy' rather than through a dedicated change management resource or programme.

While in 1993, with much optimism in establishing a dedicated management of change unit and a clear sense of purpose in forming Britain's largest and best trade union we would have intended a steady, smooth, structured change programme to integrate the three partner unions – in practice learning while doing has served us well. UNISON's strategy is 'emerging' from the growing consensus on the future direction and role of the organisation among lay members and staff, borne out of the experience of the series of major change initiatives that have helped define and shape the new organisation.

This 'emerging' strategy has as its heart the desire of UNISON to become a learning organisation. Identifying this ultimate long-term aim has a strong resonance for lay members and staff – even though there has still to be an organisation-wide, shared understanding and agreement on what this means for UNISON, how it can be achieved, and how it fits into the major change being undertaken by the organisation. Our 'intuitive', non-academic approach to O/D in UNISON has nevertheless developed within the frameworks provided by some of the main O/D and learning organisation experts – mainly Burgoyne (1999), Senge (1993) and Beckhard (1969, 1989). Since few organisations have succeeded in becoming learning organisations, UNISON's claims in this respect would be modest but optimistic! Burgoyne recently identified the key features of a learning organisation to be: close links between learning and business strategy; an organisation consciously learning from business opportunities and threats; that individuals and groups and the whole organisation are learning and continually learning how to learn; that information systems and technology support learning rather than control it; the development of processes for defining, creating, capturing, sharing and acting on knowledge; and that these various systems and dimensions are balanced and managed as a whole. On these criteria UNISON can optimistically maintain to have begun the learning/ organisation journey.

From an O/D perspective, six main mechanisms can be cited in support of this:

Developing a strategic focus

This involves the development of processes for building a more long-term strategic focus for the organisation – for forward planning and building consensus on objectives and priorities. The main vehicle for this is our union-wide Strategic Review of services to members and branches. This was a major exercise mapping and analysing our core functions and services with the aim of shifting priorities and resources to strengthen workplace organisation and provide improved services closer to the members. The key features include the following: *member education and development*, involving our membership and activist education strategy, including the UNISON Open College for members and the establishment of employer/union local education partnerships; *promoting new ways of working*, reflected in our efforts to develop and promote new ways of working in the organisation, including partnership working between lay members and staff; *encouraging member participation*, based around our work to achieve proportionality and fair representation in the lay structures; *focusing on staff training and development*, centred round our staff development programme bringing together major initiatives to develop all staff, identify learning needs and provide a comprehensive range of training and development opportunities; and *management development*, providing a focus on developing managers to achieve the union's aims and objectives.

These issues are dealt with elsewhere in this book. This chapter focuses on the O/D approach, style and work before and since 1993; the origins of O/D in the process leading up to the formation of UNISON in 1993, including the O/D 'framework' of the union's aims and values; how O/D was envisaged to work from 1993; and how it has actually developed, including work on strategy development. It examines the key principles of the union's strategic review of services to branches and members and important related staff development initiatives, including the development of women staff.

Origins of O/D in UNISON

My involvement in the merger talks began in 1989 when COHSE, the union for which I worked at that time, entered the NUPE/NALGO talks. I was one of the three executive officers from each union servicing the key UNISON merger bodies of the Joint Secretaries and Tripartite UNISON Committee. Our awareness of the sensitivities, difficulties and sheer scale of the exercise – a three way union merger, never yet attempted or achieved – meant that from the outset the discussions between the three unions focussed on the importance of the unions' traditions, cultures and histories. The need for a *new* union was recognised; it was to be a genuine merger, not a take-over by one of the partner unions. This involved, for example, a genuine recognition by both NUPE and NALGO of the COHSE fears that its membership, health care identity and particular ethos could be swallowed up by the two larger unions. Unusually in union mergers, all three unions had equal participation and representation rights on the key merger negotiating committees to ensure that no one could dominate. All three had their own academic adviser, to ensure that an awareness of history, tradition and culture was brought into all development work on structures and systems.

Different ways of working were adopted in lay member and Joint Secretaries forums: seminars to learn about each other's organisations; 'brainstorm' sessions to undertake analysis of issues and problems; contributions from outside speakers and experts; joint meetings and social gatherings of the three lay national executives, and of lay structures in the regions; project task groups comprising staff from all three unions. Much of the discussion in the merger talks centred on process issues – the 'hard' negotiations only really taking place in the final stages for agreeing the Final Report to the three national conferences, and the contents of the Rule Book. Most important of all, the union's aims and values – stated at the start of the Rule Book and providing a framework for the structure and governance of the union – represented an organisation development approach to the new union. It provided members with a clear statement on what the new union stands for, and of members' rights and the union's commitment to them.

The purpose and some of the findings of the study commissioned into the culture of the three unions (undertaken by the social anthropologist Alexandra Ouroussoff (1993)) is covered in Mike Dempsey's contribution to this volume. This study was a major innovation – another first for trade unions. It identified the key characteristics of the three union's cultures and underlined the issues that would emerge for the new union in developing its organisational culture. From an O/D perspective, and with much hindsight, its significance and effect were crucially important to the union's development. The report influenced us in three ways: first, it shaped an awareness of the importance of building a new UNISON culture to the ultimate success of UNISON and helped shape the nature of discussions and pre- and post-UNISON work; second it provided a vital opportunity for staff at all levels of the three organisations to talk to an independent consultant about their fears, anxieties and aspirations for the new organisation, rather than just discussing the practical, structural or political issues. Lay members and staff were able to say how they felt and to have their say. Third, the focus on the importance of organisational culture was a key factor in helping to develop a shared language and dialogue for change between the partner unions and into UNISON. It helped build the ability in the union to talk about and 'front up' problems, and find ways forward.

Key features of aims and values

Our aims and objectives are contained in our Rule Book, voted on and agreed by members in the successful ballot of the members to form UNISON. They stress:

- Our *commitment* to the members: to improved pay and conditions; promoting members' interests; protecting their rights; ensuring equality of treatment.
- Promoting *fair representation* in all union structures for women, member of all grades, black members, members with disabilities and lesbians and gay men.
- The importance of *partnership* working between members and staff.
- Providing 'minimum guaranteed standards' of *service to the members*; providing information; providing benefits and welfare services; offering education opportunities.
- Emphasising the *rights* of members: giving guaranteed minimum standards of advice and representation; the right to participate in the union – in elections, meetings, forums and policy development .
- The importance of *promoting public services*: of working with the Government and community to build services to the public and of *developing good relations* with employers and governments.
- Our *commitment and pledge* to staff: 'to foster good industrial relations with the union's employees through their trade unions' and 'promote equal opportunities for all employees irrespective of race, gender, sexuality, disability, age or creed'. Our aims and objectives recognise the importance of staff

training and development; of promoting equal opportunities, good pay and conditions, and a good working environment for staff.

The O/D Unit

The establishment of the O/D Unit itself was developed and agreed before Vesting Day of 1 July 1993. The emphasis on the need for the organisation to plan, develop and look ahead was embodied in the establishment of a 'Services and Development Division' , at the national centre, a lay member Development Committee, from which the O/D lay members panel developed, and an O/D staff unit (comprising the Director and secretary!). Not surprisingly in 1993 there was little understanding of O/D, and much scepticism, concern, suspicion and uncertainty, particularly among staff and managers.

UNISON's first general secretary, Alan Jinkinson, described the intended role of the unit as being

> to provide strategic input and advice to the Senior Management Team on the process and implications of organisational development and evolution, partly a think tank, partly facilitating and doing, overseeing the strategic planning process, it will act like internal consultants. Its small staff would come from among the existing staff of the three unions; ('experts' were not needed!), and its role 'advisory, facilitating and supporting' – not executive.

From 1993, the O/D Unit has comprised four staff, with the emphasis on the internal consultancy role in line with the Beckhard model which sees organisation development as a process of intervention in which consultants work with, and support, managers and policy makers in developing management processes and organisation design.

The UNISON O/D Unit undertakes work and offers advice on strategic development, management of change, staff development and internal communications. Its main role is to manage Senior Management Team (SMT) and National Executive Council (NEC) projects, working collaboratively with lay members, managers and staff on key SMT and NEC areas of work. It offers internal consultancy services in the context of the development of the organisation since merger – including project management, facilitation, team-building, information analysis, co-ordination and mediation. Its role has recently been extended to include the Personnel and Staff Industrial Relations function under a newly formed Directorate of Organisation and Staff Development.

The O/D lay member panel

The organisation-wide remit of O/D in UNISON owes much to the groundwork undertaken by the lay member O/D panel of the Interim NEC. The approach was summed up in a joint presentation by the panel chair, and myself to the Development Committee in the following terms:

- Establishing the vision and objectives
- Where the union wants to be; standing in the future
- Establishing the strategy
  the process of how we get there
- Establishing priorities
    prioritising work and projects to fit the strategy
- Building the overview
- Fitting work and projects into the work and development of the union as a whole, the strategy and vision
- Recognising the importance of planning and managing change
- Recognising the importance of building a new organisational culture – changing attitudes, beliefs, working methods.

The Development Committee and Membership Services Committees of the Interim NEC developed much innovative work on taking a 'strategic' approach to the functions and services they dealt with. Environmental 'scanning' and stakeholder, economic, technical and political analysis was undertaken – working in small groups and using SWOT and 'brainstorm' activities. This formed the basis for the development of UNISON's recruitment and organisation and membership services strategies. Four 'strategic' committees were established for UNISON's permanent committees, elected in 1995: Policy Development and Campaigns; Finance and Resource Management; Development and Organisation; and Membership Services. Today the Development and Organisation Committee is the successor to the 'interim' Development Committee, covering recruitment, organisation, branch and regional development, IT strategy, constitutional and internal structures, including the remit of the NEC's own working methods. The NEC itself holds annual review sessions following each National Delegate Conference – a mix of group and plenary work – dealing with development and decisions. At these sessions, it draws up external and internal objectives for the coming year and sets policy development priorities. These form the basis for other national committees, national departments and regions to draw up their own objectives and plans.

This objective-setting process is still in the early stages of development. The degree to which the 'high level', broad objectives of the NEC have been translated into specific aims, action and work programmes, varies considerably across the union. Some Service Groups, regional and national centre departments have undertaken valuable work in this respect. The majority of Service Groups and regions hold annual policy development/ strategy sessions to agree and plan the year's work. However, effective monitoring and evaluation processes have yet to be generally well developed and there is still mixed support for the overall process and understanding of its purpose and importance. Most important, a consistent approach across the organisation has still to be developed which matches financial resources to objectives and priorities, and establishes an integrated forward planning and development cycle and process.

Strategic Review: building local organisation

The Strategic Review, begun in 1995 following a motion carried by the National Delegate Conference called for a 5-year financial and staffing plan to build financial security, and to decentralise services and resources closer to the members. It has focused on the union's 'core' functions and purposes of negotiating, recruiting, representing, organising and servicing members. It underlines the importance of building local organisation – of ensuring that the needs of branches and members in facing the challenges and demands in the workplace are the union's number one priority. It has been spearheaded by a lay member Steering Group, bringing together representatives from the NEC, region, Service Groups and self-organised groups whose report to the 1997 Conference *Making Local Organisation Our Priority* was overwhelmingly endorsed.

During the two year period between 1995 and 1997 Conferences, the Steering Group undertook a major analysis of local organisation (branch mapping, surveys, case studies, member opinion research), alongside an extensive activist consultation programme. The emphasis was on building up an accurate picture of branch organisation and membership in the new union, and developing a consensus on future work and priorities. Around the same time a major programme of branch merger was halving the number of branches from over 3,000 in 1993 to 1,200 by 1 January 1997.

The Review has five key planning processes for improving services to branches and members:

- *Branch Development Plans*: drawn up by regions, in conjunction with branches aimed at providing the support needed to develop workplace organisation and represent members. The plans set goals for recruitment, improving local organisation, communications with members, activist education and fair representation and proportionality.
- *Regional Branch Support Plans*: 5-year plans from regions to provide administrative support to branches.
- *Regional Development Plans*: to identify medium and longer term priorities for staffing and capital investment to build 'front line' services to branches and members.
- *Shifting resources to 'front line' services*: primarily from the national centre but also within regions.
- *Decentralisation of services*: ensuring that services are provided as close to the members as possible.

Functional reviews of national departments and regions were undertaken to develop proposals over 5 years for shifting resources to local organisation and decentralisation of services. They were completed in 1999 and will result in major proposals for change in the size and role of the union's national centre and in the work and role of regions.

The Organisation Development Unit's work with the Steering Group and senior management team on the Strategic Review has been instrumental in shaping and developing the organisation-wide remit of O/D. 'Learning while doing' has again been the key approach. A way forward on the vital issue of the union's future is being developed through discussion, consultation, agreement and learning – by building the strategic skills and capability of the organisation itself and by the need in a democratic organisation to ensure full involvement of the lay member structures in work, policy development and decision making. The functional reviews are an in-house UNISON undertaking. We have not employed teams of consultants; only one outside adviser has been appointed whose role is to work with senior managers and O/D 'practitioners' to develop their analytical and managerial skills for undertaking the reviews. The consultant/mentor is adviser, facilitator and supporter, not 'doer'.

The methodology for the review, developed by the O/D support team with the consultant, is based on business process engineering. It involves analysing and costing departmental and regional core outputs, which then form the basis of the development by managers of 3–5-year plans for improving and decentralising services and building workplace organisation. These plans are measured against agreed assessment criteria covering the main development areas for the union and scrutinised by a Review Team, prior to presentation to the SMT project group. The Review Team comprises an O/D team member, national and regional managers, and an administrative staff member. Again, we have learnt as the reviews have progressed – using the experience of each phase and work with managers to develop and refine the methodology, and 'plough back' the learning experience into the process.

As the review has progressed, the roles and responsibilities between lay members and full-time staff has also clarified. The Strategic Review Steering Group has been succeeded by a lay member Implementation Group with the task of drawing up a 5-year plan for carrying out the Strategic Review. The functional reviews are being conducted as a management-led exercise, reporting progress to the group via the SMT. A special fund has been established for financing branch development pilot schemes and initiatives; regional branch support plans; branch IT development and national staffing restructuring to continue the steady shift of resources from the centre that has been taking place since 1995. The fund will become self-financing by 'accruing' savings identified from the functional reviews, savings in management costs and general efficiency measures in order to invest in branch and regional development. Pilot and feasibility studies are being undertaken on a range of services to achieve de-centralisation.

There is still much work to be done which will involve crucial choices, compromises and decisions. Nevertheless, the work so far has succeeded in building support for major change among key activists and staff, and recognition of the importance to our survival of ensuring the members needs in the workplace are met.

Building change agents among staff

Crucially, the O/D unit enjoys strong support from the SMT – and its staff work closely with the SMT and individual senior managers on a range of staff and lay member projects. The Unit organises regular review and strategy sessions for the SMT; alongside its role in the Strategic Review, it has a project management or co-ordination role in developing UNISON's information strategy, servicing our Young Members' Forum and servicing the Development and Organisation Committee. It has played a major role in staff and management development since merger, heading up the union's Women's Development Project.

Understanding of O/D has been developing among national and regional managers, although it is probably true to say that significant numbers of managers and staff – particularly in the negotiating/service group structures – remain sceptical, cynical, or unaware of the O/D role, at the same time as generally supporting the aims of the Strategic Review!

At regional level, the establishment early in UNISON of 'O/D Regional Contacts' has been one of the most significant developments for developing an identity for O/D. The group comprises a member from each of our thirteen Regional Management Teams (RMT) – usually the Deputy Regional Secretary. It meets quarterly and has an annual residential training and development session, which includes work on O/D theory and development, team-building and working, project management, facilitation, problem solving, coaching and mentoring skills, and organisational 'benchmarking'. The members are usually responsible for staff training and development remit for their region, so links with key training initiatives are strong.

As RMT members, O/D regional contacts have a major development role in the region: they organise and facilitate staff conferences and lay member strategy sessions; hold development and organisation responsibilities; as well as responsibilities for developing internal administrative and technical systems. The networking of the group is strong and supportive, the quarterly meetings a mix of strategic and process issues. They undertake a range of facilitation and internal consultancy work. For the functional reviews, they worked outside their own regions as facilitators of staff focus groups on the aims of the Strategic Review and to get feedback on staff concerns and views. Many RMT members have become NVQ developers and assessors, overseeing the introduction of the new Professional Trade Union Officers' NVQ in UNISON as part of our Regional Officer Trainee Scheme.

O/D regional contacts enjoy strong support from the Regional Secretaries and feed in ideas for policy development to the regional secretary group. They are currently undertaking the crucial role of regional 'project managers' for the functional reviews. O/D regional contacts have worked collaboratively within and across regions and with the national O/D support team to analyse work processes and produce costed 'outputs' on core regional functions. The result is that ownership and understanding of the purpose of the reviews appears to be stronger at regional than national level where managers tended to work as individuals rather than in teams. The reviews will enable the union to build a consistent picture of regional work priorities and needs and the O/D contacts will have played a major role in this.

They would certainly subscribe to the 'learning while doing' description of O/D in UNISON. Many 'O/D initiatives' in the regions – involving new ways of working, coaching, mentoring, have been pioneered by members of the group. Many of these would not be called O/D but would be done anyway! Key phrases used by the group to describe itself (from a recent feedback session) are: 'can do', 'learning atmosphere', 'group buzz', 'shared language', 'energy', 'collaborative', 'trying to change things', 'shared goal', 'non-competitive', 'non-cynical', 'a genuine desire to learn new skills'.

Staff training and development

O/D skills are being built up and developed among key staff groups, who are playing a leading role in developing overall staff training policy. In 1995, we appointed a Personnel Development Officer who, with the Staff Development and Training Unit has worked with SMT, the lay member staffing committee and key managers to build a training and development strategy aimed at gradual development towards a more open, learning-orientated organisation. The central aim of the strategy is to contribute to consistent and equitable management of all staff across the organisation by two key processes which focus on organisational objectives: development reviewing for all staff and the attainment of the Investors in People (IIP) award. The strategy has also been developed alongside a major overhaul of our recruitment and selection procedures introduced in 1995.

Development reviewing was begun in 1997 with an intensive training programme for all line managers. It involves all managers meeting on a one-to-one basis with staff, at least annually, to agree objectives, review progress and identify learning needs. These are based on departmental/regional work plans, and centred on identifying job related needs which will help build transferable skills and enhance career development. The target was for all first interview reviews to be conducted and agreed by May 1998, with the aim of building up a union wide picture of skills and training resource needs by the end of the year which will form the basis for the training programme to achieve IIP. The overall training strategy identifies four main areas of support to learning needs: integrated methods; internal and external short courses; S/NVQs; and other vocational/academic/personal development programmes. In agreement with IIP we prepared a commitment statement to achieve IIP which will be ready by the end of 1998; our first assessment will take place in our south-west region.

Women's development

Of UNISON's 1400 staff, 900 are women; but only 21 per cent of our regional officers are women; three out of thirteen regional secretaries; 82 per cent of our staff in the key grades below regional officer are women; only six out of twenty-six senior national managers are women. Thus developing women staff is crucial to the future of the union. *Women, Work and UNISON*, the first report of the Women's Development Project was published in 1998 and makes key recommendations to improve the position of women, arguing strongly that 'the organisation's future, its style and culture will come from developing women. It is good for the organisation, and the changes we can bring in will be of positive benefit to men, too. Women need to take part in developing the culture and influencing change'.

The Project is an SMT project, led by O/D, with a project group comprising grades and disciplines from across the organisation. The emphasis has been on a rolling programme of initiatives for implementation by the SMT, recognising that the development of women in any organisation, particularly in a newly merged one, is a long-haul task. While some gains can be made straight away, a radical overhaul of structure and culture takes time and commitment. The key aims of the project, around which the report's recommendations are shaped, were developed from a series of women's networking meetings across the union, bringing together regional and national staff to discuss women's development, and to map their concerns and future aspirations. UNISON women staff acted as facilitators for the meetings, preparing reports and feeding back to the project team and SMT. The report itself summarises the feedback from the meetings, attended by a third of women staff.

The six aims of the project stress the importance of career enhancement, as well of career development, of improving existing jobs carried out by women and of giving women the continuing opportunity of meeting together. Consistent development reviewing, interview skills and recruitment training for staff, and equality awareness training for managers are seen as the keys to substantial progress. The following aims and recommendations were identified:

- *Bringing women together*: continuing networking meetings, facilitated by UNISON women to plan development and review progress.
- *Developing all women*: emphasising the importance of personal development as well as career development. UNISON is the first union to pilot the Springboard Development Programme for administrative, clerical and manual staffs which has been a tremendous success.
- *Improving training and career development*: the establishment of UNISON's Regional Officer Trainee Scheme and other trainee schemes; training in job application and selection for all staff; developing and utilising women's IT skills as a key area for the future.
- *Making UNISON jobs better for women*: focusing on 'horizontal' job development and enjoyment as well as career enhancement and promotion: secondments, job swaps, shadowing, study visits.
- *Making managers equality aware*: recognising that management training and style is a major factor in developing a women-friendly working environ-

ment. Organising equality awareness training for all senior national and regional managers was one of the early tasks of the project group.

- *Building a women-friendly UNISON*: addressing the 'long hours' working culture prevalent in the union, improving job design so that jobs are more accessible to women with child and dependent care; promoting job share, part-time working, home-working, career breaks.

The report stresses that building a women-friendly UNISON is about changing the culture of the organisation, and developing 'a democratic, collaborative style of management where women are listened to, encouraged to make full use of their skills and talents and supported enough to get the 'top jobs' . . . it is important that the union says out loud what sort of culture it wants and makes all staff aware of the expectations on them.'

The UNISON Statement of Commitment to Achieving Equality, drawn up by the Project Group, and agreed by the SMT and lay member Staffing Committee spells this out, insisting that 'the development of equal opportunities is essential to achieving the aims and objectives of UNISON; it will enhance the delivery of high quality services to the members and will ensure that the staffing structure reflects the same diversity as its membership'.

To put these principles into practice, UNISON intends to develop a working environment where the contribution of all employees is valued and acknowledged, where all employees are enabled and encouraged to develop their full potential and where opportunities for movement between jobs are maximised, making the union a more friendly and supportive organisation.

References

Beckhard, R. and Pritchard, W. (1992) *Changing the Essence: the Art of Creating and Leading Fundamental Change in Organizations*, San Francisco: Jossey-Bass.

Beckhard, R. (1989) 'A model for the executive management of transformational change', in Pfeiffer, J. W. (ed.) *The 1989 Annual: Developing Human Resources*, Stamford: University Associates Inc.

Beckhard, R. (1969) *Organisation Development: Strategies and Models*, London: Addison Wesley.

Senge, P. (1993) *The Fifth Discipline*, London: Century/Arrow.

Burgoyne, J. (1999) 'Design of the times', *People Management*, 17 June.

Ouroussof, A. (1993) 'UNISON: building a new culture', unpublished presentation to UNISON Senior Management team.

6 Strategic review and organisational change in UNISON

Trevor Colling and Tim Claydon

Introduction

Key elements have differentiated public service unionism since its emergence as a force in the 1970s. While unionism in Britain's private sector had been predominantly atomised and reliant on branch and lay activist activity, public service unionism was characterised by strong central organisation which co-ordinated activity and sponsored workplace structures. Current pressures in the public services pull unions in opposing directions. Centralisation, financial stringency, and hostile local bargaining environments push them towards retaining central resources to establish frameworks or minimum floors of rights. Marketisation and the decentralisation of service delivery, managerial authority and collective bargaining, on the other hand, expose weaknesses in local organisation. So, how should public service unionism respond to these contending pressures?

Within UNISON, the issues were addressed partly by the merger. Cohering around the principle of being 'member-led', the settlement from which the union developed confirmed branches as the key unit of organisation and assured important roles for activists (Terry, 1996). Questions about the nature of professional support and how this should be structured and delivered could not be addressed effectively at that point. These have provided the focus for the union's Strategic Review initiated 2 years after merger.

This chapter examines the review in a single region which we will refer to as Region One. Fieldwork was conducted whilst the review was ongoing, between August 1998 and April 1999, and focused on local government. This is the union's largest service group, accounting for nearly two-thirds (64 per cent) of the membership overall, and it is here that the union faces the starkest organisational challenges. This discussion focuses therefore on two of the three partner unions, NALGO and NUPE. Interviews were conducted with members of the regional management team (RMT) throughout this period, with three quarters of regional organisers with local government responsibilities, and with branch officers, staff and activists in three local government branches. Two county branches were visited with sharply contrasting operating contexts: one containing several major industrial conurbations with strong union traditions, the other spread widely across large rural communities. A city branch outside these two counties and based on a recently established unitary authority was also visited.

We examine first the nature of public service unionism and elaborate on the factors which have fostered characteristics distinct from trade union practice elsewhere. The challenges facing UNISON currently are outlined briefly before attention turns to how these have been dealt with in Region One up to and during the review. The review itself is discussed in two sections. The first establishes its origins and development. Emphasised here is the context of financial stringency and the complex nature of decentralisation. We then identify the preferred elements of union organisation and practice which have emerged clearly so far. The reliance on lay activity and the reduction on full-time officer support is noted. Discussion in the concluding section focuses on whether this provides the basis for a renewal of public service unionism, particularly in the context of espoused objectives of increasing recruitment and avoiding sectional activity.

Modelling public service unionism

Though the unparalleled diversity of British trade union organisation renders attempts to generalise inherently risky, it is usually acknowledged key characteristics distinguish public service unionism from collective organisation elsewhere.

Developing from strongholds in the, historically fragmented, manufacturing and utility industries, British unionism has been predominantly decentralised and pragmatic. Defensive control over craft traditions and demarcations generated relatively large numbers of industry-based unions; general unions organising those workers excluded by such strategies; and ongoing suspicion and competition between these variously constituted unions, especially where they sought to organise the same workforces as happened frequently. The locus of activity remained local, at employer or establishment level for the most part (Sisson, 1983: 126). By the late 1960s, national bargaining had declined to the point where most substantive issues, including pay, and an increasing number of procedures (regulating disciplinary action and redundancies, for example) were agreed locally. Management and union concerns from this point focused on the proper organisation and resourcing of such activity and provided impetus to develop shop steward activity still further. The ratio of full-time officers to members was diluted further (Heery, 1996: 177) and British unions became reliant on voluntary activity to an extent 'unparalleled elsewhere in Europe' (Terry, 1995: 203).

Strengths and weaknesses derived from these structural characteristics. Closeness between members and their representatives facilitated an unusual capacity to mobilise. But fragmentation of collective organisation, within and between unions, narrowed the grounds around which mobilisation was attempted. Attachment to the notion of 'free collective bargaining' implied a separation of industrial relations from the sphere of politics and public policy (Hyman, 1989: 167). With some exceptions, steward organisations focused narrowly on the concerns of their own constituencies, often conceived in terms of the factory or particular workgroups within it (see Terry, 1995 for a fuller discussion). Criteria through which the well-being of these constituencies were judged were often similarly narrow (based on pay, for example) and relative (leading to the defence or assertion of differentials).

The resulting sectionalism and economism were disabling in three senses. First, members of the public as consumers were puzzled and often alienated by union action which they experienced consequently as victims. Second, effective enough where there were shortages of labour or specific skills, sectional demands lost their power when labour markets slackened (Hyman: ibid.). These characteristics provided shifting and insecure foundations for union activity. Finally, they left untouched managerial prerogative over work organisation, product innovation and competitive strategies. As trading circumstances became more hostile during the 1970s and 1980s, employers used and extended this prerogative to drive through significant changes in production.

Into this context emerged the increasingly important phenomenon of public service unionism. Following sustained growth through the post-war period, membership in NUPE and NALGO ballooned by 78 per cent through the 1970s (Fryer, 1989: 23). Characteristics evident in private sector unionism were shared to some extent but some distinctive ones emerged too. First, public service unions tended to be more centralised. Whitleyism, which had largely failed in the private sector, spread through the public services during the post-war period with the consequence that basic pay, holiday, hours, premium payments and allowances were determined predominantly at national level (Clegg, 1979). In comparison with health and the civil service, national bargaining in local government became comprehensive late (during the 1960s) and continued to leave scope for local adaptation even after that. Conditions for manual staff were relatively constrained. Though local discretion was given a fillip by the development of productivity bonus schemes through the 1970s, this was a partial experience. Over 80 per cent of male manual workers were covered by such a scheme by 1982 (Ingham, 1985) but services characterised by women's employment were more or less unaffected. White-collar agreements offered greater discretion, particularly over grading and therefore pay (Kessler, 1986: 162). Unions were able to negotiate minimum earnings guarantees in some areas (Fogarty and Brooks, 1986: 129) and there were general moves to secure local agreements over issues, including equal opportunities, which were not covered by national agreements.

Second, public service unions tended to be organisationally pro-active in their response to growth. NUPE's ascendancy amongst manual workers was secured by co-ordinated recruitment campaigns during the 1970s, led by full-time officers and aimed at predominantly unorganised women working in geographically dispersed services (Massey and Miles, 1984: 22). The support and sponsorship of full-time officers was also key to the development of steward systems, particularly in local government. Despite the longevity of collective bargaining, local authority shop stewards were recognised formally for the first time only in 1969. The following year, 39 per cent of NUPE's branches had no stewards at all

(Fryer, 1989: 28). Between 1971 and 1977, NUPE increased the number of accredited stewards five times to reach 10,000 and, by 1981, this number had more than doubled to 23,000 (Batstone, 1988: 78). Sponsorship by full-time officers remained vital even after steward systems were established, particularly for NUPE branches who retained relatively meagre funds. Logistical and tactical support assisted branches in maintaining an overview of the diverse and dispersed memberships they served (Kessler, 1986; Terry, 1982).

Third, and finally, conventional economistic demands in the interests of members were intertwined increasingly with *sword of justice* issues incorporating also the interests of citizens and service users (see Terry, this volume; Colling, 1997; Foster and Scott, 1998). Following the 'Winter of Discontent', when unions were vilified for apparently indiscriminate strike action, more sophisticated forms of industrial action were developed to minimise the impact on the public and, wherever possible, to enlist their sympathy and support (Colling, 1997). Campaigns broadened from industrial matters to social policy including, *inter alia,* private medicine and pay-beds, hospital and residential home closures, national and local expenditure cuts, privatisation, and social policy (Fryer, 1989). Patchy as they were, there were also attempts to form alliances with service users and pressure groups (Foster and Scott, 1998) and, following American practice (e.g., AFL–CIO, 1992), to become pro-active on issues such as restructuring and quality assurance.

Recent challenges

These distinguishing characteristics have required central co-ordination and relatively strong ligaments between levels of union activity. Recent external developments, however, have elongated the span of organisation required and disorientated internal power structures.

On the one hand, controls over important aspects of public service provision have been centralised. Increased use of performance indicators, benchmarking and the dissemination of best practice (through regulatory bodies and consultants) have generated markedly similar models of organisation and strategy. Tightened budgetary controls have created hostile bargaining environments and reduced greatly the scope for successful union mobilisation at local level (Bacon and Storey, 1993). Public sector unions have turned increasingly to the law to provide frameworks or minimum standards for local decision-making. Co-ordination, within and between unions, to identify test cases through which to establish legal precedents in domestic and European courts has become an increasingly important activity and unions have had considerable success with legal action on equal pay for work of equal value and transfer of undertakings (Colling and Dickens, 2000, forthcoming).

The need for well-resourced central structures, capable of co-ordinating activity, responses and initiatives, is heightened by pressures such as these. At the other end of the spectrum, however, relatively weak local organisation has been exposed by the decentralisation of managerial authority.

Local authority departments have always operated with some degree of autonomy, particularly those providing statutory services. Through the 1980s authorities decentralised further, first within departments to neighbourhood offices (Lowndes, 1991) and then across them so that local units assumed control over combinations of services (Flynn, 1993: 168). However, decentralisation became radical following Central Government reform to extend competition and market mechanisms into service provision. Compulsory competitive tendering (CCT) furnished the most direct vehicle by forcibly requiring authorities to invite competition for the right to provide a specified range of services and obliging them to accept the lowest-priced tender. Beyond those services covered by CCT, authorities have been required to shift from direct administration to an 'enabling' role, procuring provision from a range of suppliers. Residential and home care services have been developed increasingly through a 'mixed economy' of provision including the private and voluntary sectors in addition to directly employed workforces. Management functions in these services have been divided between clients and contractors (or purchasers and providers) with authority devolved to contractors through formal and informal mechanisms. An education market place, of a limited sort, was promoted through the attenuation of local authority influence. Influence over schools was diminished by local management of schools (LMS), the former polytechnics were incorporated as 'new universities' in 1992, and a similar process followed for further education colleges. In these cases, head teachers, executive managers and governing bodies have taken on significant new roles in relation to finance and staffing.

Though softened following the change in government in 1997, an emphasis on a plurality of service providers remains. Public–private partnerships, initiated as the *Private Finance Initiative* under the previous Conservative administration, have continued with commercial consortia bidding for the right to build and manage key local resources such as schools and roads. CCT is to be replaced by a new regime based on *Best Value*. Elements of prescription and compulsion have been removed but authorities will still be encouraged to use specialist private and voluntary sector input where appropriate and, paradoxically, the limits on doing so conjured by the CCT legislation will be removed.

Collective bargaining within local government has also been decentralised, in the light of these and other developments. Growing financial pressures combined with the transfer of responsibility for labour costs to local authorities from national government, strained the cohesion of national arrangements. Employers argued the need for greater flexibility to meet local priorities and to deal with the fragmentation generated by marketisation. Unions, though broadly anxious to retain national provisions, became increasingly aware of their limitations and costs (Kessler, 1991: 7). Nationally prescribed pay awards have carried unpredictable consequences for employment levels locally and have proved a blunt instrument in the context of discussions around CCT. These pressures culminated in the Single Status agreement signed in 1997. Though the framework remains a national one, significant new responsibilities for local negotiators are generated by the agreement. Key features include the harmonisation of the administrative, professional, technical and clerical (APT&C) with manual terms and conditions to create one new 'Green Book'; single table bargaining; a 37-hour working week; assimilation of employees onto a new pay spine; and review of grading structures all of which is to be conducted at employer level.

Developing UNISON: the regional context

Attention now turns to the manifestation of these pressures within the case study region. Region One has approximately 93,000 members organised in ninety branches and serviced by 3000 stewards. Two brief sections provide background on branch structures and on regional support for branch-based activities. Discussed then are the implications of this infrastructure for three key activities: recruitment; representation; and negotiation.

Branch structures and resourcing

Some of the organisational issues generated by environmental change had been met already by the creation of UNISON. Branches merged on the basis of single employers, effectively confirming the NALGO model as against the NUPE one based on areas. The merger settlement consolidated branches as the key unit of local organisation underpinned by the general rubric that the union should be 'member-led' and assurances enshrined within new financial regulations. These increased the resources available locally, particularly for NUPE members whose branches had retained relatively meagre funds previously. The right to collect subscription income deducted at source by employers was transferred to UNISON headquarters. In exchange, branches were able to retain their branch funds (these were substantial in the case of some NALGO branches) and were promised increases in the proportion of subscription income allocated to them, known as branch retention. Between 1993 and 1995, the union's combined branch accounts stood at some £24 million (interview notes) and, following the promised increase in branch retention, one quarter of current income now goes back to branches.

Merged branches became substantial organisations in their own right. Larger branches visited during fieldwork serviced several thousand members over large geographical areas. They were based in two or three floors of dedicated office space, employed administrative and support staff, and operated their own IT systems which enabled them to administer membership records and produce branch literature in-house. It was reported that some branches had built up significant reserves in their branch funds, amounting to several thousand pounds in some cases, particularly where they continued to enjoy sponsorship in kind from their employers (e.g. use of office space free or at below market rents).

Regional support for branch-based activities

Activists carried into the merger differing expectations of the level of service they should receive from regional staff. NUPE members relied heavily on their full-time officers who led negotiations (at all levels), were involved in first line grievance and disciplinary cases (referred to colloquially as 'rubber boots issues'), and often took an active role in day-to-day administration of the branch. NALGO activists were generally more self-reliant and some branches even restricted the grounds upon which regional organisers could visit the branch or attend meetings.

The demand for full-time officer support was said to have grown following merger, however. Diminishing branch structures were partly responsible as the NALGO position of Branch Organiser was being phased out. These branch-based staff, paid for jointly by the branch and the national union, had benefited larger branches in particular but were being transferred gradually to regional organiser positions or left unfilled when individuals left the organisation. On the other side of the equation, casework and negotiating activity continued to grow apace. Consequently, even those branches with reputations for asserting their independence acknowledged their need for full-time officer support in areas including taking casework to Employment Tribunals and managing inter-union relationships in corporate-level negotiations.

The region's ability to meet this demand was restricted, however, by the financial crisis which followed in the wake of merger and intensified gradually. Declining membership generated commensurate falls in union income, compounded by changes to the bands determining the level of subscriptions paid and repeated refusals by conference to raise subscription levels overall. Senior regional managers estimated that they had lost an average of £150,000 per annum since merger and had seen their staffing budget decline by 28 per cent. Two organisers had been transferred to a neighbouring region and a number of management positions had been deleted. Whilst the level of support required from individual organisers remained significant, branches overall had been warned of the need to be more self-reliant in the future as paid-officer support was likely to decline further.

Examined now are the implications of this scenario for three areas of branch activity; recruitment; representation; and negotiation.

Recruitment

In the context of declining membership, recruitment had become a key priority for the region. Since merger, there had been a 9 per cent drop in membership nationally and respondents estimated that Region One had lost 2 per cent of its membership every year. Some of this is merely 'paper decline', that is it is attributable to rationalisation of old data. Real decline was significant, however, and has outstripped by some way declines in employment. Respondents acknowledged that density levels in some branches had dipped below 50 per cent. This is consistent with national research indicating falls in average density in local government from 78 to 46 per cent (Waddington and Kerr, 1999). Just to retain current membership levels, the region needed to recruit 10,000 new members per annum. In the last full year prior to the research, 9,300 joiners were registered.

According to survey evidence studied by the region, three key areas were responsible for the decline. First, membership amongst managerial grades had declined in response to delayering (and subsequent job loss) and as those remaining opted for professional associations, or no representation at all, in preference to trade union membership. Second, inclination to join amongst core white-collar staff had declined, particularly amongst full-time men. Finally, the union had been unable to follow members transferred into the private sector or to recruit in the voluntary sector organisations providing services on behalf of local authorities.

Organisers were aware of the need to prioritise recruitment but methods based on their direct involvement were seen as impracticable. Partly, this was a matter of limited time but large scale recruitment exercises also provided diminishing returns. A co-ordinated exercise in one county authority had yielded only 400 members and none of these were as a result of face-to-face contact with full-time officers. At branch level, however, activities were limited generally to paper exercises. Better organised activists monitored their own membership data, responded to lists of joiners and leavers when these were offered by employers, and circulated regular newsletters, including membership application forms. Again, activities involving face-to-face contact or regular time commitments from stewards were reportedly few and far between.

Recruitment objectives remained modest in these circumstances. Respondents at branch level were aware of enormous recruitment potential in the growing voluntary sector. Securing recognition was said to be less difficult than often assumed. Small employers could be persuaded of the value of experienced advice on employment law and proper procedures. But branches were reluctant to recruit further because these employment contexts generated a disproportionate amount of casework and negotiation which they found difficult to service. Contact with members became problematic since local authority employers were reluctant to see union facility time being used to service members who were not local authority employees. Significantly, staff employed by commercial contractors under CCT arrangements were viewed in a similar way. Such was the lack of experience in this area that one branch officer interviewed was unclear as to whether such employees were even eligible for membership.

Unable to reach beyond their heartlands amongst directly employed local government staff, regional priorities cohered around 'in-fill' recruitment, that is the recruitment of non-union workers in establishments where others are members. As one senior manager put it,

> There are loads and loads of non-unionised workers in residential homes in
> this region but if 50 per cent of direct local authority employees are not

members, then I know where my priorities lie. I have to get that 50 per cent where we already have collective bargaining, facilities agreements, and deduction-at-source arrangements. No problems.

Understandable in the context of severe financial and resource constraints, priorities of this kind are likely to have ramifications for the future shape and organising capacity of the union to which we must return.

Representation

Branch mergers brought important potential benefits for the representation of members interests. Most obviously, by incorporating large proportions of local authority workforces, mergers provided the opportunity to balance their interests within one organisation, rather than across competing ones as previously. A prerequisite for realising this potential, however, is that diverse interests are represented equally and this is the issue examined in this section.

Whether attributable to a secular decline in collective activity or to the growth of a 'climate of fear', branches in region one reported significant general difficulties securing and retaining stewards in sufficient numbers. Weaknesses in organisation were particularly apparent amongst manual workers. In some areas, representation had not recovered from the damage done by the terms of branch mergers. NUPE branch officer posts were effectively eliminated once the smaller area branches were incorporated within the single employer model. Many incumbents chose not to stay on as stewards and some even resigned to join competitor unions. Diminution of personal influence appeared to be a motive in some cases but more far-reaching factors were also at play. With the focus of branch activity shifting from local areas to departments and the corporate centre, manual representatives were said to find the culture of centralised branches rather alienating. As a former NUPE organiser explained,

> The old NALGO branches, you see, . . . modelled themselves on local government so you had endless committees. Finance committee, this committee, that committee which themselves are very alienating for manual workers. Its not where they come from because a meeting to them was a meeting that anybody in the branch could come to if they wanted to. You could raise any issue you wanted to raise. Whereas the NALGO culture was, they didn't have members' meetings. Meetings were for branch committee members and it was just like receiving the papers for a city council meeting.

Manual representatives were also concerned about the loss of control over, albeit limited, financial resources at local level. NUPE branch secretaries had received previously a small honorarium based on the number of members and some were said to have used these to supplement branch funds. Though resources at branch level were increased as a consequence of merger, access to them by manual representatives was attenuated.

These internal factors had begun to diminish in importance by the time of the review, mitigated to some extent by active steps taken by branches to engage with their manual memberships. Branches visited during the fieldwork had established area committees, feeding into a department-based structure, using old NUPE branch boundaries. One had opened a satellite branch office in an outlying area which had been formerly a NUPE stronghold and another was experimenting with IT and telecommunications systems to improve remote access to branch and union systems for isolated stewards.

Such initiatives had to contend, however, with the continuing fragmentation of manual worker employment. They had been hit hardest by 'marketisation' measures which had atomised their representation, distanced them from the core interests of the branch, and multiplied the time and financial costs incurred in servicing them effectively. Branches within Education Authorities reported problems accruing from the local management of schools, for example. In the context of declining staffing levels and budgets, schools were reluctant to allow stewards facilities time for employer-wide business. One branch, alive to the need to sustain manual representation, had attempted to renegotiate facilities agreements and the some headway was made towards establishing a central fund from which schools could draw to cover for trade union activities. At the time of the fieldwork, however, the proposal had run into difficulties following political objections raised in the council chamber about the general level of 'subsidy' offered to trade unions.

Problems generated by CCT and other forms of outsourcing were still more widespread, extending way beyond schools-based staff. Problems in sustaining indigenous manual representation were particularly acute in services subject to contracting and branches clearly found it difficult to maintain contact and effective input on an 'outreach' basis. In many cases, tendering processes and contracts governing services at the time of the fieldwork had been settled prior to branch mergers and current branch officers had little knowledge of their detail or implications. Organisers suggested that branches had often focused their attentions on the remaining 'core workforce', leaving paid officers to deal with tendering and those staff subject to it. One complained,

> I dealt with one particular council where the branch just did not deal with, and did not include at all, members who had gone off under CCT . . . They had kept a lot of their members but the entire workload fell on me because the branch was not involved in, was not willing to be involved in, doing anything . . .

This was not, it was emphasised, purely a matter of branch resources.

> I don't think they have got the inclination. Even if they did have the resources, I think those resources would be used up on people within the larger employer rather than outside.

Negotiation

As discussed above, contrary to the stereotype of public sector industrial relations, decentralised bargaining is not a novel experience in local government. Indeed, as one senior manager put it, 'local bargaining had set the agenda for national initiatives as much as the other way around'. Branches had considerable experience of the kinds of activity required of them by the single status agreement and, in some senses, branch mergers had strengthened further this local capacity. By reducing the number of bodies representing staff, they diminished considerably the scope for divide and rule tactics being used against workforces and increased potentially the ability of negotiators to co-ordinate bargaining tactics. Single status was qualitatively distinct from any previous negotiations, however. Their gravity and complexity, combined with the uneven patterns of representation just noted, provided significant obstacles to the realisation of this potential.

That negotiations were conducted within a diminished national framework added considerably to the breadth and gravity of the issues dealt with locally. Experience within branches cohered around the development and implementation of procedures. Obligations to approve the operationalisation of the 37-hour week and to agree job evaluation locally, by contrast, affected the 'pounds, shillings and pence our members receive' to a far greater extent than previously (regional organiser). The context in which local agreements were reached had also changed. Bargaining had been conducted historically in the context of expansion. For some white-collar negotiators, this was true even during the difficult 1980s when fragmentation and rationalisation of manual structures was offset to some degree by increased employment in areas like social services (Colling, 1997). Current negotiating contexts, however, are austere for all groups of staff and employers approached single status negotiations with a view to driving through cost savings. Differences reported between employers appeared to be stylistic rather than substantive. Whilst some were more inclusive and sophisticated than others, most attempted to secure reform or elimination of benefits to pay for the 37-hour week, for example.

The bargaining context was also more complex than previously. At branch level, single status negotiations could be experienced as simply the latest in a bewildering array of initiatives with which they were struggling. Some larger employers were reviewing their systems in an attempt to achieve designation as 'Beacon Authorities'. Similar reviews were taking place *vis-à-vis* 'Best Value', the Government's replacement for CCT, and experimentation with Education Action Zones and the Private Finance Initiative was happening simultaneously. In those authorities affected by local government reorganisation, all of this came soon after either the excision or incorporation of large numbers of education and social services staff and all of the upheaval generated for employment structures and branch organisation alike. A branch officer from a county branch, which had lost several of their 'crack stewards' to a city authority granted unitary status, complained,

> We are in the middle of negotiating all these things which have been lumped together. Best value, private finance initiative, single status, cuts in old people's homes. It has all been brought together in one enormous lump.

In the context of austerity, 'bundling' of this kind could have quite stark ramifications. Single status negotiations in this authority were connected with 'Best Value' service reviews. Focusing in part on employment conditions, these involved comparison with private sector practice and explicit threats to outsource services where closer approximation was not achieved.

In the judgement of organisers, these contexts required tactical judgements of a kind that some branches were simply not equipped to make. With important exceptions, branches beset by internal difficulties and pressures from their employers tended to react defensively rather than adopt proactive approaches. For example, whilst acknowledging the obvious threats, female organisers stressed the opportunities afforded by single status to put employers 'on the back foot' over equal pay for work of equal value but doubted the capacity of key branches to pull this off independently. One recalled presenting the Equal Opportunities Commission Code of Practice on Equal Pay to a group of senior branch officers,

> So they say, 'oh, alright then' but they would never in a million years have picked it up and thought 'oh this is something we should put on the agenda' because it wouldn't have . . . they are very reactive in terms of what they do. They just like to have their arguments with the employer.

Decisions over the level at which to bargain also proved awkward for branches. Fearing attempts to divide and rule by manipulating weaker staff side groups in departments, some branches pushed vehemently for single corporate level nego-tiating bodies. Others were equally fearful of line management attempts to push agreements past corporate negotiators unaware of the detail of departmental arrangements and insisted on devolved bargaining. Irrespective of the approach taken, organisers were aware of the importance this placed on internal relation-ships and communications. Branches were used to balloting members on the outcome of negotiations but less practiced in how to seek mandates or determine priorities at the outset. Given uneven patterns of representation, there was a real danger key considerations for some groups of staff were simply ignored by senior negotiators because they were unaware of them or because they failed to acknowledge their importance. Some employers were willing to exploit and exacerbate such difficulties by focusing their quests for cost savings on particular services or on one of the two negotiating groups. One county authority which had retained a large, directly employed manual workforce had sought savings exclusively from APT&C staff.

> I suspect this is a political thing. They want the union to be forced into defending their better-off members. They want to operate the argument,

'look, we're doing this really important thing for low-paid manual workers, part-timers, and you're just defending your higher paid members'.

(Regional Organiser)

The overall effect of these pressures was to increase the workload of regional organisers. In part, this was demand-led. Organisers reported their branches calling them in more often for advice, to participate in negotiations, or simply so that they had, 'someone to shout at'. Were this to be the sole cause of the reported increase in workload, it might be expected to diminish as local negotiations become more routine and competence grows within the branches.

But increases were not due to demand alone. Indeed, organisers were adept at deflecting demands where they felt this would encourage or require branches to deal with problems they were capable of resolving by themselves. Important elements of organisers increased workloads came from their *active intervention* in branch decision making. Moreover, the decision to intervene was not based necessarily on inexperience amongst the negotiating team, though this was one factor. Rather, the need to ensure equity within branches or consistency between them was paramount. Organisers intervened where negotiating teams were imbalanced, in terms of gender or blue and white-collar groups, to ensure that they didn't 'leap into agreeing something that (had) more severe implications for one group of members over others' (regional organiser). Decisions were based often on professional judgements and knowledge of the branch but these were underpinned by management pressure from within the union. While managers encouraged organisers in general terms to withdraw from branches and allow them to negotiate for themselves, they were said to have specific expectations in terms of outcomes for which organisers, rather than the branches, were held accountable. For example, local managers sought to ensure that key local authorities adopted the job evaluation scheme agreed nationally, rather than others as they were entitled to do.

> There is a very, very clear responsibility that we have to inform the broader region of developments in our particular area. For example, on job evaluation, there is a reluctance on the part of some employers to accept the national scheme. . . . It has been made very clear that we have got to be out there ensuring that happens and dealing with those employers who say they are not going to accept it. And, also, informing the centre of those employers who have accepted the scheme so that we can get, you know, some peer pressure on the others.

(Regional Organiser)

Ensuring equal treatment and balancing interests across the full range of local government members are likely to remain core issues for the union in the future. In this context, co-ordination between branch and region, region and the national centre will remain a key characteristic of public service unionism, as it has been in the past. With national agreements weakening key procedural aspects of that activity, the role of professional structures, and paid organisers within them, seems set to remain critical. It is in this context that we turn now to the process and outcomes of the Region's functional review.

Functional review in Region One

The process

The strategic review was intended to address such issues systematically. Stemming from a decision of the annual delegate conference in 1995 it comprised a series of functional reviews of national departments and, subsequently, regional structures culminating in the production of 5-year plans. These were to focus on effective ways of achieving core objectives and the shifts in investment and resources required to achieve them. Space does not permit detailed discussion of the process here (see Chapters 4 and 5 of this volume for further details) but two aspects of the experience in Region One require emphasis.

First, though functional reviews of national departments had been conducted previously and some reorganisation announced, little was known at regional level about the likely shape and extent of decentralisation from national headquarters to the regions. Indeed, the very notion of decentralisation had become somewhat obscured by the time of the regional review. The original motion to conference contained an explicit brief to recommend, 'the appropriate allocation of resources to regions, proportionate to the level and depth of work undertaken at that level' (internal documents: 1996). Principles underpinning the review included an acknowledgement that UNISON, 'is at present over-centralised and grossly bureaucratic' and that this required 'a planned and ordered movement of staffing resources from national to regional level' (ibid.). Terms of reference for the regional reviews, by contrast, referred only to ensuring 'that services are provided closer to the members wherever possible' and looking at options to 'free resources to strengthen local workplace organisation' (UNISON, 1997: 10). Nobody interviewed entertained any prospect of additional financial or staffing resources being transferred from national offices. As one organiser reflected, 'there weren't vast functions being moved from national to region where everyone could say, "oh, isn't that great," you know.' Senior managers referred to discussions about devolution of functions and budgetary controls but stressed that these were aimed at the medium term and assumptions about them had not been built into 5-year plans.

Second, because of this and the general context of financial stringency, emphasis was attached to the achievement of objectives within current, and possibly declining, budgets. Particular attention was paid, as per the original motion, to further possible savings from management structures. Beyond this, local perspectives became preoccupied with the distribution of funding between professional structures and the branches and the apparent paradox of substantial branch funds co-existing with requirements for cuts in professional structures. Unable to recoup or access these funds directly, lateral thinking was required.

As a senior manager suggested, the central motif for the exercise became, 'if you can't move the money, then move responsibility for the service to where the money is.'

The model

It should be noted that the model of organisation emerging from the reviews has yet to be confirmed in full. At the conclusion of the research, the region's 5-year plan had been accepted but specific initiatives within it were subject still to approval by senior management at national level and by the NEC. Regional managers had prepared their ground carefully, however and they were confident that key elements would be established in due course.

Reorganisation of branches

A critical role was posited for branches within region one's review. The central motif for the review, discussed above, required that they take on responsibility for an expanded range of membership services. But devolution was to be managed carefully. Plans to decrease officer involvement in day to day branch matters were matched by increased influence over longer term development and direction.

Quid pro quo's secured previously at Annual Conference had provided some of the groundwork for devolution. In exchange for increased branch retention, branches had assumed responsibility for some costs borne previously by the region including printing, distribution and education/training. Elements of the 5-year plan depended on the extension of this principle to other areas. It was envisaged that branches would pay for selected regional campaigns, meetings of regional working groups. Depending upon changes to financial regulations, it was also envisaged that branches may be able to contribute directly to the salary costs for additional regional organising staff.

Branch activities and responsibilities were also to be expanded. Organising staff were given clearer roles in monitoring branches' strategic development and direction. These were embodied within Branch Development Plans. Responsibility for completing these rested explicitly not with the branch but with the full-time officer and, once agreed, they were subject to approval by regional committees. Though the formats adopted varied from branch to branch, they were to be used to encourage branches to take on increased responsibility for recruiting, collective bargaining, and 'rubber boots' issues (grievance and disciplinary hearings) with objectives set, once again, by core outputs.

For the longer term, the 5-year plan referred to the need to develop workplace trade unionism and, specifically, to improve representation amongst manual groups. The focus of communications within the region was adjusted from the branch to the workplace and the broader membership. Provision was made for ten bulletins per year delivered directly to stewards and three or four bulletins were planned for the membership as a whole. For the longer term, managers hoped to benefit from the extension of UNISON*direct* into the region. A pilot scheme in the London area had linked members to stewards via a call centre, the number for which was publicised using internal literature and public advertising.

Reorganisation of regional professional structures

Commensurate with encouragement of lay activists to take on additional tasks, direct support from paid officers was reduced. Employment within the region was cut back and organising staff remaining were encouraged to focus on broad development and organisational work rather than 'rubber boots' issues. Changes in the composition of the region's workforce and in management style reinforced such orientations.

Consistent with the overall context of financial stringency, proposals were founded upon an aggregate decline in employment within the region. As a member of the Regional Management Team put it,

> At the end of the day, however I try to dress this up, there will be fewer officers and the Five Year Plan . . . makes that clear. If . . . everything we are planning is applicable in a year's time, there has to be fewer organisers.

The number of organising staff overall was reduced from thirty-three at the time of merger to twenty-nine projected within the proposals. Incorporated within this, as required, was significant pruning of the management structure from twelve at the time of the merger to five.

Below management level, the organising workload was redistributed. The number of paid staff engaged on organising tasks actually increased from twenty-one to twenty-four but this involved three fewer Regional Organisers. Those remaining were encouraged to withdraw from providing direct support to branches and to focus instead on broader development and organisational issues. Four innovations stemming from the review were designed to support such a shift. First, organising staff were redeployed in three cross-functional teams. That is, teams were based for the first time on geographical areas, rather than services, with an expectation that individual organisers would work with branches from a range of service groups. The gravitational pull exerted on organisers by individual branches was expected to weaken in this context; '[we want to] break the brick walls we have built around branches, having one officer responsible for everything than happens in that one branch' (RMT member). Second, routine casework, handled previously by organisers, was to be passed to a specialist team of three caseworkers. Third, organisers and regional managers were also to be released from servicing lay committees. Instead, regional secretarial staff were to undertake such functions and they were also to be deployed within branches to advise on aspects of office and branch administration.

All of this took place within an increased emphasis on proactive management of the union including the closer management of organisers. Following rational-isation of management structures, key roles were envisaged for the three remaining Senior Regional Organisers. Each one was to take on regional responsibility for a specific service area and lead one of the multi-functional teams. Team performance was to be evaluated against targets derived from the core outputs and SRO's were given discretion over how staff should be deployed to meet them. Decisions over the nature of cross-service working and the pace at which it was to be introduced were devolved to this level. Significant budgetary discretion was also anticipated for the future with team based budgeting used eventually as the basis for staffing decisions.

Discussion and conclusions

Public service unionism has been distinguished by three key characteristics. Relatively centralised structures, in terms of authority and resources, mirrored those prevailing for collective bargaining purposes and facilitated coherent responses to public policy debates. Public service unions, NALGO and NUPE prominent amongst them, tended to be organisationally pro-active. Professional structures were geared towards sponsoring and developing effective lay representation. Finally, the work undertaken by public service workers required their unions to engage in political debate and activity to a greater extent than unions elsewhere. Onslaughts on the very concept of public service provision eroded distinctions between the interests of service users and service providers and was reflected in more sophisticated campaigning and industrial action.

Pressures mounting over the last two decades, however, have destabilised these structures and orientations. Intensified central controls over policy and finance have limited the exercise of strategic choice by employers. Bargaining tactics available locally have been restricted in these circumstances and unions have turned increasingly to public policy and the law to establish minimum floors of rights. On the other hand, particularly in local government, service provision at employer level has been decentralised, fragmented and dispersed to an increasing number of administrative centres, within and beyond the public sector. Collective bargaining has been adjusted accordingly with national agreements providing frameworks within which local negotiators are able to exercise significant discretion.

These contending pressures pull unions in quite different directions. Developments at employer level highlight that the need for well-resourced local organisation, always acknowledged, has now become acute. Arguably, this should foster devolved approaches to bargaining and representation similar to those found traditionally in the private sector. On the other hand, UNISON's central mission to represent all elements of large and diverse public workforces, makes it especially important to avoid economistic and sectional perspectives. Richard Hyman's advocacy of a cure to the 'sickness' of British trade unionism is apposite in this context.

> It is essential to co-ordinate activity; to avoid divisive demands and strategies; to relate particularistic interests to broader class interests; to show special

consideration for those . . . whose oppression by capital is matched by subordination within trade unionism itself.

(1989: 185)

Connections between levels of activity are critical in the complex environments described. Local objectives are strengthened by the availability of national policy and legal frameworks covering, *inter alia*, minimum earnings, pay equality, and rights under transfer of undertakings. For these to provide minimum standards in any meaningful sense, however, co-ordination is required to ensure that they are applied consistently and developed appropriately. Ligaments provided by professional structures become critical in this scenario.

These issues were addressed in part by UNISON's merger. The NALGO model of large, independent branch structures based on single employers was confirmed and resources were skewed towards branches to a greater extent than had been the case in NUPE previously. The strategic review, begun 2 years after the merger, reviewed the kind of professional support structures required by these branches. It was not undertaken in a vacuum, however, and the context of severe financial crisis has been influential. The basic framework emerging from the review is clear, though some aspects awaited confirmation at the conclusion of fieldwork. Branch autonomy is confirmed and extended, with lay activists undertaking functions formerly the responsibility of full-time officers. Recruitment, representation and negotiating in particular are to become the primary responsibility of the branch. Aspects of branch administration and routine representation at Employment Tribunals is to be undertaken by specialist staff. Withdrawing organisers from direct involvement in these tasks, it is envisaged, will facilitate some reductions in their number and a more strategic role for those remaining. Priorities cohere now around developing and sustaining organisation. Using mechansims such as Branch Development Plans, it is expected that organisers will become mentors to branches; monitoring their medium-term development and advising occasionally on tactical matters. Savings realised as a result of restructuring of this kind will be ploughed back into support functions, particularly at regional level.

Does this model meet the requirements of a contemporary public service union? Does it provide strong units of local organisation and the ligaments between them necessary to ensure consistency and equality? This research highlighted both the continuing demand for regional organiser input at branch level and, thereby some of the possible costs involved in its reduction.

First, recruitment efforts may be weakened. This is not to say that current targets are unachievable, though the difficulties are significant and well-known. Rather, they will remain confined to 'in-fill' recruitment leaving open key questions about the representation of workers delivering public services through third parties. We know that British unions are notoriously poor at approaching non-union workplaces. Millward and Stevens found that 85 per cent of establishments with non-union manual workforces and 90 per cent of establishments with non-union white collar workforces had not been approached by a union official in the previous five years (Kelly, 1990: 41). More recent findings suggest that unions are poor at following their members when they change jobs. More than a quarter of members relinquish their membership when changing employers even where a union is recognised in their new organisation. Where there is no recognition, the figure climbs to 75 per cent (Woodland and Cully, 1997). These findings find resonance in this study. Branches were prevented from extending recruitment beyond current heartlands not by opportunity but by the time and resources required to service them subsequently. This presents particular problems to public service unions affected by a significant amount of contracting and inter-agency working. Currently waiting in the wings, PFI and best value threaten to extend the fragmentation of membership, which has been so damaging in manual areas, into core areas of professional and technical services. How to recruit and retain members in these settings are questions yet to be resolved at regional level but this will almost certainly depend on paid officer input.

Second, withdrawal of organisers from direct involvement in branches may have consequences for attempts to ensure equality within representative structures. Surveys have revealed paid staff according higher priority than lay members to issues such women's representation (Kelly and Heery, 1994). In this study, ensuring appropriate accommodations between manual and non-manual members, in hostile bargaining environments, was also seen to require the intervention of paid officers. Representation amongst manual staff, a key factor in this study, is acknowledged within UNISON as being generally problematic (Williams, 1997: 504). Sometimes despite the best efforts of branches, members affected by local management of schools and by CCT have become distanced from the union. That lay representatives find it difficult to service such members effectively is reflected in surveys. Waddington and Kerr (1999) found that between one third and one half of UNISON's membership expresses dissatisfaction with some aspect of organisation. Infrequent contact with branch and full-time officers is a particular grievance cited by 20 per cent of those leaving the union (see chapter by Waddington, this volume). Where these problems stem from poor organisation, branch development plans co-ordinated by regional organisers, may offer important guidelines. Where they stem from an inability, or from a refusal, to address the issues, direct input from regional organisers may still be required if the consequences of uneven representation at branch level are to be avoided.

Finally, as has been apparent already in health (Lloyd, 1997), decentralised bargaining increases the calls on paid officers. Limited experience is a factor in some instances and, where this is the case, may be expected to abate once local bargaining becomes routine. Intervention to ensure diverse membership interests are treated equally was also common, however. Women officers reported having to encourage branches directly to pursue gender equality issues, for example. Consistency between branches also provided imperatives for organisers' intervention. Whilst generally encouraging withdrawal from negotiating activity, UNISON managers required organisers to ensure that particular precedents were set and others avoided. Intervention on these latter two grounds is entirely consistent with the unions broader mission and the need for it, therefore, is less likely to abate.

The strategic review process remains incomplete at the time of writing. There is important evidence of innovation and the potential for reinvestment following the realisation of savings will clearly be a critical issue as the organisation develops further. If public service unionism is to remain distinctive and appropriate to the context in which its members work, a greater degree of cohesion is required than that achieved by the private sector model apparent generally in the UK. Regional full-time officers play an important part in securing that. The next key test for UNISON's organisation will be whether resources devolved to branches as a consequence of the merger can be matched by support for local professional structures. Paradoxically, as has always been the case in the public services, properly resourced professional structures are a pre-requisite for effective workplace organisation.

Acknowledgements

The authors would like to thank staff and activists in Region One for their generous assistance with this research. We are also thankful to members of the Industrial Relations Research Unit (where the original version of this paper was first presented) and to the editor of this volume, Mike Terry. Their comments have helped us to improve the chapter considerably. Responsibility for errors and omissions remains of course with us.

References

AFL-CIO (Public Employee Department) (1992) *Reinvigorating the Public Service: Union Innovations to Improve Government*, Washington DC: AFL-CIO.

Bacon, N. and Storey, J. (1993) 'Individualisation of the employment relationship and the implications for trade unions', *Employee Relations*, 15:1.

Batstone, E. (1988) *The Reform of Workplace Industrial Relations: Theory, Myth and Evidence*, Oxford: Clarendon Press.

Clegg, H. (1979) *The Changing System of Industrial Relations in Great Britain*, Oxford: Blackwell.

Colling, T. (1997) 'Managing human resources in the public sector' in Beardwell, I. and Holden, L. (eds) *Human Resource Management: A Contemporary Perspective*, London: Pitman.

Colling, T. and Dickens, L. (2000) 'Gender equality and trade unions: a new basis for mobilisation' in Noon, M. and Ogbonna, E. (eds) *Equality and Diversity in Employment*, London: Macmillan, forthcoming.

Flynn, N. (1993) *Public Sector Management*, London: Harvester Wheatsheaf.

Fogarty, M. and Brooks, D. (1986) *Trade Unions and British Industrial Development*, Policy Studies Institute Research Report, London: PSI.

Foster, D. and Scott, P. (1998) 'Conceptualising union responses to contracting-out municipal services, 1997–97', *Industrial Relations Journal*, 29: 2.

Fryer, R. (1989) 'Public service trade unionism in the twentieth century', in Mailly, R., Dimmock, S. J. and Sethi, A. S. (eds) *Industrial Relations in the Public Services*, London: Routledge.

Heery, E. (1996) 'The new, new unionism', in Beardwell, I. (ed.) *Contemporary Industrial Relations: A Critical Analysis*, Oxford: Oxford University Press.

Hyman, R. (1989) 'The sickness of British trade unionism: is there a cure?', in Hyman, R. (ed.) *The Political Economy of Industrial Relations: Theory and Practice in a Cold Climate*, London: MacMillan.

Kelly, J. (1990) 'British trade unionism 1979–89: change, continuity and contradictions', *Work, Employment and Society*, May, special issue.

Kelly, J. and Heery, E. (1994) *Working for the Union: British Trade Union Officers*, Cambridge: Cambridge University Press.

Kessler, I. (1986) 'Shop stewards in local government revisited', *British Journal of Industrial Relations*, 24: 3.

Kessler, I. (1991) 'Workplace industrial relations in local government', *Employee Relations*, Special Edition 13: 2.

Lloyd, C. (1997) 'Decentralisation in the NHS: prospects for workplace unionism', *British Journal of Industrial Relations*, 35: 3.

Lowndes, V. (1991) 'Decentralisation: the potential and the pitfalls', *Local Government Policy Making*, 18: 2.

Massey, D. and Miles, N. (1984) 'Mapping out the unions', *Marxism Today* (May).

Sisson, K. (1983) 'Employers' organisations', in Bain, G. S. (ed.) *Industrial Relations in Britain*, Oxford: Blackwell.

Terry, M. (1982) 'Organising a fragmented workforce: shop stewards in local government', *British Journal of Industrial Relations*, 20.

Terry, M. (1995) 'Trade unions: shop stewards and the workplace', in Edwards, P. K. (ed.) *Industrial Relations: Theory and Practice in Great Britain*, Oxford: Blackwell.

Terry, M. (1996) 'Negotiating the government of UNISON: union democracy in theory and practice', *British Journal of Industrial Relations*, 34: 1.

UNISON (1997) *Strategic Review: Making Local Organisation our Priority*, NEC Report Number One.

Waddington, J. and Kerr, A. (1999) 'Membership retention in the public sector', *Industrial Relations Journal*, 30: 2.

Williams, S. (1997) 'The nature of some recent trade union modernization policies in the UK', *British Journal of Industrial Relations*, 35: 4.

Woodland, S. and Cully, M. (1997) 'Swings, roundabouts and slides: changes in union membership 1995–6'. Paper at British Universities Industrial Relations Association Conference, University of Bath, July.

7 Promoting representation of women within UNISON[1]

Anne McBride

Introduction

During the creation of UNISON, it was agreed that 'the promotion of equal opportunities and fair representation should be central to the union's organisation and structure at all levels' (COHSE, NALGO, NUPE, undated: 18). One of the founding principles of UNISON is the representation of 'women, members of all grades, black members, members with disabilities and lesbians and gay men' (UNISON, undated: 2). This is a very ambitious aim – particularly as UNISON is also the largest UK union representing workers across a number of very distinct public sector organisations. In one rule, UNISON is promising that its structures will recognise that over two-thirds of its members are women, that its members work in a very wide range of occupations and that a high proportion of its membership share aspects of exclusion and oppression in wider society. It would be an ambitious aim to discuss how UNISON has dealt with all of these aspects in one chapter. Instead, this chapter looks at the representation of one marginalized group and discusses how representation has been promoted for women as a distinct group of members.[2] It is based on case study material collected at national and regional levels within UNISON over a 2-year period (ending November 1995).

Drawing on feminist political theory, this chapter identifies a democratic need distinct to women – the need for a guaranteed role in policy formulation. The chapter presents two strategies for addressing this specific democratic need in society and voluntary organisations. One strategy seeks to guarantee a minimum number of women representatives on policy-making bodies. The other strategy seeks to guarantee that women, as a group, will be represented in the policy-making processes. The chapter makes a number of distinctions between the two strategies. The distinction used in subsequent analysis is that the former strategy identifies women as individuals in a sex-category and that the latter strategy identifies women as an oppressed social group (Cockburn, 1996). The potential of either strategy to guarantee women a role in policy formulation is noted, as too the possibility that both could operate at the same time. This framework is applied to trade unions and the chapter argues that genuine inclusion in union interest representation requires representation by individual women and representation of women as an oppressed social group.

Using the above framework, the chapter analyses the introduction and impact of proportionality and self-organisation. The chapter is based on research collected over a 2-year period using an in-depth case study approach. Research was conducted through the analysis of five committee structures and elections; observation of fifty-six union meetings at national, regional and service group level; and thirty-eight semi-structured interviews with members and paid officers. The chapter explains how two rulebook commitments have the potential to facilitate representation by individual women and of women as a group. It then indicates how this has been pursued in practice. In particular, the chapter illustrates how proportionality has pushed and pulled women into representative positions, thus achieving representation by individual women. Illustrations are also provided of how the priorities of women can be determined through self-organisation. However, despite these positive signs of representation by and of women, at the time of the research, committee agendas did not reflect the priorities raised by women as a group. Although proportionality had guaranteed individual women a role in policy formulation, this was not the same as guaranteeing women, as a group, a role in policy formulation. Whilst it could be argued that this discrepancy will diminish over time, the research raises a number of key obstacles to fundamental change. The chapter argues that a primary source of this discrepancy is UNISON's structure. Whilst it provides considerable support for women as a social group it does not support the representation of women as a social group. In the absence of rights to group representation, UNISON relies too heavily on women representatives to push women's priorities forward. In particular, this strategy takes insufficient account of men's responsibilities to their mixed constituencies, the multiple roles of representatives and the norm of discussing issues in gender-neutral terms. The chapter argues for a re-assessment of the links between self-organised groups and policy-making committees. For trade unions more generally, the chapter illustrates the importance of distinguishing between strategies supporting representation by individual women and those supporting representation of women as an oppressed social group.

Democracy and power

Women's distinct democratic need

A number of feminist political theorists have argued that women's marginalized position within society provides them with a distinct democratic need within society. This section summarises the debate and identifies this democratic need. For the purposes of this discussion, representative democracy is defined as 'a political system in which the people elect representatives to act for them for certain purposes' (Holden, 1993: 58). Participatory democracy is defined as a system in which 'the basic determining decisions (and perhaps other decisions) are made by the people actively participating in the political process' (Holden, 1993: 127). In the context of trade unionism, representative democracy will be used to refer to the system in which union members elect representatives to act for them at a number of levels within the union. Participatory democracy will be used to refer to the system in which union members actively engage in policy formulation and decision-making processes at an informal and local level.[3]

Feminist political theorists are in agreement that women need a guaranteed role in policy formulation (see Pateman, 1988; Young, 1990; Phillips, 1991, 1993). Although women have the right to vote and stand for election, they are consistently under-represented in national politics in most liberal democracies. A primary explanation for this phenomenon is that traditional conceptions of representative and participatory democracy make an artificial division between public and private spheres of life and ignore women's greater participation in the home. However, although Pateman (1983) argues that radical changes are required at home if women are to be equal and full citizens in society, the main strategies for increasing women's access to decision making relate to the structures of democracy themselves. Cockburn (1996) has usefully categorised these strategies into those that encourage the representation of women as 'individuals in a sex-category' and those that encourage the representation of women 'as an oppressed social group' (ibid.: 76–82).

Strategies for representing women as individuals in a sex-category

These strategies recognise that women, as a biological group, are under-represented in most policy-making bodies. The purpose of these strategies is to guarantee that a minimum number of women representatives will be present on those bodies. To achieve this, women are distinguished from others by their biological sex (Cockburn, 1996). Representative seats can be reserved for women in specific, absolute numbers (often referred to as 'quotas'), or in proportion to the number of women in the constituency (often referred to as 'proportionality'). The reservation of seats for women is an acceptance that a bias acts against the election of women and a belief that changing structures can enforce an improved presence of women (ibid.: 77).

As noted by Phillips (1991) and Cockburn (1996), it is important to remember that women who occupy reserved seats do so because of their biological status as women, not because they are philosophically committed to the priorities of women as a group (although they might be at the same time). Cockburn (1996) argues that since women elected as members of a sex-category have a constituency of men and women, they are not obliged to speak for women only. Put another way, it cannot be assumed that representation by women is the same as representation of women. Thus strategies that identify women as individuals in a sex-category will be addressing arguments for representatives to reflect the gender make-up of the represented, but will not be addressing arguments that call for women as a marginalised group to be represented. A number of writers argue that if society and organisations genuinely wish to include marginalised constituencies, they need to start from an appreciation of what it is to be a member of an oppressed social group.

Strategies for representing women as an oppressed social group

Such strategies recognise that it is not only women as a biological group who are under-represented on policy-making bodies, but women as a social group. When women are conceptualised as a social rather than a biological group, it is possible to focus on the social outcomes of marginalisation, rather than the numerical outcome. In other words, these strategies focus on the missing priorities of women, rather than on the missing women per se. Young (1990: 44) argues that social groups are not aggregates of individuals, but are defined through their social status, and the common history that social status produces. It is very important to note that the social group of women is defined through their sense of identity and not through shared biological attributes. Young (1990) identifies women as an oppressed social group because they are subject to 'gender-based exploitation, powerlessness, cultural imperialism and violence' (ibid.: 64). The definition of women as an 'oppressed group' enables recognition of the effects of that marginalization. In Young's words,

> Where some groups are materially privileged and exercise cultural imperialism, formally democratic processes often elevate the particular experiences and perspectives of the privileged groups, silencing or denigrating those of oppressed groups.
>
> (ibid.: 184–2)

A key distinction between this set of strategies and those identifying women as a sex-category, is that representation is not dependent on the election of individual women. Nor, does the concept rely entirely on structures of representative democracy. Instead, there is an emphasis on representation through women's active involvement in participatory democracy. There are two processes for guaranteeing the representation of women as a social group. Young (1990) discusses the first process and Cockburn (1996) and Briskin (1999) discuss the second.

Young (1990) believes it is possible to counteract the bias towards privileged groups by providing 'mechanisms for the effective recognition and representation of the distinct voices and perspectives of those of its constituent groups that are oppressed or disadvantaged' (ibid.: 184). From Young's perspective, women could be genuinely included if societies and organisations provided,

> (1) self-organization of group members so that they achieve collective empowerment and a reflective understanding of their collective experience and interests in the context of the society; (2) group analysis and group generation of policy proposals in institutionalized contexts where decisionmakers are obliged to show that their deliberations have taken group perspectives into consideration; and (3) group veto power regarding specific policies that affect a group directly, such as reproductive rights policy for women, or land use policy for Indian reservations.
>
> (ibid.: 184)

The importance of self-organisation lies in the space it provides for oppressed groups to determine their own interests away from the influence of the privileged group. The importance of the latter two mechanisms lies in the rights they provide to representation. The policy-making committees are seen as the 'mainstream' committees to which self-organised groups have rights of representation. From Young's (1990) perspective, this representation is exercised through the obligation of decisionmakers to take group policy proposals into account and through group veto. Thus, this three-dimensional process of self-organisation, consideration of group proposals and group veto suggests that women, as a group, would be guaranteed a role in policy formulation through their active involvement in informal, women-only groups.

Another mechanism for the representation of a social group on mainstream committees is the inclusion of a representative of the self-organised group on the mainstream committee (Cockburn, 1996; Briskin, 1999). Any women who were elected to represent a women's self-organised group on a mainstream committee would be expressly elected to represent the concerns of women as a social group (Cockburn, 1996: 90–3). As noted above, this is different to women elected to mainstream committees from mixed-sex constituencies who may well bring a woman's perspective to the committee but are not obliged to speak for women as a group. Irrespective of which mechanism is used to provide groups with rights to representation on mainstream committees, it is important to note they provide for the representation of social groups, not individuals. This is distinct from the earlier set of strategies that provide for representation by individuals. Thus, one way of distinguishing between the two sets of strategies for increasing women's access is to note that the former set emphasises representation by individual women and the latter set emphasises the representation of women as a group.

Cockburn (ibid.: 89) argues that it is possible, and desirable, to provide for representation by individual women and representation of women as a social group. Certainly a number of commentators agree that increasing the number of individual women representatives on policy-making bodies is a necessary but not sufficient condition for guaranteeing women a full role in policy formulation. Whilst increasing the number of women on policy-making groups empowers individual women, it does not empower the social group of women. In other words, changing the sex of the players does not guarantee a change in the power relations between men and women. From this perspective, until fundamental change takes place in society, men will continue to be members of a materially privileged group and women will continue to be members of a socially oppressed group. The relevance of this perspective to trade union democracy is discussed in the next section.

Meeting women's democratic need in trade unions

A number of studies illustrate how women have been excluded from policy-making in unions and how their concerns have been suppressed (see Beale, 1982;

Cockburn, 1983, 1991; Colling and Dickens, 1989; Cunnison and Stageman, 1993). In particular, the studies provide a number of graphic illustrations of Young's (1990) argument that the perspectives of privileged groups (in this case men) are often elevated and the perspectives of oppressed groups (in this case women) are silenced. The pervasive nature of this exclusion can be seen in Cyba and Papouschek's (1996) study of female workers in four sectors in Austria. Their research revealed that a large proportion of problems mentioned by women never went beyond the preliminary stages of 'confused discontent, dissatisfaction or assessment of the problem' (ibid.: 71). They noted that a number of 'objectively' disadvantageous workplace situations were frequently leading to no reaction from the women themselves (ibid.: 69). By reconstructing the manner in which problems were articulated, Cyba and Papouschek were able to conclude that the process was blocked from the outset by 'inner barriers' (ibid.: 69). They attributed these inner barriers to women's lack of social identity in the world of work and argued for new forms of workplace representation which start from 'women's real life problems and experiences' (ibid.: 67–79).

The above studies stress the importance of who determines what is a legitimate trade union issue and underline the need for women to have an active role in the articulation and promotion of their interests. This is an important point at which to reiterate Cockburn's (1996) distinction between the representation of women as individuals in a sex-category and the representation of women as an oppressed social group. Cunnison and Stageman (1993) argue that a strategy that only seeks to increase the number of women in representative positions 'still leaves the pervasive hold of male culture, the underpinning of formal and informal male power' (ibid.: 167–8). This analysis suggests that unions would ideally pursue both strategies to ensure that women as individuals, and as a group, are guaranteed a role in policy formulation. In practice, few unions have developed both strategies to the same extent. A number of unions in the UK have recognised the importance of women's self-organisation. In a recent survey, fourteen of thirty unions surveyed provided some form of women-only structures (SERTUC, 1997). This compares with only six using reserved seats for women on their executive committees (ibid.). UNISON is one of the few unions providing for the representation of individual women at the same time as women's self-organisation.

Although unions are more likely to provide women-only structures, this is not the same as providing rights of representation to women as a social group. The latter is a problematic strategy. Whilst women's self-organisation enables women as a social group to determine their own priorities, providing such groups rights to representation challenges some of the basic principles of democracy. In particular, it challenges the idea that decisions are made by individual representatives elected by the whole people. Instead, it provides self-organised groups with an explicit role in decision making. Moreover, groups gain access to decision making because of their societal status not through their election by the whole people. Phillips (1991) sees the basis of this access as problematic. Phillips (ibid.) notes that present forms of representative democracy are based on political rather than social groups. She argues that this ensures that there are few mechanisms for enabling women's voices to be heard or women's perspectives to be agreed. In the absence of effective mechanisms for interest aggregation amongst women, Phillips concludes that the representation of women, as a group, rests 'too exclusively on trust' (ibid.: 91). As will be seen later, some UNISON activists echo these views. For Phillips, genuine inclusion of women starts from a major redistribution of household tasks and responsibilities and involves mechanisms to ensure that representatives mirror the national composition of society as a whole (ibid.: 152–7).

A more positive view of interest aggregation amongst women can be seen in trade union studies by Cockburn (1991), Cunnison and Stageman (1993), Briskin and McDermott (1993), and Briskin (1999). Whilst Phillips' (1991) work throws doubt on the capacity of democratic mechanisms to discover what women want as a social group, the above works are full of references to the effective use of such mechanisms. Given that Phillips' (ibid.) work concerns politics in society as a whole and the above studies relate to trade unions, it is tempting to conclude that trade unions are more able to organise suitable structures for social groups. Briskin's (1999) conception of self-organisation is based on a belief that it must take account of institutional realities of the trade union. For Briskin, the legitimacy of self-organisation depends upon 'maintaining a strategic balance between autonomy from the structures and practices of the labour movement, and integration (or mainstreaming) into those structures' (ibid.).

Briskin (ibid.) identifies resource control, decision-making powers and an organised and politicised constituency as essential elements of autonomy. Integration is dependent on protective mandates for women's committees; direct input into organisational decision-making; links to the collective bargaining process and union-wide communication potential (ibid.). Briskin's work indicates that women's voices and perspectives are heard when unions provide the aforementioned structures and processes. Moreover, this and similar studies provide illustrations of the ability of women's self-organisation to challenge male assumptions underpinning present forms of trade unionism and transform organisations so that they go beyond 'letting women in' (Briskin and McDermott, 1993: 6). Briskin's autonomy – integration framework can be used to demonstrate the considerable support that UNISON's rulebook provides for women's self-organised groups.

Representation by and of women within UNISON

Proportionality is an example of women being identified as individuals in a sex-category, defined as 'the representation of women and men in fair proportion to the relevant number of female and male members comprising the electorate' (UNISON, undated: 66). At the time of merger, women made up 80 per cent of COHSE, 74 per cent of NUPE and 51 per cent of NALGO but were under-represented on many committees. Using proportionality UNISON is encouraging an increase in representation by individual women and enabling (or enforcing) a process whereby representatives reflect the gender make-up of the represented.[4]

Self-organisation is an example of women being identified as members of an oppressed social group. UNISON rules provide for self-organisation of four disadvantaged groups within the union. The rules indicate considerable support for black members, lesbian and gay members, members with disabilities and women members. The rulebook states that self-organised groups should have resource control, decision-making powers and support for an organised and politicised constituency – all elements of autonomy cited as essential by Briskin (1999). Self-organised groups also have protective mandates; the potential for union-wide communication and direct input into organisational decision-making at branch, regional and national level – again, all elements of integration cited as essential by Briskin (1999). By supporting women's involvement in representative and participatory forms of democracy, UNISON's rule book is making it less likely that women will be silenced by men and more likely that women will be heard. These intentions are expressed in a UNISON recruitment leaflet aimed at women:

> We all joined a union because we want a better deal. Demands vital to women's working lives are already high on UNISON's agenda, but it will take women to push them through – and to develop new ones.
>
> (UNISON, 1994)

Given these clear intentions, UNISON provides an important site in which to explore the potential for unions to support representation by individual women and of women as a social group.

Supporting representation by women

This section looks at the way in which UNISON's rulebook supports representation by women at national and regional level.[5] The purpose of proportionality is to guarantee a minimum number of women representatives on policy-making bodies in UNISON. UNISON's proposals for meeting this aim are indicated in the structure of the National Executive Council (NEC), which is the only committee structure to be detailed in the rule book. UNISON makes a distinction between men and women members in the NEC structure.[6] Each constituency within the NEC is multi-representative so that more than one seat is contested per constituency. The representative seats within each constituency are variously reserved for female members, low-paid female members, male members, and female and male members (known respectively as 'women's seats', 'low-paid women's seats', 'men's seats' and 'general seats'). A minimum number of seats are reserved for women in each constituency. When aggregated across the NEC, this minimum represents 62 per cent. of all NEC seats and compares favourably with women's membership of UNISON in 1993 which stood at approximately 67 per cent. If every women's seat is filled and women win all the general seats, women could make up 75 per cent of the NEC. Given that UNISON now comprises 72 per cent women (TUC, 1999), this elasticity is an important feature of the constitution.

Within UNISON, the framework of direct elections; multi-representative constituencies; categorisation of seats by sex and low pay, facilitated the achievement of proportionality on three of five committees which the author studied (McBride, 1997). The effect of guaranteeing women's representation is illustrated most dramatically by the election of the first national Local Government Service Group Executive (LG SGE). Before the first UNISON Local Government service group elections, former NALGO and NUPE members were operating within interim sector committees based on the executives of their former unions. The interim sector committee for white-collar workers (primarily based on former-NALGO executive members) consisted of 25 per cent women and the interim sector committee for manual and craft workers (primarily based on former-NUPE executive members) consisted of 35 per cent women. The UNISON LG SGE brought together white collar and manual and craft workers. The proportion of women elected to the first LG SGE was 66 per cent. This compared favourably with the 65 per cent female membership in the Local Government service group and represented a dramatic increase in women's access to decision making at a national level in relation to both former partner unions. A key factor in the achievement of proportionality on committees was the inclusion of proportionality in the rulebook (together with the NEC template). The importance of creating these spaces is that it sent out positive messages to women and encouraged the demand for, and supply of, women representatives. Unfortunately, it is not possible to detail in this chapter the processes which made representation by women more likely to be realised or frustrated – this is provided elsewhere McBride (forthcoming). The important issue for this chapter is to note that, through its rulebook, UNISON is able to guarantee individual women a role in policy formulation.

Supporting representation of women

This section looks at the way in which UNISON's rulebook supports representation of women as a social group. This section explains how the structure supports debate amongst women at branch, regional and national level and indicates the implications of this for interest representation. It uses material collected from two regional women's self-organised groups (indicated in the text as Region X and Region Y) and material collected from the national women's committee and national women's conference.

The purpose of self-organisation in UNISON is to enable members of four identified groups – including women – to establish their own priorities. As noted earlier, UNISON's rulebook provides considerable support for groups whereby they have space to be autonomous and opportunities to be integrated. Although Region X and Region Y used this support in different ways, they both provided mechanisms to enable women's voices to be heard and women's perspectives to be agreed. Region X concentrated their resources on building a branch-based regional network of women activists. The intention was that the activists would organise women's shop-steward committees at branch level. Views expressed at this level would be represented at the regional women's committee consisting of representatives from across the region. The regional women's committee developed a 12-month programme of training for women shop stewards attracting a high number of new shop stewards. The delivery of shop steward training in women-only courses was seen as a way of teaching and enabling women to run the union and 'making it possible for them to intervene'. Women involved in developing this structure saw it as a way of supporting individual women representatives and providing for the representation of women as a group.

Region Y, by contrast, concentrated their resources on facilitating the participation of all women and providing an alternative way of doing things to mainstream activities to encourage members to determine their own activity within self-organisation. Regional Forums were held at which women discussed issues such as pensions; domestic violence; harassment; work-related stress; and personal development. These forums were expressly open to all women members so non-activist women would be encouraged to attend. The traditional standing orders of meetings were changed so questions could be posed on paper, rather than orally. The women's self-organised group also produced a quarterly regional Women's Newsletter that was direct-mailed to individual women across the Region and bulk-mailed to all branches.

However, despite women's self-organised groups providing opportunities to support women, the research indicated that this was not the same as supporting representation of women as a social group. UNISON has recognised that women are members of an oppressed social group but self-organised groups are not organised around service groups, nor do they have rights of representation on service group issues (with the exception of the national service group conference). In addition decisionmakers are not obliged to show their deliberations have taken group perspectives into account. Nor do social groups have veto power regarding specific policies that affect a group directly. Instead, the rulebook reaffirms the need for self-organised groups to 'work within the established policies, rules and constitutional provisions of the Union' (UNISON, undated: 20).

Although mainstream committees and conferences did consider motions from women's self-organised groups, this was the exception. In general, issues raised in women-only events were not visible on agendas or heard in meetings. Table 7.1 illustrates this phenomenon. It contains issues raised by women participating in the regional women's self-organised group in Region X. Only the issues in the right-hand column were also discussed in the mainstream Regional Committee or Council.

The table implies that a number of women's workplace concerns were not making their way to mainstream agendas and that women's investment in articulating these concerns was not being rewarded. Rather than interacting with mainstream structures, women's self-organised groups seemed to be running in parallel to them. Issues discussed within women's self-organised groups were

Table 7.1 Workplace causes of concern to women in region X

Discussed in women's self-organised group	Discussed in women's self-organised group and Regional Committee/Council
New employee rights for part-time workers	National minimum wage
Sexual harassment	Boycott of employer in dispute
Gender implications of CCT	Support for strike action: renewal of
Maternity/paternity leave	contracts
Difficulties of childcare for shiftworkers	Timing of meetings
Impact of multi-skilling on women	Facilities time
Job segregation	Time off for meetings (health;
Job evaluation/study of wage differentials	nightworkers)
Equal pay	Proportionality at branch level
Promotion	Inaccurate membership records
Positive action training	Pensions
Sickness policies	
Breast cancer screening scheme	
Fair representation of black women	
Direct mailings of women-only courses	
Training for local bargaining/CCT and TUPE	

seldom discussed in mainstream structures and issues discussed in mainstream structures were generally not discussed within the women's self-organised groups. Whilst this limited overlap may be construed as evidence of complementary processes, this distance – or parallelism – does have serious implications for the representation of women within the union. If concerns raised by women are not discussed in mainstream committees, they are unlikely to be pursued by the union.

This latter point is very important. Research by Waddington and Kerr (see Chapter 17 in this volume) indicates that UNISON women members at workplace level are more likely than men to be dissatisfied. This research reveals that women are more likely to say that they left UNISON because there was 'not enough help to members with problems' and because they 'received little information from UNISON'. The regional women's forum in Region Y provides another illustration of women 'missing out' at branch level. Women welcomed the opportunity to discuss a number of issues in regional women-only events as they did not discuss such issues at branches – despite their desire to do so. If concerns raised by women are not pursued at branch level, then it may be difficult to retain women members, or they may be more likely to embrace groups who are prepared to take militant action on their behalf. A female interviewee argued that women's self-organisation was a 'self-indulgent wank'. If women's self-organisation is unable to produce something fundamentally different, despite its many activities, this might be considered an apt description. Put more politely, women's self-organisation could be interpreted as an expensive way of marginalising some women within UNISON.

It could be argued that it takes time for self-organised groups to organise themselves so that their concerns are projected onto mainstream agenda. Indeed, prior to merger, the Final Report (COHSE, NALGO, NUPE, undated: 18) noted that tackling barriers to participation and ending exclusion would not be achieved overnight. However, the year-long observation of mainstream committees and women's self-organised groups suggests that there are fundamental barriers to the genuine representation of women as a social group within UNISON. The following section argues that, as constituted, women's self-organisation has insufficient access to represent women as a group. As a consequence, there is too much reliance on individual women representatives to represent women as a group. The section indicates reasons for this being a limited strategy.

Barriers to the representation of women

Noting that there are barriers to the representation of women within UNISON is not to say that UNISON has not supported women as a social group – the above evidence shows that it has. In Briskin's (1999) terms, UNISON has provided women's self-organised groups with resource control and decision-making powers. It has provided protective mandates for women's committees, direct input into organisational decision making, and union-wide communication potential. What it has not provided are effective links to the collective bargaining process. Whilst encouraging members to participate in the union through local, informal groups is a necessary strategy, it does leave a potential vacuum for the representation of that group – particularly along service group lines. UNISON's guidelines on self-organisation note that 'the relationship between self-organised groups and service groups is crucial' (UNISON, 1998: 9) and that 'service groups at all levels . . . have a responsibility to ensure that the self-organised groups are able to participate in setting and discussing those [negotiating and service conditions] priorities' (ibid.: 10). However, these are guidelines, not rules. As noted above, group representation is possible through the representation of social groups on mainstream committees. That women's self-organised groups do not have seats on all mainstream committees, suggests that the primary function of self-organised groups in UNISON is to support members rather than to guarantee these social groups a role in policy formulation.

The argument that UNISON is supporting women as a social group, rather than their representation, can also be made using Young's conceptualisation of democracy for oppressed groups. As noted earlier, Young (1990) argued that the voices of oppressed groups could be heard if three mechanisms were instituted. Self-organisation was the first. The second was that decisionmakers should be obliged to show their deliberations have taken perspectives of oppressed groups into account and the third, that oppressed groups should have veto power regarding specific policies that affect them directly (ibid.: 184). Using these criteria, an overall assessment of UNISON's attempt to provide for representation of women would be that UNISON is achieving representation by individual women but not of women as an oppressed social group.

A UNISON recruitment leaflet noted that 'it will take women' to push the demands vital to women's working lives through the agenda. In the absence of representation of women as a group, UNISON is relying too much on individual women to push things through. Besides the point that men too should bear responsibility for pushing these issues through because many are representatives of female-dominated constituencies, this statement is limited for other reasons. Reference was made above to the conceptual difference between women elected by mixed constituencies and women elected by women. Although women elected by mixed constituencies may speak on women's issues, they are not obliged to speak on behalf of women because they are members of the same sex-category. It is only women elected by women who are obliged to represent women but, as noted above, women-only representation is not permitted on all mainstream committees. The research revealed limitations to the reliance on individual women to represent women as a group. They are constrained, first, by the multiple representative roles they perform and secondly, by the norm of discussing issues in gender neutral terms.

The multiple roles of women representatives

UNISON's perception that it would require women to push women's demands through to fruition assumes that women will primarily push women's demands, but ignores the reality of their multiple roles. The research showed that whilst women do share some common lived experiences concerning their subordinate position within society, they chose not always to prioritise these concerns all the time. Woman representatives might speak simultaneously, or separately, for a geographical region, for an occupational group, for women and for a political group. Raising women's concerns was only one of their roles. Indeed according to one interviewee, proportionality may even lessen the need to speak for women:

> I do not feel the same compulsion to raise 'women's needs' as there are plenty of other women who would raise or do raise the issues.

Whilst this phenomenon is not specific to women, it needs to be built into UNISON's strategy for ensuring that women's demands move onto mainstream agendas. First, male representatives need to be aware that they too need to represent the views of their female constituents. Second, it is important to note when members are more likely to raise women's concerns and ensure that meetings provide the requisite environment. The non-participant observation of mainstream committees indicated that the relationship between women representatives and their pursuit of women's concerns is contingent. The study identified three of these contingencies. First, women speak explicitly for women when they are the elected representatives from a women's self-organised group. Second, they speak explicitly for women when they speak about issues arising from the domestic sphere. Lastly, women often speak for women when they discuss workplace issues – although this is often implicit, because they refer to the experiences of 'their members' rather than to those of 'their women members'. However, at the time of this research, these opportunities were limited and there was a strong tendency for agendas and committee discussions to be gender-neutral.

Gender-neutral discussions

Women did speak for women when they discussed domestic and workplace issues. However, such issues were not regularly discussed on the national and regional mainstream committees. Research on the Local Government National Service Group Executive and Region X's Committee and Council indicated a bias against discussing workplace issues and towards discussing wider policy-based issues in a non-gendered way. It was only when workplace issues were raised by women that women's experiences were fully articulated and distinguished from the experience of 'gender-neutral' members. These workplace issues explicitly or implicitly related to women because women were relating their experiences from all-women workplaces. It tended to be newly active women who spoke specifically about workplace issues but interviews and observations indicated that workplace-based discussions were not seen as a 'good thing' on national committees. Instead, a higher value seemed to be placed on those contributions that showed a breadth and depth of experience. In addition, the wider, policy-based issues tended to be discussed from a gender-neutral perspective. This was particularly noticeable in relation to discussions about trade union democracy; work organisation and issues such as Compulsory Competitive Tendering (McBride, forthcoming).

Given that the workplace is one source of the material differences between men and women, it is important to note the infrequency of discussion of workplace issues on mainstream committees. Hyman (1984: 181–2) talks about decision making being detached from members' experiences and it is possible to see this happening in mainstream regional and national meetings. Earlier studies and debates illustrate that this detachment from members' experiences is not a gendered phenomenon, but it could be argued that it has a gendered outcome. Although the process is the same for everyone, it has adverse implications for women because they are being distanced from discussing the very issues that are the basis of their subordination at work, for example, job segregation. This process of 'distancing' is a double-blow for women because it distances them from the key institutions which, from their point of view, need to be changed. It might be possible for these effects to be ameliorated by representatives from the women's self-organised groups but, as noted above, they do not have access to all mainstream committees.

All this confirms why individual women may not push the concerns of women. Given the research findings of Waddington and Kerr, this is a risky strategy. Providing women with rights to group representation on all mainstream committees would be one way of addressing this issue. However, this is not a simple matter of changing the constitution. Group representation is a challenging issue that requires fundamental changes in attitudes and expectations from all participants.

Making women's participation count

Structures of representation are based on the principle that individuals gain access to decision making through their election. Group representation challenges this view as it provides socially oppressed groups access to decision making because of their societal status. Perhaps it is not surprising that UNISON has not provided for the representation of women as a social group – it does constitute a radically different form of democracy. Young (1990) argues that decision makers should be obliged to show that their deliberations have taken group perspectives into consideration. In addition, she argues that groups should have veto power regarding specific policies that affect them (ibid.: 184). Are UNISON members prepared to give the self-organised groups such rights to representation? Are they prepared to make provision for the representation of women's self-organised groups on all service group committees. Are they prepared to change their guidelines on self-organisation into rules?

Taking such a radical step is further complicated by the nature of UNISON. The rationale for group representation is that this is the only way in which the experiences and perspectives of the oppressed groups will be heard by the privileged. However, with women taking up the majority of representative seats in UNISON questions are inevitably raised about whether this changes the status of women. Is it still possible to argue that women are an oppressed social group within UNISON? Is it still possible to argue that individual women representatives do not understand the particular experience and perspectives of women as a social group?

These are important questions for which the empirical evidence has some answers. That union business tended to be discussed in gender-neutral terms does suggest that the tendency to silence the perspectives of women is still strong. This is not to say that women representatives did not elevate the particular experiences of women from time to time. They did. However, given their multiple roles, their commitment could never be the same as that of a women's self-organised group representative, who had been specifically elected to talk for women. This is illustrated by the regional women's committee representative on the mainstream Regional Committee in Region X,

> My role is to progress wherever possible women's point of view. . . . my role is the voice of the women of the region.

Having a women's self-organised representative on every committee is not a guarantee that all of women's concerns will be discussed in mainstream committees (see Table 7.1) but it is a necessary and not sufficient condition for supporting the representation of women as a social group.

Another important condition is the presence of an organised and politicised constituency of women (Briskin, 1999). Phillips (1991) argues that there are few mechanisms in society for enabling women's voices to be heard or women's perspectives to be agreed. This argument was echoed by activists in UNISON concerned about the accountability of women's self-organisation:

> who do the self-organised women speak for. . . . their democratic account-ability is suspect and they are not necessarily mandated.

> I worry that self-organisation encourages self-selection and is therefore not democratic. . . . If there are no women at a local level, where is the accountability of women to the branch?

That women are uneasy about self-organisation should not be a surprise (see Colgan and Ledwith, 1996). Colgan and Ledwith attribute women's resistance to women's self-organisation to the environment in which they 'learned their trade unionism' (ibid.: 171). Certainly, this is a different model of trade unionism – but it is still one underpinned with elements of participatory democracy. UNISON has provided considerable support for women as a social group. Studies in Region X and Y confirm the ability of women's self-organisation to raise women's voices and concerns. The challenge is to channel the energies of this constituency of women into mainstream participatory and representative structures. In the long term this could be addressed through the constitution. In the short term, this could be addressed through existing structures.

Whilst women-only groups were encouraging women to become active within women's self-organised groups, they did not regularly engage with the mainstream representative policy structures. This implies that women-only groups need to identify the purpose and function of their groups in the context of the mainstream representative and participatory structures. Effective integration within the representative and participatory structures can be through two points of access. Given that women are members of an oppressed social group, gaining access through either point is not likely to be easy but, in the absence of rights to group representation on all mainstream committees, it is a necessary strategy.

First, women-only groups can gain access by supporting the election of their colleagues to mainstream committees. Active involvement in women's self-organised groups does not preclude women from being representatives on mainstream committees. Proportionality opens the door dramatically for all women. In addition, if more women compete for general seats, as well as women's seats, the possibility of achieving proportionality increases. If women are elected from women's self-organised groups, they will still be required to represent mixed constituencies. However, if they have been elected on the women's self-organised group 'platform', they also have a clear mandate to speak of women's concerns.

Second, women-only groups can gain access by participating at a local level just as any other interest group. In the absence of group representation, it is important that men and women representatives are aware of women's concerns. Activists in women's self-organised groups at branch level can formulate policy proposals for consideration at a number of levels. Within the service group structure, policy proposals could be sent to regional service group committees for onward transmission to the national service group executive. Alternatively, the proposal could be sent direct to the national service group conference. Within the non-service group structure, proposals could be sent to regional council for onward transmission to the national executive council. Again, the proposal could be sent direct to the national delegate conference.

If the primary purpose of women's self-organisation were participation in policy formulation at a local level, this could have a beneficial effect on levels of participation generally. Pateman (1970) argues that participation at a local level provides practice in democratic skills and procedures. The women's self-organised group in Region X was specifically training women to 'run the union' through women-only education groups. The benefit of learning such skills in a women-only environment is that 'expertise' and 'democratic skills' can be conceptualised in a manner that is useful, rather than prohibitive, to women. If women participate in policy formulation at a local level, they will be in a stronger position to mobilise support for women's concerns should they decide to become a mainstream committee representative. Although the above may sound overly prescriptive for organisations that are 'free' to determine their own interests, in the absence of strong mechanisms for their representation, anything less than the above would suggest that women as a social group are still being marginalised. Some may argue that this makes women fit into the structure, rather than the structure fitting round the women. However, the different approaches of Region X and Y imply a certain amount of flexibility in how self-organisation is pursued.

This chapter has argued that genuine inclusion of women requires representation by women *and* representation of women as a social group. Research has indicated that UNISON's structure does support representation by women. It does guarantee individual women a role in policy formulation. More specifically, this chapter has shown how proportionality can be used to overcome a bias against the election of women at national and regional level. Supporting the representation of women as a social group presents a different set of challenges. At the time of this research, UNISON's structure did not provide for the representation of women as a social group. In the absence of rights to group representation, UNISON has relied too much on individual women to represent women as a group. Not only does this ignore men and women's responsibilities to their mixed constituencies it suffers from two limitations. The strategy is limited by the multiple roles of women representatives and the tendency to discuss issues in gender neutral terms. Together, the structure and the strategy reduce the potential for women as a social group to have a guaranteed role in policy formulation.

This analysis has implications for all unions in the UK. Few unions support the reservation of seats for women on their policy-making committees. Given the potential for constitutions to support the election of individual women, is it defensible that many union committees do not yet reflect the gender make-up of their constituencies? In addition, unions are more likely to support women-only structures than reserved seats. Are these structures being used to support the representation of women as a social group, or are they merely supportive? Given the research in UNISON, it is likely to be the latter. Unions need to discuss whether they have the political will to support the representation of women as a social group and women need to organise themselves according to that response.

Notes

1   This research is part of a three-year study of UNISON funded by the Economic and Social Research Council. I would like to thank all members and officers within UNISON who gave so freely of their time and opinions during the study. Thanks also to Mike Terry, Linda Dickens, Cynthia Cockburn and John Kelly for their constructive comments on this work.
2   It is not the purpose of this chapter to deal with the diversity of women as a group. This is dealt with elsewhere (see McBride, forthcoming).
3   This equates to the phrase 'participative democracy' (e.g. Hyman, 1975: 76).
4   Another dimension of representativeness dealt with in the rulebook is 'fair representation' (UNISON, undated: 15). The purpose and implementation of this concept are discussed in McBride (forthcoming).
5   The implications of supporting representation by women at branch level are different and are discussed in McBride (forthcoming).
6   A distinction is also made between low paid women and other women. UNISON defines a 'low-paid woman' in relation to her earnings and thereby her subscription band.

References

Beale, J. (1982) *Getting it together: Women as Trade Unionists*, London: Pluto Press.
Briskin, L. (1999) 'Autonomy, diversity and integration: Union women's separate organizing in the context of restructuring and globalization', *Women's Studies International Forum*, 22: 5: 543–54.
Briskin, L. and McDermott, P. (1993) *Women Challenging Unions*, Toronto: University of Toronto Press.
Cockburn, C. (1983) *Brothers: Male Dominance and Technological Change*, London: Pluto Press.
Cockburn, C. (1991) *In the Way of Women*, London: Macmillan.
Cockburn, C. (1996) *Strategies for Gender Democracy: Women and the European Social Dialogue*, European Commission, Employment, Industrial Relations and Social Affairs, Supplement, 4: 95.
Colgan, F. and Ledwith, S. (1996) 'Sisters organising – women and their trade unions', in Ledwith, S. and Colgan, F. (eds) *Women in Organisations – Challenging Gender Politics*, Basingstoke: Macmillan.
COHSE, NALGO, NUPE (undated) *The Final Report: Final Report of the COHSE, NALGO, and NUPE National Executives to the 1992 Annual Conferences*, London: UNISON.
Colling, T. and Dickens, L. (1989) *Equality Bargaining – Why not?*, London: HMSO.
Cunnison, S. and Stageman, J. (1993) *Feminizing the Unions: Challenging the Culture of Masculinity*, Aldershot: Avebury.

Cyba, E. and Papouschek, U. (1996) 'Women's interests in the workplace. Between delegation and self-representation', *Transfer*, 1: 61–81.

Holden, B. (1993) *Understanding Liberal Democracy*, Hemel Hempstead: Harvester Wheatsheaf.

Hyman, R. (1984) 'Die Krankheit de britishen Gewerkshaften: Gibt es ein Heilmittel?' reproduced as 'The Sickness of British Trade Unionism: is there a cure?', in Hyman, R. (1989) *The Political Economy of Industrial Relations: Theory and Practice in a Cold Climate*, Basingstoke: Macmillan.

Labour Research (1998) 'Are women out of proportion?', 87(3): 12–14.

McBride, A. (1997) 'Re-shaping trade union democracy: developing effective representation for women in UNISON', unpublished Ph.D. thesis, Coventry: University of Warwick.

McBride, A. (forthcoming) *Making a Difference? Gender Democracy in Trade Unions*, Aldershot: Ashgate.

Pateman, C. (1970) *Participation and Democratic Theory*, London: Cambridge University Press.

Pateman, C. (1988) *The Sexual Contract*, Cambridge: Polity Press.

Phillips, A. (1991) *Engendering Democracy*, Cambridge: Polity Press.

Phillips, A. (1993) *Democracy and Difference*, Cambridge: Polity Press.

SERTUC (1997) *Inching* (*extremely slowly) towards equality*, London: Southern & Eastern Region TUC.

TUC (1999) *1999 Directory*, London: TUC.

UNISON (undated) *UNISON Rules As at Vesting Day 1993*, London: UNISON.

UNISON (1994) *It's our union!*, London: UNISON.

UNISON (1998) *Get yourself organised, UNISON guidelines on self-organisation*, London: UNISON.

Young, I. M. (1990) *Justice and the Politics of Difference*, Princeton: Princeton University Press.

8   Working with Labour

The impact of UNISON's political settlement

Maggie Jones

This chapter sets out to explain the background and implications of UNISON's unique political compromise, brought about by the necessity to release deadlocked negotiations over UNISON's political role but proving to be a rather more enduring feature of the union's development. The paper then analyses the impact of the internal political settlement on the union's relations with government and the Labour Party and identifies a range of opportunities and challenges for the future.

A difficult conception

In 1992 the negotiations to create the new union had cleared several major hurdles, but had failed to resolve the critical issue of whether or not the new union should be affiliated to the Labour Party. Both NUPE and COHSE had long histories of affiliation, whilst in 1988 NALGO had voted to establish a political fund but had agreed not to seek affiliation to the Labour Party. Indeed, it had promised its members that the merger would protect the tradition of non-affiliation valued by many of them.

This issue proved to be divisive not only on the relatively simple constitutional issue of Labour Party affiliation, but also because as time went on more deeply held concerns about the general political direction which the union might take began to surface. There was, on the one hand, a view, that NUPE and COHSE were too close to Labour policies and had too easily compromised in the past. Whereas, on the other hand some felt that NALGO was prone to taking up oppositionalist stances fuelled by unrepresentative left groups who were not sympathetic to the Labour Party.

The outcome of these tensions was a compromise designed to ensure that these two political traditions – essentially both affiliation and non-affiliation – would be allowed to continue within the new union. It became encapsulated in the new rule book's Aims and Objectives as a commitment 'to maintain a political fund and the relationships which reflect the traditions of COHSE, NALGO and NUPE'. This compromise was a necessity as without it the merger talks would have foundered. Nevertheless, at the time there were many who worried that the concept of one union actively pursuing two political agendas might tear the union apart over time. There was also concern that this would have an adverse impact on the relatively stable relationship which NUPE and COHSE had previously enjoyed with the Labour Party, with no one able to confidently predict how this merger would affect votes on policy decisions within the Party in the future.

In addition to the broad political compromise, further negotiations, including consultations with the Certification Officer, produced a chapter of the rule book which sets out the detailed management of the two traditions. Two political fund sections were created, one to be known as the Affiliated Political Fund (APF), based on the old COHSE and NUPE members, and the other to be known as the General Political Fund (GPF), based on the old NALGO members. The former would remain affiliated to the Labour Party, the latter would be independent of any political party. Management of the two funds would be through the exclusive control of two committees of the National Executive Committee (NEC) made up of members contributing to the relevant fund and, until 1 January 1996 no existing members were able to transfer from one fund to another nor to join both funds. In other words, membership of the two funds was ring fenced for a period of time to allow both to become established. This protective ring was reinforced in the run up to Vesting Day with the appointment of two members of staff to head up the work of the two funds with a clear message to remaining staff that they should not interfere in the work of the other political tradition to the partner union from which they were employed.

From concept into action

The relatively late agreement on the political structures meant that in the run up to Vesting Day there was a scramble to set up the framework of the new arrangements. This was less problematic for the General Political Fund as their functions in the previous partner union (NALGO) had been administered by an NEC committee which oversaw the union's political fund expenditure, so they were able to adapt with relative ease.

The new arrangements for the Affiliated Political Fund were much more challenging. In both COHSE and NUPE political fund business including all matters relating to Labour Party activities had been integrated into the mainstream union structure. This applied at all levels, from branches discussing local affiliation to high profile debates on Labour Party issues at their annual conferences. Within the new union this was no longer possible. There was therefore a need to set up separate arrangements at all levels within UNISON for members paying the affiliated political levy to meet and make decisions separately. This required two things. Firstly, an internal democratic structure to broaden involvement was needed to ensure that Labour Party issues were not solely the preserve of a committee of UNISON's NEC. Secondly, and perhaps more problematically, an agreement had to be reached on which political issues were the legitimate business of the APF and which issues were appropriate to be considered by UNISON as a whole.

The National Affiliated Political Committee, which was elected by the out-going NUPE and COHSE NECs to take responsibility for the APF in UNISON, moved quickly to agree a branch, regional and national structure. At its heart was a commitment to the central UNISON principles of proportionality and fair representation; principles that ensured both that women were represented in numbers that reflected their share of overall UNISON membership (propor-tionality) and that other groups such as disabled, gay and lesbian, and black members, and manual/low-paid members were also guaranteed representation ('fair representation' – see Chapter 6 by McBride in this volume). It also sought to mirror the policy-making developments taking place in the Labour Party at the time with a greater emphasis on detailed policy discussions and less concern for passing resolutions. The new structure culminated in an annual National Political Forum at which the Labour Party Conference delegation also attended so that they were able to take forward the APF's views direct to the Labour Party.

One of the key elements of the new structure, endorsed by the first Forum, was that to hold office or represent the APF at any level beyond the branch a member had to be an individual member of the Labour Party as well as contributing to the APF. This policy was more easily justifiable precisely because of the existence of the two political fund sections. It was argued that if members wanted to play a role in the political affairs of the union, but did not want to join the Labour Party, uniquely compared with other unions, they had the simple option of belonging to the non-affiliated (general) political fund. Whilst this view has never been endorsed by the union as a whole, neither has it been effectively challenged and its operation remains in force to date. This is a great strength of the APF compared to other unions as all its decisions taken at regional and national level are taken by members who are committed to the Labour Party.

Defining the responsibilities of the APF

From Vesting Day onwards, intense discussions took place to try to reach agree-ment on the scope and limits of the APF's political role within the union. There was concern that the APF was trying to prescribe its boundaries of responsibility too widely, limiting the ability of the union to comment on political issues. Meanwhile, the APF was determined that any matters that related to its relation-ship with the Labour Party, including how its delegates voted at Labour Party Conference, should be the sole preserve of APF levy payers. These discussions took place in the year running up to the first UNISON Conference and included representatives from the two political funds and senior officers up to the General Secretary, but an acceptable compromise was not agreed.

As a result, the stage was set for a major row on this issue at the first Confer-ence. The focus of the disagreement was a decision of the Conference Standing Orders Committee (SOC) to rule out of order resolutions which tried to instruct the union on positions to be taken up with the Labour Party. The SOC argued that under the terms of UNISON's rules such matters should be dealt with by the APF. This issue proved to be massively controversial amongst the delegates.

However, it also had the effect of galvanising the ex-NUPE and -COHSE delegates at the Conference who felt that the APF was one of the few remaining forums in UNISON where manual workers and the low-paid had a dominant voice. It became much more than a debate about a Standing Orders ruling, and in a moment of passion they organised to protect the APF's autonomy within the Labour Party. In the end they won over many ex-NALGO delegates who could see the damage that this confrontation was causing and secured their position at the Conference.

This was a watershed in the development of the two political fund sections. The APF accepted that it needed to take account of the political views of UNISON members as a whole, whilst retaining control over how these issues were pursued within the Labour Party. This became part of the political settlement at the heart of UNISON and is still broadly operable at the current time.

The end of the political fund 'ring fence'

The UNISON Rule Book had always defined an interim period for the two political funds during which time members of the previous partner unions would remain in their original funds. The interim period ended on 1 January 1996 and there was some concern that there would be massive movements between the funds after that date. In particular, there was the potential for UNISON to completely dominate the block vote at Labour Party Conference if large sections of the GPF membership were to switch to the APF. There were even rumours that the APF was making arrangements to alter its decision making timescales to disenfranchise incoming levy payers who had previously been members of the GPF.

In reality, the APF adopted a different strategy and set about encouraging and welcoming ordinary members to join the APF arguing that they could be vital recruits to help Labour win the next election. As soon as it became clear that the APF was not a closed organisation, the political imperative to join from some sections of the union was lost, whilst others failed to grasp the new opportunities that were now available and the anticipated block movements did not occur. The result is that in 1998 the membership of the union was still broadly split down the middle between the two funds and the UNISON affiliation to the Labour Party (and hence its block vote) actually dropped for the first time in that year.

The lack of grassroots change was not reflected among the leading GPF activists at national and regional level, many of whom have made a point of joining both funds or switching to the APF causing some particular disparities and problems. Throughout its history, the APF has maintained a strong commitment to proportionality and fair representation. For example, the Labour Party Conference delegation is composed of two-thirds women, has representatives from the disabled, black and lesbian and gay self organised groups, and has a manual worker quota of 50 per cent of the delegation. Similarly, the national and regional APF committees have quotas for women and manual workers. The influx of activists from the GPF has put particular pressure on the manual workers' quotas in the key positions and has, on occasions, been the source of particular conflict. This remains an unresolved issue for UNISON as a whole, but given the history of the APF and its manual worker roots, it has a particular resonance in this sector which will continue to create tensions until a wider settlement is achieved within the union.

Perceptions of the membership

In 1995 the union was required to ballot all members on the continuation of its political fund. The Certification Officer agreed a dispensation to allow the ballot paper to be accompanied by an explanatory statement specifying that in UNISON's case this would mean the continuation of one political fund divided into two political fund sections – one affiliated to the Party and one independent of any political party. The members voted overwhelmingly to endorse the current arrangements, with 75 per cent voting in favour and only 25 per cent voting against. This reinforced the continuation of the existing arrangements for ten years unless a further all-member ballot was held.

In 1996 and 1997 the APF conducted two MORI surveys of APF levy payers. The results showed that 80 per cent were Labour supporters and the majority of these were fairly or very strong supporters. However, when asked about the Affiliated Political Fund a large majority knew very little or nothing about it and did not make the link between their payments to the union's political fund and their support of Labour. They did, however, support the idea of the union's links with the Labour Party, although this rarely appeared to be discussed at branch level. This lack of information about the unique political fund arrangements is also apparent amongst new recruits where around 20 per cent do not tick either box on their UNISON application form indicating their choice to of a fund. Of those who do select 45 per cent are choosing the APF and 51 per cent are choosing the GPF, with the remaining opting out, but it is not clear on what basis these choices are being made. From this it is clear that more work is necessary to understand how the members want to express their political preferences for the union and far more information and education is required to ensure that members are aware of their options within the union.

Advantages of the two-fund system

Several years into UNISON the story of the two political funds, which had such inauspicious beginnings, can be seen to be more successful than might initially have been imagined. It has demonstrated that bringing three unions together with very different political histories and aspirations can be made to work.

At the heart of the success is the extra choice available to members. In other unions, if members want their union to have a political role the choice is simple and stark; the union either affiliates to the Labour Party or it does not. In UNISON the choice is a more sophisticated one but arguably a more valid one. Moreover, as time goes by and the union becomes dominated by those who have joined since Vesting Day the APF will have the added credibility within the Party of arguing that those members who are affiliated to the Party have made an explicit choice to be in the affiliated fund giving money to the Party (although the MORI surveys mentioned above indicate the need for caution). It could be argued that the basic system adopted by UNISON should become a model for use elsewhere.

At the same time, the political fund rules, which concentrate control of the two budgets in the hands of committees of UNISON NEC have brought about another advantage. The rules prevent branches having their own access to political fund money and all branch requests for expenditure have to be channelled upwards. At the same time, the rules specify that APF money can only be used in support of the Labour Party and GPF money has to be spent on non-party political activities. The result is that the union, and in particular its branches, are unable to spend money in support of political parties other than the Labour Party.

This has been the source of a considerable battle with a number of 'front' organisations and party political newspapers such as the *Campaign for a Fighting Democratic UNISON* and the *Socialist Worker* newspapers. UNISON's NEC, quite rightly, have taken a hard line on this based on legal advice and rulings from the Certification Officer. The union has been forced to confront some of the more undemocratic elements in its ranks and whilst this issue remains at the forefront of controversy within UNISON and is unlikely to go away, undoubtedly the political fund rules have helped to strengthen the NEC's hand in keeping UNISON aligned with the mainstream left in British politics.

The impact of a New Labour government

In the run up to the General Election the APF allocated significant resources to supporting Labour's election campaign. The GPF used its resources in parallel to run a non-party political advertising campaign raising the importance of public service issues. Neither position was in open conflict with the other. The subsequent election of a Labour government has raised new political dilemmas for the union but in other respects has helped to clarify the roles of the two political funds for the future. The onus of the union's political work is now to influence and relate to the Labour government (this is discussed at length in Sawyer's contribution to this collection). This is accepted as a legitimate function of the union as a whole in representing its members' interests, so all the different sections of UNISON's membership are able to form their own relationships with the relevant government departments including the civil servants and Labour Ministers (i.e. this set of relationships is not restricted to the APF). Beyond this, the two political funds play a mutually supportive role and often work together on joint initiatives. This includes funding campaigns, facilitating meetings and lobbies, co-ordinating the UNISON group of MPs and targeting individual MPs with specialisms. There is scope for this work of the two committees to be further integrated in the future.

As distinct from our relationships with government, the APF maintains a separate link with the Labour Party. This was important in the run up to the election when the manifesto was being agreed and will gradually pick up in importance again as the next tranche of policies for the medium-term work their way through the Labour Party machinery. New methods of liaising on these policies in UNISON are being developed to complement the radically changed policy-making procedures now in use in the Labour Party based on their 'Partnership in Power' proposals. These require the APF representatives on local, regional and the national policy forums to contribute detailed policy ideas through to the Party on a regular basis as the 'rolling programme' of policy is developed. This requires well-briefed and articulate proponents of our members' case who are able to negotiate and win allies for our position.

The new government is also a cause for the GPF to rethink its role. The original NALGO political fund was created to run campaigns opposing the then Tory government's attacks on public services. Since that time, the GPF have continued to fund anti-cuts, pro-public services campaigns. These have been tacitly seen as helpful to the Labour Party. The GPF now have a new dilemma in terms of how its non-Party political stance should be positioned in relation to the new government. In due course there will be pressure for it to use its funds to continue pro-public service, anti-government advertising. This has not reached a critical stage as yet and it currently retains a neutral stance. However, if the GPF at any time started to use its funds to campaign against the Labour government, it could for the first time cause a real political rift between the two political funds. Whilst the operation of the two political fund sections has remained remarkably resilient through UNISON's formative years and more recently with a change of government, it is equally likely that there will be a need for change and renewal in the future. These changes could be brought about by the pressures of external forces; they could also arise from the need to rationalise and integrate our internal structures.

Organising in UNISON

There are a number of levels at which UNISON's political fund organisation should be reviewed and strengthened. At a basic level, as shown by the MORI survey, there is a need to inform members much more clearly about the role of the two funds. There is still a great deal of ignorance and apathy about this part of the union's activity. More specifically, there is a particular need for the APF to improve its branch organisation which is, at best, patchy. The branch merger process has left a situation where only half of the branches have an APF officer (and therefore receive materials from the APF) and even fewer have APF sectional meetings.

This leads on to the bigger issue about the two political fund structures. It could be argued that in an attempt to protect and retain the two political traditions we have created separate ring-fenced activities in a way which is artificial and which does not easily blend in with the mainstream union concerns of organising and representing members. There is a case for maintaining member choice but within more integrated structures.

However, one major barrier to re-examining the operation of the two funds derives not from their operation as such but from a structural issue of much wider relevance to the union. This is the continuing problem of fair representation for particular groups in UNISON. More specifically, the APF continues to provide a forum for low-paid manual workers in UNISON in a way which is denied to them elsewhere; in effect, on all other major committees the representatives of manual workers are in a minority and there is a widespread feeling that their interests are not being adequately reflected. Until this problem is addressed and resolved within the wider union, it is unlikely that a proper analysis of the political organisation of the union can take place. This weakens our political operation and therefore the effectiveness of UNISON as a whole. This is one of the real challenges which confronts us for the future.

Changing role in the Labour Party

At various stages of the Party's history it has been rumoured that attempts would be made to sever the links between the unions and the Party. These rumours were again proved wrong when the Labour Party agreed its submission to the Neill Enquiry. The submission restated the vital contribution which the unions make to the Party and basically endorses the current affiliation arrangements. The main thrust of the Party's case is directed at tightening up company funding and private donations, rather than affecting the status of the unions as integral to the Labour Party structures so it is anticipated that the Labour/trade union links will remain in place for the foreseeable future.

Other Party changes such as the new policy forums and the rolling policy programme continue to give the unions a major voice. The unions continue to face a challenge to maximise their input into these new structures and ensure a continued voice for our members. This requires a different way of working and style of operation which is taking time to implement. The impact of these changes could, in time, have a major influence on the way that policy is made within UNISON.

Changing relationships with government

In the years of opposition much was said and written about the need to learn the lessons from the strained relations between government and unions which characterised the 1970s. The Labour Party's *Partnership in Power* project partly arose from a need to address these concerns and set up new mechanisms for dialogue for the future. It is too early to say whether this will achieve its aim. However, notwithstanding the internal party changes, there are issues about the relationships between the unions, the TUC and government which remain to be resolved. Undeniably, the unions have legitimate concerns on behalf of their members which they have to pursue, and finding the most appropriate method and style to achieve this presents us all with a challenge which has major implications for the work of the political funds.

In several quarters within UNISON and the trade union movement more broadly there is considerable unease about the union's relationships with government, particularly on the macro level. The much-trailed models of social partnership have not been wholeheartedly embraced and the TUC is still struggling to establish its role. At the same time, on a day-to-day basis, contact with ministers and civil servants is working at an unprecedented level with a real warmth, and effective dialogue is taking place. Across the government decisions are being taken that will improve the lives of our members and we are able to exert real influence and impact on those decisions.

This is a bigger issue for the union than one relating to the future of the political funds but resolving the tensions around these relationships will undoubtedly have an impact on the campaigning and parliamentary activities of the two funds and, in the longer term, could have a fundamental impact on how UNISON relates to the Labour Party.

9 UNISON and New Labour
Searching for new relationships

Tom Sawyer

Although my main subject is the relationship between UNISON and the Labour Party, my interest in UNISON, my union, goes far beyond the political aspects. I care passionately about the union. I hope it is what people want it to be and that it turns out to be what members want from it. As one of the 'founding fathers' of the union, and one who tried to develop a clear vision and sense of purpose for the union, which Bob Fryer's contribution has analysed in detail, I am both delighted by the fact of the merger and on occasion saddened that the union has not always lived up to my ambitious personal expectations. But I firmly believe that the merger was necessary and in every way justifiable and there is no sense in which I would want to turn the clock back. It is already an enormously successful union; the most successful, powerful, influential, and professional union in the British labour movement and one that is still only in the foothills of its life.

This contribution concerns the relationships between two of the loves of my life: my love of the union and my love of the Labour Party. I joined my union – NUPE – when I was 15 years old and I worked for it for 24 years as a full-time official. I have been a member of the Labour Party for over 30 years and am only the second person this century, after Arthur Henderson, to hold the office of both Chairman and Secretary of the Labour Party. I have always seen these two aspects of my own life as directly and intimately connected and that personal vision translates then and now into a vision of the *organisational* relationships between the two. At present, the most striking feature of the relationship is the speed and intensity of *change* both within the union and the Party, often at a speed which makes it difficult to find the space and time to reflect on change and accommodate to it in the ways democratic organisations like to do. At this moment it is impossible to predict the kind of change that will affect the two organisations and their relationship, but it is clear that change is both rapid and profound. In the next 20 years than we will all need to travel faster that we have done in the earlier part of the century. We have to be aware of that.

But the change does not and cannot obscure the fact that the union and the Party continue to operate in ways that are underpinned by very important and highly-valued relationships. A system of shared values has kept us together and still does. We still share the same social goals, and although we talk about and apply them in different ways, those shared values and goals remain of central importance to all of us. When our relationship hits bad times, as has happened and may well happen more often as we go through the first period of the Labour government, it is those shared values and goals that keep us together.

Our shared values lead me to conclude that, despite the current arguments concerning the future relationships between the Labour Party and the trade unions in general, and UNISON in particular, I am assuming that a close relationship between this union and the Labour Party will continue for the foreseeable future. The relationship is based fundamentally on those shared values which have not changed in 100 years and I do not expect to change in the next 100 years.

The shared values are reflected in our close relationships and in the very many practical and important ways we have developed of working together. The Party has to recognise, and I certainly do recognise, the enormous support and help that we continue to get from the trade union movement, and in particular, from UNISON. In terms of helping the Party UNISON more than punches its weight at local, regional and national levels as was clear from the contribution that UNISON members made in the General Election campaign. Large numbers of UNISON officers and lay activists in effect gave up their 'union job' and worked for the Party for 3 or 4 weeks; some staff were seconded to work for the Party, while others volunteered to work. During the election campaign there were perhaps 250 people working at Party headquarters at Millbank, and as many as thirty or more came from UNISON, and similar UNISON contributions could have been found at all levels up and down the country. UNISON members are also involved in ongoing Party activity all the time, at every level: there are more Labour councillors in UNISON than any other trade union; more UNISON Labour Party officials such as branch secretaries and constituency secretaries than from any other trade union. UNISON members have played a key role in the Labour Party policy forums, on the National Executive; all the time you can see UNISON playing a very helpful and constructive role within the Party. I certainly treasure that and welcome it and have a high regard for the contribution that people make, and that it is widely echoed within the Party – I do not know whether the Party leaders say this publicly often enough. But it is certainly true that leading Cabinet members respect and recognise the vital contribution made by UNISON and that is very important. And it's not just a kind of, a shared values thing – it's a practice thing as well. In effect in all these ways, and of course through a major financial contribution, UNISON helps us maintain a political party. When I became General Secretary of the Party we had to run a major political party on an income of £11–12 million a year. Since then we have pushed that figure towards £20–25 million, through the efforts of professional fund-raisers and we know that although the headlines reflect the big 'one-off' donations, what really counts still is the member fundraising, the constant telephone calls at election times asking for more cash for the election fund. It still works, and it helped us defeat the Tories and get back into power. And we rely on UNISON and other union activists for much of this.

Maggie Jones' paper asks UNISON to confront a major challenge because she is in effect asking the union to adopt and work within a twin-track approach in its dealings with government and in doing so to be absolutely clear about the distinctions between the two tracks. The first track is affiliation to the Party through the Affiliated Political Fund whose creation was such a key innovation at the time of the merger and since. This means quite clearly affiliating to the *Party* and supporting the Party's organisation or, if I can personalise it, helping *me* and my successor as Party Secretary without necessarily liking the government. Facing up to this distinction is important; the funds go to the people who run the Labour Party, not to those who run the Labour government. The Party is not responsible for every – or indeed any – decision made by the government. But there is a role there for supporting the Party because the Party is independently important. Governments come and go but political parties remain. For that reason sustaining a strong party with a big membership that is active in the community, representing the community, working with local councils and community organisations, is very important. The second 'track' is the relationship between the *Government* and the trade unions as Social Partners, notably through the agency of the TUC. So the adoption of the twin-track approach is in effect to act to support the Party and play a constructive and important role in the Party, and at the same time but distinctly to operate as a Social Partner in working with government. The twin-track approach also implies that the two processes and institutions should not get mixed up because they are slightly different roles. In particular unions should not bring their 'Social Partner' issues through the Party via affiliation, but take them up with John Monks and through the TUC team to the government. This has never happened before in relationships between previous Labour governments and the unions. In the past the rules were very mixed up and it was not exactly clear what was supposed to happen. Quite often a union might approach the government as a Social Partner and ask for something and if the government refused the union would revert to the Party affiliation 'track' and there would be a resolution on the subject at the National Executive Committee, backed by a group of politicians to create pressure on the issue within the Party, and hence the Government. The Prime Minister was caught in a vice between what he was trying to do as a Social Partner and what he was trying to do as a Party leader. This was a way of trapping the Prime Minister, making life difficult for the Prime Minister and perhaps, at the end of the day, getting what the union wanted. The approach was 'get what you want' and do not worry too much about the rules and procedures, even if that makes life difficult for a Labour government. Maggie Jones' paper is asking UNISON to uncouple these two elements in the relationship, to be clear about uncoupling them and to pursue them in different ways but to be constructive about both routes. That is a bold initiative about which few unions have thought as much as UNISON, although most unions are having to practise it in one way or another because that is the way both the Party leader and the leadership of the Party want it to be done. Large, powerful and creative trade unions such as UNISON should grasp this new approach and the opportunities it offers and integrate it into their political agenda. In this way they may be able to derive positive benefits from the approach, which is far less likely if unions wait to be pushed reluctantly in this new direction, because it will happen in any case.

In considering how UNISON will need to think about reconstructing its approach to Labour – the Party and the government – it is necessary to spell out a number of new factors affecting those relationships that may be difficult for the union to confront and accept. New Labour is difficult for some people, to the extent that at least before the 1997 election there was a great deal of internal debate as to who was 'New' or 'Old' Labour, often heavily tinged with the cynicism and sarcasm that often appear in political parties. At least Tony Blair was quite unambiguous that the Party had campaigned as New Labour and would therefore govern as New Labour. He and the senior politicians around him now all recognise, even if it is against their political instincts to do so, that the New Labour concept did have a powerful impact on the electorate, and that it would be sensible to govern in a way that we had promised before we were elected. New Labour does mean something different and that means that UNISON, as with the rest of the trade union movement, has to respond to that. I would not want to try to define New Labour precisely, but I want to identify four elements that are important to recognise if the new relationships to which I referred are to work to the unions' advantage.

First, New Labour demands strong central leadership of the Party and it does mean the leader is very powerful. There is nothing new in the rule book that indicates that, and there have been no formal proposals that have created it. But it is a continuation of the centralised power that has been developed under the leadership of Neil Kinnock, that was then developed by John Smith, that Tony Blair has elaborated in order to win elections and to convince the voters of the mission and the vision of the Party. In this the leader becomes very important as the embodiment of this vision. Whatever one may think of this it is a fact that in the British political system, at the present time, there is very little one can do about that. Tony Blair will campaign on these terms for as long as he is leader which will certainly be for another term, maybe two. But the style and approach are now established as necessary levers for success, and it therefore appears inevitable that whatever follows Blair will be in the same vein. In that sense at least there is no turning back to 'Old Labour'.

Second, New Labour is, intentionally, very light on ideology and, so Tony Blair and his colleagues would argue, it is strong on values. But certainly he does not sell an ideologically based Party. He sells a Party that is very pragmatic, capable of responding flexibly to situations, and strong on values such as community and solidarity and fairness, although these are stated in terms significantly different from the traditional collectivism of 'Old Labour'. Nevertheless, in terms of social and economic policy they do present opportunities for establishing dialogue with unions and others interested in these matters. But the unions will have to frame their agenda and approaches along these new lines, not the old, if that dialogue is to succeed.

Third, it is a *Centre–Left* Party. This may be a particular problem for people in UNISON who, I think, may have been among those who hoped that, the election won, Labour would revert to its more traditional role, policies and relationships. Clearly UNISON has emerged as a union which would see itself and would be defined by others as a union of the Left. For those who, like myself, see these words as more than empty slogans, NUPE certainly can be identified prior to the merger as a Leftish union, COHSE a Rightist union, and NALGO as having moved to a Left position at least on its NEC and amongst its activists. So, I would see UNISON as a union that sees itself on and of the Left, and which sees certain principles as being important, certain values as needing constant emphasis. Rodney Bickerstaffe, the General Secretary, is an embodiment of what UNISON stands for. He speaks for the downtrodden, the low paid, and oppressed, and UNISON feels politically most comfortable and united when it campaigning on such issues. For this reason if no other, a Centre–Left Party might not be so easy to live with. But it is a Centre–Left Party and Blair has made it absolutely clear that while he wants to extend a hand to the trade unions he also wishes to establish the same kind of relationship with business. He wants to govern and be re-elected on that basis and UNISON again will have to come to terms with that.

The fourth comment in this brief comment on New Labour is that inside the Party, the organisational as well as the rhetorical emphasis is on partnership not conflict. Tony Blair likes the policy forums, the debates, and the idea of the reformed conference. He does not like our traditional idea of a conference involving set-piece confrontational debates between 'composite 1', 'composite 2', and 'composite 3' where the outcome is often a form of 'winner takes all' even though there may be substantial support for the 'losing' motions. He wants a different kind of relationship with both Party members and unions which I would categorise as a 'partnership agreement'.

These are just elements that I think are important components in the complex political and organisational mix that I would describe as New Labour and I have gone through them because I am not certain that UNISON has really acknow-ledged, still less bought into, this new approach. I think the union needs to understand the significance of what has been going on. There is still a discernible feeling, in UNISON as elsewhere that the entire approach and agenda will change either if or when Tony Blair loses the leadership, for whatever reason, or if he were defeated in the Party on two or three big issues and then realise that he has got it all wrong and has to go back to how it used to be. I have to say that I think the first of these is impossible for several years and the second is at most highly improbable. The approach will stay as it is and it is important for UNISON to face up to that and to make clear that, while it may not have any intention of becoming a 'New Labour' trade union (whatever that may mean), it does intend to operate as a 'new union' in the John Monks mould that will work with New Labour.

Four issues need to be addressed if UNISON is to develop an effective relationship with New Labour. First it is necessary for UNISON to make clear its unambiguous rather than its partial and suspicious commitment to working with Labour on that basis. This is perhaps particularly an issue for UNISON more than other unions, partly because it is the largest and most influential trade union in the country, and partly because there is a deep uncertainty about UNISON's position felt at the highest levels of the Party. People often ask where does the union really stand on many key issues. Part of the reason for that is that there appears to be no consistent message coming from those who represent UNISON within the Labour Party. Some representatives articulate a very responsive, perhaps even a 'New Labour' message while others hang back a little and give the clear impression that they are not on the same wavelength, not signed up to the new approach. Clarity on that from the union would enhance your standing within the Party and your opportunity to influence policy in the ways I have indicated.

Clearly related to this issue is the second key question of who speaks for UNISON and who leads it? In part this question derives from the debates that took place during the merger talks concerning whether we were creating a union led by the lay membership and what that meant. The union needs to understand that its influence within the relationships I have been describing may be reduced if, for example, the General Secretary appears on television to articulate UNISON policy while at the same time others, also claiming to speak on behalf of the union, are saying fundamentally different things. Such behaviour immediately raises the issue of who speaks for UNISON and who leads it, and this question assumes a great significance in the context of developing relationships with Party and government along the 'twin tracks' I have been outlining. My strong advice to the union would be to trust the key national officers – the General Secretary and the President – and to make clear that they speak for and articulate the policy of the union. Equally, when the union sends representatives to the Party, make it clear that those representatives have the responsibility to speak to UNISON's policy and position but equally do not mandate them to vote the union 'line' irrespective of debate and other considerations. Because when unions participate in the activities of the Party, they have to take on board the views of other unions and of the politicians. UNISON must trust its representatives enough to give them some flexibility and the opportunity when appropriate to make compromises and to move forward. This approach is developing but the union still needs to go further in trusting the people elected or selected to speak for it and to try and minimise the other, unrepresentative, voices.

The third issue is perhaps more uncomfortable but it also needs to be looked at, and it might be described as the problem of the hostility and unfriendliness both towards the wider official labour movement and to the Party shown by individuals and groups operating within UNISON who are not signed up either to the union or the Party. One clear example of this can be seen at the UNISON conference which is seen as quite threatening to the Labour Party and certainly to the Labour leadership. The importance of this should not be exaggerated since many unions, and perhaps again UNISON in particular, are past masters of the techniques that enable conference decisions to be somehow 'forgotten' or glossed over in practice. These are traditions that we all share. While they can be accepted and lived with they do constitute a rather ramshackle approach to making policy in a modern union. It would be much better if UNISON could move towards a conference where people came from the membership, articulated real members' views and opinions and made decisions on that basis instead of allowing it to be hijacked in the way it sometimes is. If the union could do something about that, it would make a significant positive contribution to relationships with the Labour government, so it is a clear challenge for the future.

Fourth, and finally there is a linking undercurrent to many of these ideas which I would describe as a feeling, rarely explicitly articulated, that parts of the union would be more comfortable by reverting to a more traditional 'oppositional' role again, not least since that would avoid the need to confront the difficult attitudinal and structural changes I have outlined. From my own personal experience of 24 years as a union official I know that working with a Labour government is not easy. But if UNISON were able to create the structures and environment that will enable it to make clear decisions about the Labour government, and to express and carry through a determinination to support it and work with it whilst at the same time being critical of it when necessary, that would work to the immense benefit of the union, the Party, and, ultimately, government. Recently I was at a policy forum at which UNISON's representatives gave the Secretary of State who was also present no room for doubt about what they felt about one of the particular policy options. But that was done in a closed room, in private, and in a comradely, friendly, open, honest way. That is likely to have had, and to continue to have, a great deal more influence on government policy than if somebody had passed a resolution at the conference to which the government felt to need to reply and could easily ignore. The job of Labour Party General Secretary in the policy forum process is to try and lock ministers and Party members in together so they cannot escape and they have to talk and listen to each other, and it is to that process that a united and single-minded UNISON can make a major contribution.

Finally I do want to applaud the efforts that are being made this time by UNISON: the new structures and the ideas; the energy and the goodwill are absolutely first-class. I have no doubt that we can achieve all that the Party promised at the last election and more, and be re-elected for a second term. We can change things in a way that we perhaps did not even imagine we could, if we can continue to work together. UNISON needs to play a constructive role in that dialogue and be a really respected player. My ideas as to how that might be achieved have been sketched out above, and if the union is prepared to work towards them then there is a very positive future to look forward to.

Part II
The UNISON agenda

10 UNISON and changes in collective bargaining in health and local government

Carole Thornley, Mike Ironside and Roger Seifert

This chapter focuses on UNISON's key role in the rapidly moving collective bargaining arena in the public sector, with an emphasis on its heartlands of the National Health Service and local government.[1] These two sectors jointly employ over two and a half million people (Salamon, 1998: 283–4), a majority of whom are women,[2] and account for just under half of all public sector employment and around a tenth of the total national workforce. They also span a very wide range of clerical, professional, technical, administrative and manual occupations, with relatively high levels of union density, multi-union representation, and correspondingly complex institutional arrangements for collective bargaining.

On its formation in 1993, UNISON became not just the largest union in the country but also the most significant representative of public sector workers, with 440,000 members in health and 800,000 in local government. It is thus the largest single union in both sectors: within health, it is the major union for ambulance, ancillary, managerial, administrative and technical staff and is one of the two leading unions for nurses; within local government it represents administrative, professional, technical, clerical and manual employees covered by the new single status agreement.

Collective bargaining is the central trade union method of protecting and improving the conditions of service of its members. This chapter has a particular emphasis on the issues of pay and performance, which are the most important aspects of the employment relationship. Following a brief overview of collective bargaining and changes to it prior to 1979 for both health and local government, we analyse the recent context to UNISON's formation within each sector. It is argued that the merger is best seen as a necessary response to political and institutional changes in public sector employment and collective bargaining. The unions' arguments in favour of the merger, which was strongly supported by the membership of the three unions in the merger ballot, included the need to unite to fight the main issues facing the majority of the combined membership: job loss, relative low pay, increased workloads, managerial initiatives to cheapen work, and an overall loss of power and control over job regulation. In a final section, both the potential for, and challenges to, the new union, UNISON, are discussed.

The background to collective bargaining in health and local government before 1979

The first half of the twentieth century saw a piecemeal and partial growth of representation of health workers in both trade unions and professional associations, with concurrent attempts to influence the terms and conditions of work in a health care system that was itself deeply class-based and fragmented, and which carried the heavy burden of Victorian hypocrisy to the care of the wretched. In contrast local government had emerged from the Victorian purpose of the avoidance of nuisances, under the influence of gas and water socialists, to become an increasingly coherent state service with aspirations to adopt the Whitley national collective bargaining mechanisms with their local joint consultation wing (Clay, 1929). Both NALGO and NUPE had clear policies to fight for the permanent establishment of national bargaining in local government.

Between the Wars the health care system was in financial and institutional chaos. As far as the staff were concerned working conditions were arbitrary and frequently dreadful, and this was in no small part due to collective bargaining arrangements which were both local and patchy. In local authority hospitals, for example, domestic, manual, clerical and administrative employees were only partially covered by locally negotiated agreements, with the majority of nurses outside the scope of collective bargaining altogether. In voluntary hospitals 'collective agreements were virtually unknown . . . and trade unions had met with little success in their attempts to organize' (Clegg and Chester, 1957: 4). Public attention focused then, as now, particularly on the plight of nurses, and successive enquiries into endemic shortages highlighted low pay, poor terms and conditions and lack of national collective bargaining and pay arrangements as major explanatory factors (for a full review see Thornley, 1994).

National bargaining, in the form of Whitleyism, arrived in local government when the National Joint Councils (NJCs) were established in 1946. This was followed in the health services when the National Health Service (NHS) was formed in 1948, with a General Whitley Council and a number of Functional Whitley Councils comprised of Staff Sides and Management Sides.[3] This was largely the result of years of agitation by the three main unions, and it was followed by rapid union growth – by 1950 NUPE had 170,000 members, COHSE had over 40,000 and NALGO had over 140,000 in local government and 10,000 in health. Although much-criticised throughout its history from a variety of perspectives (see Seifert, 1992; Thornley, 1993; for the health service), this system survived in broadly similar form until the early 1980s, and still plays an important, albeit reduced, role in local government and health.

Until the mid-1960s the view that Whitley ruled OK within local government and health was to some extent accurate. On the one hand, national agreements were usually secured between increasingly large and well-represented unions and their employers. At the same time, the agreements provided for increasing levels of real pay for some occupational groups, improved conditions of service for most and were nationally implemented resulting in limited industrial relations at local level. On the other hand, dissatisfaction grew amongst those occupational groups who failed to enjoy growth in real rates of pay: for example, around this period real rates of pay stagnated or fell for nurses (Thornley, 1993). Moreover, this period of relative calm hid many deeper failings both in these services and in the wider economy.

Several developments came together to undermine the system, creating much more active and militant unions, and start the long process of destabilisation of both the services and their industrial relations. First, was the increasing use of incomes policies by successive governments, which effectively bypassed Whitley and in practice eroded public sector pay relative to other groups. Second, was a shift in the patterns of service delivery, in part due to technology and in part due to the changing nature of user expectations, causing staff shortages and altering traditional power relations within and between the various staff side groups. Moreover, uneven funding by central government created uncertainty, put pressure on local managers and added to the frustrations of staff. Finally, the recognition that the system itself had failed to eradicate endemic low pay lent a continuing impetus towards union activism.

Two outcomes followed: the increasing use of special pay reviews, for example by the National Board for Prices and Incomes (NBPI) and Lord Halsbury for nurses in 1968 and 1974 respectively, and then by Clegg across local government and health in 1979, and of industrial action. This was a period of a general increase in public sector strikes and demonstrations, notably including teachers, miners, and railway workers, as well as nurses (Winchester, 1983). The 1970 'dirty jobs' strike by manual workers against low pay, led by NUPE, was the first major national strike in local government. NALGO members in London took that union's first major industrial action in 1974, to win their London weighting claim. And in the same year health workers held a major national dispute. This was followed by the 1978–79 'Winter of Discontent' as manual workers, again led by NUPE, engaged in a bitter struggle against low pay. The strike ended with the setting up of the Standing Commission on Pay Comparability under Professor Clegg (Clegg, 1980), which included reports on health workers and local government staff. The year 1980 saw industrial action by the entire NALGO membership in local government, as the 1979 pay negotiations based on comparability broke down. The incoming Conservative government was faced with a demoralised management in local government and health, and an angry and frustrated staff.

Changes in the public sector bargaining environment

We do not share the view of many academics that the late 1970s saw a break with a golden age of public service employment, in which the state acted as a 'model employer' (Fredman and Morris, 1989; see Thornley, 1995 for a critique). For many state employees the reality of their exploitation had always been that of low pay, poor conditions of work, and oppressive line management. Nevertheless, the nature of public service work was altered significantly under the successive

Thatcher governments, which set about changing the structures of local government, the health and education services, the civil service, and the nationalised industries and utilities. The first Thatcher government came to office in 1979 with a programme to tackle the perceived problems of British capitalism buoyed up by the rhetoric of *laissez-faire* free market economics. Private enterprise, powered by the motor of profit, was viewed both as the sole source of wealth and as the best means of distributing that wealth throughout the population. Public spending was consequently seen as a drain on wealth creation – every pound spent on public services 'crowding out' capital that could be invested more profitably elsewhere (Bacon and Eltis, 1976). The public sector was treated not as a means of increasing the resources available to the general population, but as a source of inefficiency, waste and dependency. Therefore, the government set about reducing its scope, damning its contributions, and undermining its staff and their unions.

This was to be achieved by the twin methods of transferring activities from the public sector to the private through a variety of mechanisms, and by reducing the cost of what remained via cuts in financial support and changes in the management of labour. In health and local government this involved the hiving-off of some services to private companies, and contracting out of other services to private contractors. Local authority and health authority spending was brought under stricter central government control through successive changes in the funding arrangements, strengthening the audit and inspection functions, and deciding how funds should be spent through target setting. Cost reduction was also to be achieved through greater 'efficiency', resulting in better 'value for money', which meant in reality maintaining a politically acceptable level of services while reducing labour costs by getting fewer workers to do more work for less money or by substituting cheaper workers for more expensive.

Thus public service costs were driven down through a general decline in funding streams and the creation of market-like systems, in which providers competed against each other for these scarce resources – a beggar-my-neighbour system. However, while managers in the private sector faced with declining revenues can respond by shutting down all or part of their business, or through diversification and/or a shift in core activities, or by cutting prices to expand the overall market, in the public services these options were largely unavailable, so that the main basis for 'competition' between managed units was that of lowering unit labour costs, especially since such services were typically labour intensive. But with the majority of staff on national wage rates and with key performance targets set by central government, local managers were left with a very limited range of choices as to the management of their existing labour.

The drive to cheapen local services by cheapening the workforce therefore meant a tightening of management control over labour, with the government blowing the managerialist trumpet over the slogan of the right to manage, and a loosening of trade union control through collective bargaining over pay and conditions. The 1980s saw a series of attacks on trade unions, through a general attack on their capacity to organise lawful industrial action, by deliberately creating permanently high levels of unemployment, and by investing heavily in the defeat of significant trade union action in the civil service and in the steel and coal industries (Kessler and Bayliss, 1998: chapter 7).

All this was supported by a general strengthening of labour management through the use of human resource management techniques, including total quality management initiatives that had been tried and tested in private companies. The managerialism often employed in an attempt to ensure that private companies generate maximum profits was being applied in public services. For the employees, working for a health trust or local authority was becoming more like working for a capitalist, cutting across their traditional notions of performing a service for the people.

The managerialist drive for flexibility and control, along with the installation of the new information technologies, brought about major changes in the organisation of public service work. It resulted in a general degradation of front-line public service work, as the division of labour between grades was altered. In particular, decisions about the organisation and planning of work were transferred into the hands of managers, while in many cases subordinate grades found their jobs being routinised and checklist-driven through the performance management techniques of work study and job evaluation. The workforce profile shifted, as higher graded jobs associated with higher levels of formal qualifications and autonomy were substituted by lower graded jobs where skills and experience remain largely unacknowledged and unrewarded.

More and more jobs were badly paid and insecure as managers imposed a new industrial order on staff, under conditions that made it difficult for both individual workers and their collective organisations to mount effective opposition. The birth of UNISON, then, represents the best collective solution to the problems of millions of individual workers confronted by what were for them largely new management devices to curtail their earnings, worsen their conditions, undermine their job security and attack the basis of their working lives, namely the recognition of their skills and experience, the service they provide and their union organisation.

Changes in collective bargaining in the NHS

Despite some attrition in numbers over the past two decades,[4] the NHS, through its constituent parts, is still one of the major employers of labour in Europe. Around a million people are directly employed, mainly in Trusts, with many more indirectly employed through private contractors supplying services or private firms supplying goods. By far the largest single occupational group, accounting for over half the workforce, is nursing and direct patient care support staff.[5] Administrative and estate staff account for a further fifth of the workforce, with scientific, therapeutic, technical and ambulance staff accounting for around 15 per cent. Despite a high public profile, medical and dental staff only account for around 7 per cent of the health workforce.

Wages and salaries constitute the largest single item of revenue expenditure,[6] with the nursing paybill constituting the largest element in wages and salaries at around £8 billion. Collective bargaining over pay is therefore a central issue for all those involved. Governments interested in restraining expenditure on the NHS must necessarily be concerned with holding back health service workers' pay – and nurses are here a prime target. However, the objective of pay restraint sits uneasily with both recruitment and retention requirements of management and the desire of trade unions to obtain the best available pay deal for their members. In addition, pressures on managers to reduce the unit labour costs of delivering the service to patients requires the introduction, with or without union agreement, of changes to working practices which may be in direct conflict with unions' desires to maintain 'decent' working conditions and quality of service provision.

The history of collective bargaining arrangements and outcomes can only be understood in the light of these conflicting issues and objectives, and here, if anything at all is to be learned from history, it is that old ideas often parade in new clothes. This is particularly pertinent to recent and current policy debates about the form and level of institutional arrangements for collective bargaining in health, which tend to run alongside a traditional neglect of the relevance and importance of the material outcomes of these processes: namely, pay levels which will recruit, retain, and motivate staff as well as being acceptable to them in terms of 'felt fair' comparability. The other important and neglected outcome of the conflict, sometimes hidden and sometimes open, between management and staff is control over the labour process itself and therefore over the frontier of management rights to manage.

UNISON, and its forerunner unions, have played a vital role in keeping public attention and public policy firmly engaged with pay and staffing outcomes. In particular, the issues of low pay and associated poor conditions of service have been linked with negotiations over the future forms and levels of pay determination so as to ensure the best possible representation for UNISON members.

NHS collective bargaining under the Conservatives

By 1979, the TUC-affiliated forerunners of UNISON were achieving very high levels of membership: notably, COHSE and NUPE outstripped the Royal College of Nursing (RCN) for nurse membership alone in 1980. This was based on increased effectiveness in organisational terms and more especially in the political and industrial campaigns for better treatment and representation of health workers' interests. The incoming Conservative government posed immediate challenges for the unions: it was swift to abolish the pay comparability commission chaired by Professor Clegg, and to embark on the wholescale revisions to the public sector previously described. The first major change in collective bargaining arrangements in the NHS came very quickly. In the autumn of 1981, health service workers decided to combine forces in a campaign, co-ordinated by the TUC Health Services Committee, to gain increases in pay, which for 2 years had been below the rate of inflation. Government intransigence then led to industrial unrest which lasted through most of 1982 and constituted the 'most sustained and severe disruption ever seen in the service (nearly a million days were lost)' (Salvage, 1985: 140). A Pay Review Body for nurses emerged as one solution, serving to 'divide the unity of health staffs' (Carpenter, 1988: 379) as the RCN accepted this offer.

Much has been made by some commentators of the fact that the Review Body system in theory removed half a million staff from 'collective bargaining' arrangements (Millward *et al.*, 1992: 231–4). However, the Review Body system in practice still strongly resembled a negotiating process, stimulating, if anything, a greater production and dissemination of evidence by unions, and, paradoxically, greater Staff Side unity on a number of occasions (Thornley, 1993). In this respect, though the pay determination system for nurses was conceived with an inbuilt bias that 'favoured' the more conservative RCN and aimed to undermine the potential for industrial action more generally, not least by splitting nursing staff from the rest of the non-medical workforce, COHSE, NUPE and NALGO were still highly active and influential within and without the review body system. The mid- to late-1980s saw industrial unrest on the part of most functional groups of health service workers, including nurses and ambulance workers, with sustained union pressure across the pay determination system for improved pay outcomes. Within the Review Body itself this led to the Clinical Grading exercise in 1988 giving an uplift in pay to registered nurses – a kind of 'review within a review' – but poor pay outcomes remained problematic within the service as a whole, both for nurses and other occupational groups.

A second dimension to the Conservative agenda for reform of health service collective bargaining was more pernicious and continued into the 1990s, namely an attempt to decentralise and further fragment pay determination in a context of privatisation, while also attempting to intensify work (Seifert, 1992; Lloyd and Seifert, 1995) and to substitute cheaper labour for more expensive. Ancillary staff formed an important target for workforce reductions, labour intensification and Compulsory Competitive Tendering (CCT) from the early 1980s onwards, and from the mid- to late-1980s nurses became a key target group for pay decentralisation, driven through the medium of the Review Body, and grademix changes, driven centrally and imposed by resource constraints at local level (Seifert, 1992; Thornley and Winchester, 1994; Thornley, 1996, 1998a). These changes were to coalesce following the 1989 White Paper, *Working for Patients*, proposing the creation of NHS Trusts and an 'internal market'.

To the extent that health service unionism had 'come of age' in the 1970s and changed tactics to survive in the 1980s, the 1990s were quickly to provide a strong impetus for merger and the creation of UNISON. The NHS and Community Care Act of 1990 marked the strongest challenge to Whitley – and national collective bargaining and pay determination – in its history. It thereby also marked the strongest challenge to the gains made by unions and their future potential to represent members' interests. The key components of the Act have tended to be neglected by commentators obsessed with the 'purchaser–provider' divide and contractual implications of an 'internal market', namely the new freedoms for Trusts to set pay locally: these were given added impetus by the creation of a new, locally-paid, grade of staff called variously Health Care Assistants or Support Workers. Taken together with repeated proposals for performance-related pay and extended private provision of services, this new system offered the potential to fragment, decentralise and individualise pay (Thornley, 1993) and opened the way to Trust managers seeking to bypass unions and collective bargaining altogether (Seifert, 1992).

Early progress by Trusts in establishing local systems was very slow (Bach and Winchester, 1994) while the merger and formation of UNISON in 1993 was rather fast. The merger itself was fuelled not just by the pace and extent of Conservative reforms in the 1980s and early 1990s, but also by the legacy of union co-operation and relative unity in confronting them, experienced both in industrial actions and within the pay determination systems. A proximate influence was the ambulance workers' dispute of 1989–90 where 'all the unions agreed from the start for the need for the closest possible co-ordination of action and statement' (Seifert, 1992), and which provided perceptions of inter-union co-operation at the time merger talks were getting off the ground.[7] Moreover, the logic of pay decentralisation – and the necessity for national co-ordination to combat it and of local co-ordination to fight for the best possible deal where necessary – provided an equally strong logic for forging a strong and powerful union with joint resources.[8] The new union was well in place by the time that central exhortations to Trusts to use the new machinery turned into diktats, once again using the nurses' Review Body to drive through change, alongside further privatisation initiatives. In June 1994 the now-famous instruction from the NHS chief executive to senior managers (the 'Langlands' letter) outlined the pursuit at national level of enabling agreements with NHS unions and required all Trusts to have local pay machinery set up by February 1995. The Review Body played a vital role in getting the process under way, giving basic national recommendations for nurses' awards in the 1995–6 and 1996–7 pay rounds, while leaving pay 'top-ups' to be decided locally in the context of a hybrid 'two-tier' system (Thornley, 1998a).

The reaction from health service staff and their unions was strong, largely united, and effective, at both national and local levels, with UNISON playing a key role. The nursing unions and associations, for example, presented an 'almost unprecedented . . . united front' in calling for the retention and improvement of national machinery, before launching a 'joint national offensive' (*Nursing Times*, 1995). Commissioned survey and case study research on the 'local pay experiment' (Thornley, 1998a) found that local pay paradoxically tended to reunite staff groups at local level, not least because the great majority of Trusts opted for a unique percentage increase across staff groups. UNISON was well-placed to emerge as the largest union with the strongest local steward network, leading negotiations in the majority of Trusts: the union's lead negotiators overwhelmingly reported perceptions of Staff Side unity, while noting in a majority of cases that managers lacked experience in pay negotiation, and were sometimes hostile to the principle of bargaining.[9] The frustration created by protracted pay negotiations over often small amounts of centrally-resource-constrained money, with generally poor pay outcomes, undoubtedly increased both conflict and union membership in most Trusts – early indications were that this was leading to membership shifts in favour of UNISON (Thornley, 1998a). Working in combination and individually, the NHS unions managed to gain maximum publicity for their concerns and the exercise in 'local pay' was abruptly truncated in an historic U-turn by the Conservative government before the General Election. Even the nurses' Review Body reporting in February 1997 included a vigorous indictment of the conduct of the local pay experiment, though its members still seem wedded to the principle.

If the Conservative U-turn on local pay could be seen as an historic achievement for the new union, then the last few years have seen an equally concerted attempt by UNISON to address the second strand of the 1990 NHS Act, namely the incremental, and rapid, increase in the use of locally paid Health Care Assistants and Support Workers. It has commissioned major research exercises into their terms and conditions of work (Thornley, 1997), which are not collated or published in official national sources. These research exercises have revealed appalling initial pay outcomes which often undercut Whitley rates for equivalent staff, alongside inadequate training provision. They have also shown that this grade is being actively exploited to substitute for extant nursing staff. UNISON has been vigorously campaigning on all issues of their employment, with a particular focus on pay and conditions and training, both at national and local levels, and has achieved some notable successes at each level in obtaining improvements or getting health care assistants (HCAs) put firmly on the agenda for inclusion in the nurses' Review Body or a new pay system.

If there have been past successes for the new union, the challenges ahead are also significant. UNISON has campaigned widely for public recognition of the plight of its low paid members not least through its submissions to the Low Pay Commission, the Health Select Committee, and the nurses' Review Body. However, low pay and unequal pay will remain crucial issues for UNISON, particularly for support staff, administrative and clerical staff, and nursing staff,[10] who equally suffer poor conditions of service and a relative lack of control over their own labour. This high degree of exploitation is exacerbated by the overwhelmingly feminised nature of the health service workforce, and by continuing divisions on the staff side. In addition, the increasing use by managers of HRM practices closely related to quality management initiatives has meant a constant pressure on local union activists, supported by their full-time officials, to counter their more oppressive aspects.[11] At the same time, UNISON's advocacy of 'quality' in terms of service provision and patient care in the NHS provides an apt example of the ways in which unions confronted by such initiatives are able to impose a competing understanding of the meaning and basis of such terms with respect to pay and conditions of work: low pay and degradation of work have deleterious consequences for the quality of patient care. However, this struggle also puts strains on union resources.

Today, much remains of the old Conservative policies: the pay system is fragmented and chaotic, the nurses' Review Body has been progressively undermined and devalued as an 'independent' arbiter, a significant minority of staff still remain on Trust contracts while the rapid growth of HCAs exacerbates this tendency, differentials have widened dramatically, and many health service workers remain locked in poverty pay. More pernicious still has been the growth of private provision, with associated poorer pay and conditions, both through the massive expansion of nursing homes and through CCT and, more recently, the Private Finance Initiative (PFI). In this context, the formation of UNISON has been of vital importance, and we turn to look at future prospects after a discussion of changes in collective bargaining in local government.

Changes in collective bargaining in local government

Local government is a central industry in the nation's economic and social life. The 410 local authorities in England and Wales employed 1.9 million people in 1998, down from 2.1 million in 1979. Local government annual spending of over £50 billion accounts for a quarter of all public spending. Councils vary widely in size, from the small district councils employing fewer than 200 to the large unitary, metropolitan district and shire county councils employing up to 50,000. Between 1979 and 1997 all councils had to deal with the violent attentions of Conservative governments aimed at weakening local political power, at undermining local government trade unions and collective bargaining, and at privatising services in the name of efficiency and customer benefit but really to provide more profits for private business.

In 1979 there were about forty national negotiating councils and committees, involving more than sixty separate, recognised trade unions and professional associations. Some covered small groups of employees such as the 300 justices' clerks, while others covered larger groups as with the 6,000 probation service staff and the 7,000 magistrates courts staff. The largest and most important bargaining units were the National Joint Council for Administrative, Professional, Technical and Clerical Services (NJC-APT&C), covering over half a million non-manual employees, and the National Joint Council for Local Authorities' Services – Manual Workers (NJC-MW), covering over a million manual employees. NALGO, Managerial, Administrative, Technical Staff Association (MATSA), NUPE, Association of Clerical, Technical and Supervisory Staff (ACTSS) and COHSE were recognised for non-manual negotiations, and General, Municipal, Boilermakers (GMB), NUPE and Transport and General Workers Union (TGWU) were recognised for manuals. NALGO had around 450,000 members in local government, mostly APT&C, and dominated the NJC-APT&C as the majority union. NUPE's membership of 400,000 was considerably higher than the other two manual worker unions combined.

The 1997 'Single Status' agreement brought the remaining directly employed 1.5 million manual and white collar employees under the umbrella of the National Joint Council for Local Authority Services, the largest bargaining unit in the UK with a 1996 paybill of £13.13 billion (*Local Government Management*,

1997). By this time UNISON had been formed and the three local authority associations had merged to form the Local Government Association. We are therefore concerned to show the changes in employment and work which radically altered the relationships within local government of white collar and manual staff, and how those changes wrought by government policies created the circumstances to forge a united organisation to defend and progress the conditions of service of all members under the new regime.

Local government collective bargaining under the Conservatives

The first Thatcher government had no clear policies to transform local government, as Secretary of State Michael Heseltine continued his Labour predecessor's policy of imposing cash limits on local authority funds and interfering in an increasing number of policy areas. The employers began a process of cutting back on capital programmes and making piecemeal closures of small units such as residential establishments. Responding with a 'business as usual' approach, the unions continued negotiating over pay and conditions, protecting the national agreements, and campaigning to defend both local services and local democracy. The main burden of the cuts fell on manual employees, and this pushed NUPE as well as the TGWU and GMB onto the back foot in terms of responses to such massive job losses. Employer bargaining objectives at national level aimed to tie pay settlements to the principle of 'affordability' rather than comparability, looking for increased productivity, weaker national agreements and more local flexibility (Kessler, 1989). NALGO spent £1 million on its 'Put People First' campaign at the time of the 1983 general election.

By the late 1980s the cuts in local government funding became deeper, and the attack on manual employees more severe. Nationally imposed cuts were locally implemented, and the impact on collective bargaining was substantial. Although the Whitley national bargaining structure was untouched, with bargaining over pay rates continuing as normal, the reality was that many actual terms and conditions were being determined at the level of the local authority or, in an increasing number of cases, at the level of the service unit such as direct labour organisations. In some local authorities changes in terms and conditions were imposed unilaterally, but in most they were implemented through locally negotiated agreements. Both the level and scope of bargaining were shifting, and bargaining itself was becoming fragmented between a growing number of smaller bargaining units. The unions' traditional strength had been in negotiating and then defending national agreements within a context of job security, relatively low pay and limited changes to skills hierarchies. All of this was linked to a public service ethos. As the central government and local employers turned away from national agreements, undermined job security, maintained low pay with the additional ingredient of more part time work, and deliberately broke down skills, so the unions found it difficult to maintain their membership base and their bargaining position.[12]

It was during this period that the foundations were laid for the Conservatives' final attack on local government through CCT and the poll tax. These actions persuaded both NALGO and NUPE to cooperate on a range of issues and to liaise more closely with each other.[13] The defence of local government became a key political issue within the TUC as the balance of membership and power shifted towards the large public sector unions (Marsh, 1992: 152), and this was also reflected in the importance for Labour councillors of finding a way out of their funding dilemmas. NALGO's second £1 million campaign, for the 1987 election period, was stopped by the courts, resulting in their decision to create a political fund, which brought NALGO even closer in its general alignment with NUPE and COHSE.

The poll tax, implemented during the third Thatcher administration, had a profound impact on local government. Each successive local election saw another tranche of Tory activists driven out of politics as Labour took over the council chambers and the Conservatives became the third party in local government. Fearful of electoral collapse, the Conservatives finally ditched both the tax and Mrs Thatcher, although the new Council Tax retained the same centralising principles of its discredited predecessor.

NALGO tapped into the deep unpopularity of the Thatcher government in 1989 with its first ever national strike involving all local government members, over pay and in defence of the national agreement. The employers misjudged both the mood of the employees and the determination of the NALGO leadership. However, they were now quite clear that local flexibility was a priority issue in coming to terms with the declining level of funding. With labour costs making up over 70 per cent of total spending, significant savings could only be made by cutting the wage bill. CCT was proving quite effective in reducing labour costs – where contracts were won by the council workforce this was invariably on the back of a mixture of reduced staffing levels, reduced working hours, increased intensity of work, less job security, worse conditions of service, and tighter management control.

These developments drove forward the momentum for merger. First there were clear advantages to be gained by pooling resources to enhance the national capacity to negotiate with the employers and to campaign to defend local government. Second, the labour markets for manual and non-manual employees were becoming similar as the APT&C internal labour market broke up between business/service provider units. Third, the majority of NALGO members were now managed just like NUPE members, challenging the traditional NUPE members' view of NALGO as the bosses' union. Fourth, there was a shared commitment to tackle low pay, and fifth, the urgency of unity was apparent from the future plans of government in terms of white collar CCT. All of these pressures were becoming acute in the workplaces, as local managers embraced the triumphalist rhetoric of 'New Public Management' (Pollitt, 1993) with its three Es: efficiency, effectiveness and economy. When the NALGO and NUPE conferences voted for merger they did so in order to mount the best defence of their respective memberships in the difficult times ahead.

By the time UNISON came into being, a year after the Tories won their fourth general election victory, all the main local government reforms were in place. CCT was extended into white collar areas, deepening the exposure of the council workforce to external competition. Internal markets, established under the community care provisions, became widely accepted as a model for local authority organisation. Under pressure from the Audit Commission and the District Auditor, more and more councils chased 'value for money' through the establishment of business units and through a 'mixed economy' of competing providers owned by local authorities, by private companies and by not-for-profit private voluntary organisations. New funding arrangements hamstrung the councils yet further – the PFI tied councils more tightly to business logic, and a proliferation of piecemeal initiatives set councils in competition with each other to submit bids for funds for government-decided projects. Local councils became less concerned with the democratic control of services and yet more concerned with the management of resources (and human resources in particular) to meet government criteria.

Pressures on collective bargaining systems and outcomes were clear. National bargaining was waning in importance, and the employers were clearly prepared to take the initiative to secure greater freedom to decide on labour management issues at local level. NALGO and NUPE branches had been tested in their resolve to ensure that negotiations took place over these issues, resulting in a series of local strikes, some of which were long and drawn out trials of strength. These bitter struggles helped to cement the merger at local level, as co-operation over anti-cuts campaigns in the 1980s grew into joint action against oppressive management in the 1990s. Where branch mergers had been unthinkable only 10 years earlier, local government had changed so much that they could now be achieved with only a very small number of problems.

A further crucial factor in consolidating the merger nationally and locally was the 'Single Status' agreement, under negotiation since the early 1990s and signed in 1997 (Industrial Relations Services, 1997). As with the UNISON merger itself, the logic towards single status was strong – it embraced the unions' desire to protect national bargaining and to maintain a basic set of negotiating principles while recognising the employers' aim for local flexibility and the reality of fragmentation. The merger of the three employers' associations into the Local Government Association also followed this logic. In local authorities the result has been the establishment of formal negotiations at the levels of the employer, the department and the business unit, bringing together the former NALGO and NUPE negotiators who previously bargained separately over most issues. Conditions have been created for greater unity between different membership groups over a range of bargaining issues.

Future prospects for collective bargaining and UNISON in health and local government

May 1997 saw the Labour Party back in government as the consequences of the Tory reforms became apparent to the electorate. The landslide vote for new

Labour was a massive rejection of the completed Tory project, leaving the Conservative Party as a small rump in both national and local politics. However, the new government has yet to take any significant steps towards a renewal of Britain's political economy. Indeed in three relevant areas policies appear no better: CCT, PFI and collective bargaining.

The CCT regime in local government is to be replaced by 'best value', which will cover a full range of council services and which retains the competitive elements of CCT. Councils are still expected, under the watchful eye of the Audit Commission, to ensure a 'mixed economy' of public and private service providers. Proposals to reform council structures will distance councillors yet further from control over the nature of service provision, further enhancing the policy-making role of the expert managers. In this way local authorities are becoming less the democratically accountable political representatives of local communities and more the 'partners' of private businesses. This apparent depoliticisation of local government is an attempt to treat political issues as if they were administrative and technical difficulties. Hence, rule by experts is seen as more efficient, effective and economical as they are unencumbered by the nuisance of democratic accountability and local councillors responding, however imperfectly, to their electorate.

Nowhere is this clearer than in current government support for the Conservative policy of PFI which entails a small-print potential for widespread privatisation of service provision. This is a key concern for UNISON, in both health and local government, as is the plight of those already 'contracted-out', and UNISON is already taking a lead role in the fight to protect both terms and conditions of the service deliverers and the rights of service users. This issue is likely to provoke very widespread public concern and carries very heavy risks for Labour in the future.

In local government, where UNISON has very deep roots in the workforce, branch and workplace activists are sure to continue the classic trade union activity of engaging in collective bargaining wherever and whenever they can find an opportunity. Seemingly, the government has not thought through the consequences of pushing measures that can only result in further speed-up and degradation of work, and in more oppressive management, among a highly unionised workforce with a growing tradition of militant resistance. The government is apparently unaware of the extent to which local government employees expect their employers to involve their trade union in negotiations over change in the workplace, and this failure to involve the collective side of public sector work provides the basis for both government policy to flounder in practice and for the union to counter crude private sector nostrums of good management with its own version of how to run a public service.

In health, the Labour government is undoubtedly more open to consultation with the unions than former Conservative administrations, but has demonstrated a worrying ambiguity over collective bargaining. Its new NHS pay proposals, for example, are at best confused and at worst may prolong or even exacerbate problems already experienced. At the present time, negotiations are unlikely to produce a swift or lasting settlement. Part of the problem here, of course, is a traditional concern by this government as with previous governments with pay processes, combined with an equally traditional unwillingness to accept the evidence of staff shortages and discontent over pay outcomes and other related work issues. Cash limits, pay freezes and the purchaser provider split were initially continued and, although the February 1999 settlement for nurses made some extra provision for newly-qualified registered nurses, it did little for nursing as a whole.[14] Early settlements and offers for non-Review Body staff have been even poorer. UNISON is conducting a major campaign this year for a large uplift for non-Review Body staff as well as keeping up pressure through the Review Body for significant rises to nurses' pay, including the now urgent case of Nursing Auxiliaries (Thornley, 1998b).

UNISON now has the capacity to recruit and represent a majority of health service workers as well as those in local government and to provide a strong and unified staff side at both local and national levels for the first time in history. Part of the opportunity ahead lies in publicising this strength and capacity in major recruitment drives, along with highlighting successes in combating the endemic problem of low pay and linking this explicitly to recruitment and retention problems, challenging gender-based inequalities, and in not letting labour substitution pass unnoticed. More generally, UNISON's great strength lies in its size, commitment to national pay arrangements, allowing for some local flexibility where necessary, and the ability to co-ordinate national and local activity and gain public sympathy and support.

Local negotiators are likely to be ever more hard pressed in the future with both negotiations over pay and pay-related conditions, along with the bewildering increase in non-pay issues around training, human resource management initiatives, privatisation, grademix changes, absence and service provision changes. These duties will add to existing grievance, disciplinary, health and safety and equal opportunities work. UNISON is already addressing the strengthening of branch structures and fulltime officer support for future battles ahead. Ultimately, UNISON and its forerunner unions have always had a high degree of success in handling the potentially thorny issue of pay negotiations for different occupations and grades and UNISON is the only union which can operate on the 'ratcheting' principle. Future successes will undoubtedly hinge both on fulfilling the large potential for increased recruitment and in changing the *nature* of health service and local government unionism.

While governments retain the view that markets are the best way to allocate resources, and that the managerial techniques that are used to accumulate profits should also be used to run public services, the challenges are likely to be strong. A strong streak of managerialism explains governmental support for stronger individual employment rights alongside a rejection of stronger trade union rights – both labour market flexibility and managerial prerogative are perceived to be threatened by trade union organisation, while stronger individual employment rights are less of a threat because they are difficult to uphold in the absence of trade unions. We are seeing a renewed emphasis on performance management, supported by an array of management information-gathering techniques through computers, video cameras and generally tighter supervision. The search for 'best practice' smacks of the worst forms of scientific management, as service delivery becomes a set of technical issues driven by the stopwatch and the performance indicator rather than a set of social, political and economic issues involving human beings.

UNISON, like NALGO, NUPE and COHSE before it, has not embraced the market model and has retained its commitment to public ownership. The achievement of the National Minimum Wage underpins bargaining over national rates of pay. As the biggest TUC affiliate it has the capacity to launch influential campaigns over important questions of workers' rights, not least their collective rights to organise and to mobilise. These two trade union functions of political campaigning for workers' rights as citizens and collective bargaining over workers' rights as employees at work are the very foundations of trade unionism, and will help ensure that UNISON members in these two crucial services receive strong and representative support from the main organisation protecting their rights as workers as well as the rights of the service users.

Notes

1 This chapter discusses local government, excluding education, in England and Wales. Scotland has a slightly different system, and Northern Ireland has a significantly different one, each with its own collective bargaining arrangements.
2 Around 60 per cent of local government workers (UNISONfaq, 1998) and around 80 per cent of the non-medical workforce in Health (DoH, 1998: 4).
3 Doctors and dentists are a notable exception and were granted a Review Body from the early 1960s.
4 Due in no small part to the reduction in numbers of ancillary workers, both through direct reduction and contracting out.
5 Current official figures leave a lot to be desired, but 'nurses, midwives and health visitors' are shown as constituting 44 per cent of the workforce with a further 11 per cent being defined as 'health care assistants and support staff' (DoH, 1998). For a detailed review of problems with these figures and definitions, see Thornley, 1997 where it is shown that many of this latter group are engaged in a wide range of nursing duties.
6 NHS accounting methods have undergone a number of changes and now tend to understate the significance of pay. On current accounting pay would stand at some 65 per cent of revenue expenditure – however, different accounting methods would show this at closer to 70–80 per cent.
7 Terry, 1996 refers to the 'control and discipline exercised in the ambulance workers' dispute, in which NUPE and the other unions involved hardly put a tactical foot wrong'.
8 See in particular Terry, 1996 in which the increasing recognition by NUPE and COHSE in particular of the need for national co-ordination and strength in the face of the limitations of local action in fighting privatisation and contracting out is discussed.
9 The perceptions of 'management' here largely refer to senior managers. Clearly an important area for future research concerns the extent to which junior and middle managers in particular, many of whom may be UNISON members, have accommodated the potential conflict between their roles as unionised employees and as managers.

10 For detailed reviews of pay, see UNISON (1997) and Thornley (1998c).
11 For example, the misuse of 'flexible' contracts, the secretive use of sensitive information, and a disregard for trade unions and collective agreements.
12 Between 1982 and 1992 NUPE membership fell by 160,000. See Fryer and Williams (1993: 142).
13 NALGO and NUPE joined with the GMB and TGWU to produce the booklet *Who Dares Wins*, a trade union guide to CCT, and NALGO, NUPE and the Council of Civil Service Unions established the Public Services Privatisation Research Unit, based at NUPE's head office.
14 Rodney Bickerstaffe noted that it was 'bittersweet', and UNISON noted that it was 'unlikely' that the increase would be enough 'to raise morale and stem the exodus from nursing' (Bickerstaffe, 1999).

References

Bach, S. and Winchester, D. (1994) 'Opting out of pay devolution? The prospects for local pay bargaining in UK public services', *British Journal of Industrial Relations*, 32: 2.

Bacon, R. and Eltis, W. A. (1976) *Britain's Economic Problems: Too Few Producers*, London: Macmillan.

Bickerstaffe, R. (1999) *Internet News* (May), London: UNISON.

Carpenter, M. (1988) *Working for Health: the History of COHSE*, London: Lawrence & Wishart.

Clay, H. (1929) *The Problem of Industrial Relations*, London: Macmillan.

Clegg, H. (1980) *Standing Commission on Pay Comparability*, Cmnd 7880, London: HMSO.

Clegg, H. and Chester, T. E. (1957) *Wage Policy and the Health Service*, Oxford: Basil Blackwell.

DoH (1998) *Statistical Bulletin* (May), London: Department of Health.

Fredman, S. and Morris, G. (1989) 'The state as employer: setting a new example', *Personnel Management*, August.

Fryer, R. and Williams, S. (1993) *A Century of Service: An Illustrated History of NUPE 1889–1993*, London: Lawrence & Wishart.

Industrial Relations Services (1997) 'Historic single-status deal in local government', *IRS Employment Trends*, 639.

Kessler, I. (1989) 'Bargaining strategies in local government', in Mailly, R., Dimmock, S. J. and Sethi, A. S. (eds) *Industrial Relations in the Public Services*, London: Routledge.

Kessler, S. and Bayliss, F. (1998) *Contemporary British Industrial Relations*, 3rd edn, London: Macmillan.

Lloyd, C. and Seifert, R. (1995) 'Restructuring in the NHS: the impact of the 1990 reforms on the management of labour', *Work, Employment and Society*, 9: 2.

Local Government Management (1997) Autumn.

Marsh, D. (1992) *The New Politics of British Trade Unionism*, London: Macmillan.

Millward, N. *et al.* (1992) *Workplace Industrial Relations in Transition: The ED/ESRC/PSI/ACAS Surveys*, Aldershot: Dartmouth.

Nursing Times (1995) 91: 10.

Pollitt, C. (1993) *Managerialism and the Public Services: Cuts or Cultural Change in the 1990s?*, Oxford: Blackwell.

Salamon, M. (1998) *Industrial Relations: Theory and Practice*, Hemel Hempstead: Prentice Hall Europe.

Salvage, J. (1985) *The Politics of Nursing*, London: Heinemann.

Seifert, R. (1992) *Industrial Relations in the NHS*, London: Chapman & Hall.

Terry, M. (1996) 'Negotiating the government of UNISON: union democracy in theory and practice', *British Journal of Industrial Relations*, 34: 1.

Thornley, C. (1993) 'Pay determination for nurses: pay review, grading and training in the 1980s', PhD Thesis, Warwick University.

Thornley, C. (1994) *Back to the Future*, London: UNISON.

Thornley, C. (1995) *The 'Model Employer' Myth: The Need for Theoretical Renewal in Public Sector Industrial Relations*, 13th Annual Labour Process Conference.

Thornley, C. (1996) 'Segmentation and inequality in the nursing workforce: re-evaluating the evaluation of skills' in Crompton, R., Gallie, D. and Purcell, K. (eds), *Changing Forms of Employment: Organisation, Skills and Gender*, London: Routledge.

Thornley, C. (1997) *Invisible Workers*, London: UNISON.

Thornley, C. (1998a) 'Contesting local pay: the decentralization of collective bargaining in the NHS', *British Journal of Industrial Relations*, 36: 3.

Thornley, C. (1998b) *Neglected Nurses, Hidden Work*, London: UNISON.

Thornley, C. (1998c) *A Question of Fairness: Nurses' Pay Trends 1979–1998*, London: UNISON.

Thornley, C. and Winchester, D. (1994) 'The remuneration of nursing personnel in the UK' in Marsden, D. (ed.), *The Remuneration of Nursing Personnel*, Geneva: ILO.

UNISON (1997) *Submission to the Low Pay Commission*, London: UNISON.

UNISONfaq (1998) (January) Information Resource Centre, Policy and Research Department, UNISON.

Winchester, D. (1983) 'Industrial relations in the public sector', in Bain, G. (ed.), *Industrial Relations in Britain*, Oxford: Blackwell.

11 UNISON and low pay policy

Peter Morris

This chapter describes the development of UNISON's strategies on low pay. Its centrepiece has been the National Minimum Wage. The detailed argument and supporting evidence for the union's policy is largely contained in the evidence to the Low Pay Commission and not covered here. The focus is on how the policy evolved and the dynamics and tensions it has produced.

The chapter is in three parts. The first describes the formation of the policy. The case for a minimum wage law emerged in NUPE largely as a consequence of the failure of collective bargaining to deal with the problem of low pay in the public services. It led to a campaign over 25 years to secure support within the TUC and the Labour Party. It became part of a larger argument about economic policy that valued labour as a resource to be maximised rather than a cost to be minimised.

The second part examines how the policy was developed within UNISON. At one level it provided a clear, radical agenda around which the new union could unite. But, at another it has provoked tensions about what it means in terms of internal relativities and wage inequalities. The consistent advocacy for a particular figure, uprated in line with the increase in earnings throughout the economy, has kept alive the case for a higher rather than a lower level of minimum wage, an instrument of labour market policy as much as social policy.

The third section describes the emergence of bargaining strategies around low pay within UNISON. These developed less as part of a coherent, union-wide approach and more as a consequence of the internal logic of sectoral negotiations. Significant gains have been made, both through national and local bargaining, usually as part of a wider wage restructuring, often the principles of equal pay for work of equal value.

Forming the policy

In its early stages, UNISON's policy is largely the story of NUPE's campaign for a National Minimum Wage. During the late 1960s and early 1970s, the union evolved a range of strategies for tackling low pay, through a series of strikes involving refuse collectors, street cleaners, hospital workers, and especially, women, mostly part timers, working as cleaners, cooks and care workers. The failure of collective bargaining to resolve the problems of low pay led the union to argue for a minimum wage law to underpin the wages structure. In 1973, NUPE put a resolution to the Labour Party conference, calling for a legally enforceable minimum wage. It was defeated by 3 to 1 on the basis that it would represent interference by the Government in free collective bargaining.

As a result of the Social Contract in 1974, Local Authority and Health Service male manual workers minimum pay rates, for the first and only time since the war, reached the then TUC low pay target of £30 a week, or two-thirds of male manual earnings. The deal was largely the work of Jack Jones, the General Secretary of the TGWU, a powerful advocate for the low paid, but opposed to statutory intervention. During the Winter of Discontent, in 1978–9, union opposition to a minimum wage, and more generally to redistributive low pay policies, resurfaced especially among the craft unions. Government pay policy could contain neither the demands from the better paid that differentials be maintained; nor the need for new voices, particularly those of female, part-time, marginal workers in the public services, to be heard at the bargaining table. The Conservatives were elected on a programme to curb union power and make the market the main determinant of pay.

For a number of interlinked reasons, trade union attitudes began to shift in the early 1980s. The first was the experience of the Government's programme of deregulation, especially in the field of employment law, where the legislative protection of most value to those outside the mainstream of collective bargaining was scrapped. Revocation of the Fair Wages Resolution, changes in unfair dismissal law, contracting-out legislation in public services, alongside the restrictions on secondary strike action meant that the low paid in unorganised or weakly organised firms became increasingly detached from the economic bargaining power of the union at sector or company level.

Second, the high levels of unemployment that followed the Government's monetarist policies both eroded union power and led to an unprecedented growth in a fragmented, casualised, low-wage sector. A 50-year trend towards wage equality was reversed; and the position of the low paid further undermined by the gradual removal of the floor of rights in social security. Third, union experience over equal pay – combined with the sheer complexity of the Equal Value Regulations – led unions to re-evaluate their approach to the law, developing dual strategies more along European lines, based on an inter-action between the law and bargaining. The *Julie Hayward* [1984] equal pay case sparked major pay restructuring in a number of sectors, including local government, universities and the health service.

Winning support

NUPE skilfully built support for the National Minimum Wage. At the 1983 TUC, the union won support for a consultative study, seconded by the Association of Scientific, Technical and Managerial Staff (ASTMS), who had previously opposed the policy. At the Labour Party, Rodney Bickerstaffe, the newly appointed General Secretary, moving a resolution for a statutory national minimum wage, set at not less than two thirds of average earnings, said:

> Still on the same issue – the outrage, the humiliation in one of the world's richest countries of low pay endured by seven million working poor to whom a dream ticket means enough food and proper clothing; freedom from the need to borrow; safety from the indignity of their nightmare reality – degrading, destroying poverty . . .

> . . . There are some pluses. More and more unions, constituencies and MPs now hold that a genuine, determined, a planned attack on low pay must be underwritten by the will of the entire community in the form of a statutory minimum wage under which no employer shall force and exploit any one of our people.

While the resolution was passed, it did not get the two-thirds majority needed to entrench it as policy. The Low Pay Unit, and staunch advocates like the Civil Service Union, worked untiringly to build support within the unions and the Labour Party. In the following year, the National Union of Tailor and Garment Workers, almost all of whose members were covered by Wages Councils, changed their position, saying that a National Minimum Wage might help them toward the two-thirds target, which negotiations never would.

The problem remained the opposition of the TGWU. They feared that minimum wage legislation could undermine union organisation and become a Trojan horse for incomes policy. However, at the 1985 Labour Party conference, a NUPE-led composite calling for consultation on the implementation of a minimum wage (as agreed in 1983) alongside strategies to end poverty pay based on strong union organisation, underpinned by legal rights, won overwhelming support. In 1986, it was supported by the TUC. COHSE supported the policy and deployed it effectively as part of a broader bargaining strategy within the Health Service.

The argument evolved that the minimum wage should be an instrument of economic efficiency as well as social justice, a spur to improved productivity and training, and changes in job design and work organisation. Low pay was increasingly seen as integrally linked to the undervaluing of women's work, especially of those skills associated with work at home, like cooking, caring or cleaning, or requiring particular dexterity. Implementation of a minimum wage could and should involve a redistribution of wages. If it did not, it was argued, it would merely increase prices, possibly reduce employment and not help the low paid.

Labour and the Minimum Wage

The minimum wage scarcely featured in the 1987 General Election campaign but following the election in that year Labour set up a working group under John Smith MP, the Shadow Chancellor, to consider the details of its implementation.

Agreement was reached on how the formula for half male median earnings should be calculated, dividing earnings including overtime by 39 hours to produce an hourly rate. The £3.40 an hour used by Labour in the 1992 election campaign was derived from these calculations. A second working group was formed to draft a brief on the form that minimum wage legislation might take, defining who should be covered, what should be included within the wage and how it should be enforced. It included representatives from Labour's secretariat, officers from NUPE and the GMB, academic lawyers and practitioners. A paper drafted on behalf of the group by Bob Simpson from the London School of Economics was sent to Tony Blair, the then Shadow Employment Secretary, in December 1991.

The driving force behind Labour's policy was John Smith who was committed to the minimum wage as much on moral grounds as on economic. He did not (as some unions feared) see it as part of a wider deal with the trade unions. Indeed, he doubted their capacity to deliver on any accord. If introduced at £3.40 an hour he did not envisage a minimum wage rising significantly towards the two-thirds target over the lifetime of a Labour government. On Smith's election as leader in 1993 the minimum wage became a central element of Labour's economic programme. He argued that there was a false antithesis between social justice and economic success. Ending poverty pay and bringing Britain up to the European level would be a substantial and overdue measure of justice of immediate and lasting benefit to millions of people whose needs and interests, and those of their families, had been so badly neglected.

UNISON and the National Minimum Wage

From its formation in July 1993 it was clear that the National Minimum Wage would be a central policy for UNISON. Although only adopted by NALGO in the year before the creation of UNISON it had the virtue of providing a clear, radical programme around which the new union could unite. With some hesitancy, a dual strategy began to emerge, with UNISON both pursuing the introduction of national minimum wage legislation through the Labour Party and the TUC, and developing a bargaining agenda to present to employers to secure guaranteed minimum pay levels in the collective agreements negotiated by the union.

The virtues of intransigence

The first two UNISON Conferences adopted, without significant debate, NUPE's formula for a minimum wage of male median earnings rising over time to two-thirds of average earnings. But whereas the earlier discussions had set the minimum wage within a fairly complex context of pay bargaining, inequality and redistribution, the argument within UNISON tended be more formulaic, focusing particularly on a non-negotiable set of demands relating primarily to the monetary level at which it should be introduced.

The critical debates were at the 1996 Conference. The year before, the Labour Party had significantly modified its approach. If elected, Labour would introduce a National Minimum Wage as soon as was practicable, but it would not campaign on a specific figure, nor on a formula in relation to average earnings from which a figure might be derived. Instead it would establish a Low Pay Commission, following the election, involving employers and unions. The TUC meeting a month before UNISON's 1996 conference had recognised and accepted that Labour would determine the National Minimum Wage in the light of all the economic circumstances prevailing at the time, and that it would set up a Commission, involving the social partners. The TUC called for a target based on the established formula that a National Minimum Wage should be initially introduced at half male median earnings, rising in time to two-thirds male median earnings.

The debate at UNISON's 1996 Conference defined the union's approach in relation, first, to difficult tensions around internal pay differentials; and second, to the TUC's position and the growing union consensus that was being sought around a £4 per hour figure for the minimum wage. A central composite on the Minimum Wage and Social Benefits, advocating a figure of £4.26 linked to benefit reforms, was overwhelmingly supported. One amendment '[accepted] that all service groups will need to ensure that achieving [the national minimum wage] will require all other pay elements to be secondary to our central objective. Achieving this target will be vital in convincing our lowest-paid, part-time, women manual workers that their interests are also the interests of our better-paid members. We must show with solidarity that we are a campaigning union as well as a caring union.' It was moved by a school meals worker who said:

> 15 months ago I'd never even been to a union meeting. . . . But as a cook in the school kitchens I feel very strongly about low pay. The council pay settlement resulted in some of our members receiving an extra £25 a week. Some of our kitchen staff don't even earn that for a week's wage. . . . This amendment is about differentials: the dreaded word. If our low-paid workers are to achieve £4.26 those who are higher paid cannot insist on keeping the existing pay differentials. . . . We need the help and support of all UNISON members, especially the higher-paid, if we are to win our fight. So I ask Conference please support the amendment . . . with your hearts and your heads as well as your votes.

She was supported by another low-paid, part-time, female manual worker speaking on behalf of the National Executive Council, arguing that now was the time to give the minimum wage priority m wage negotiations.

The case against the *priorities* identified in the amendment was put by a male, white-collar delegate. He argued that the figure of £4.26 could unite the Conference and needed to be vigorously fought for through the TUC. But he also argued strongly against the view that low pay should be the dominant priority, since the wording of the amendment that argued for this sought to make other pay elements secondary to this demand rather than arguing that implementation of the minimum wage be fully funded across the public sector.

> Put simply, the amendment argues the minimum wage be funded by redistribution of earnings between public service workers rather than funded by government and employer . . . the amendment opens up the prospect [of pay restraint]. I would ask you to reject it. It cannot be achieved at lower living standards.

The amendment was defeated by a significant majority. That the argument may not be conclusive (and indeed will continue to be a necessary debate within the union) is suggested by the single status deal in local government in 1997 which embodied a redistributive policy over the whole pay range. A second amendment – which was passed – required the union to submit to the TUC a motion based on the union's policy of a minimum wage of £4.26 per hour.

The TUC had been careful to build a coalition in support of a minimum wage policy but they feared too high a figure could open up damaging divisions between unions and risk the opposition in particular of craft unions concerned about differentials. While affirming commitment to the formula, no minimum wage figure had been on the agenda for debate at the previous two Congresses. UNISON's call for this precise figure led to last-minute negotiations at Congress House, involving the withdrawal of UNISON's representatives on the General Council and telephone discussions with the miners' leader Arthur Scargill who was on Doncaster railway station. These in turn led to two separate composites, one from UNISON and the National Union of Mineworkers in support of £4.26; and a second led by the GMB representing the TUC consensus for a £4 wage target. In addition there was a General Council statement supporting half male median earnings but noting this provided figures in the range between £3.80 and £4.26.

There was a fierce clash on the floor of the TUC Congress between John Edmonds of the GMB and Rodney Bickerstaffe, UNISON's General Secretary. In the event both composites and the General Council statement were passed. Although the resulting ambiguity caused some difficulty to the TUC, it was important within UNISON that the General Secretary had demonstrated through his passionate speech that he kept faith with conference commitments and would not temper the union's demands for a level that represented a decent living wage. More generally, UNISON's commitment to a particular formula, despite its statistical flaws, meant that over a period of years the discussion of the level was kept in line with the increase in earnings. This in turn enabled the union to maintain its argument for a higher rather than a lower level, and for a minimum wage that was primarily an instrument of labour market policy designed to increase productivity and efficiency and to connect the pay of the lowest paid to that of higher-paid workers, rather than simply a safety net.

Evidence to the Low Pay Commission

With Ian McCartney's appointment as Shadow Minister for Employment in 1996, the Labour Party once again had a strong advocate for the minimum wage. He launched a two-pronged attack: an onslaught against the salaries of acquisitive top management through the 'Fat Cats campaign'; and detailed planning of the implementation of a minimum wage. He actively involved unions and employers in his approach and UNISON facilitated joint discussion with the leading private contractors.

Following Labour's election victory on 1 May 1997, a nine-member Low Pay Commission was formed under the chairmanship of Professor George Bain. Rita Donaghy from UNISON's National Executive Council was one of the three trade union representatives. They began taking evidence in the autumn. UNISON had both undertaken and sponsored significant research on the minimum wage, developing the social and economic argument in support, and analysing in particular its regional impact. It drew on this evidence in its submission to the Low Pay Commission in October 1997. Three assumptions about the purpose and the form of the National Minimum Wage underlay the approach:

1   Employment should enable people to earn a decent living. If a minimum wage is going to be effective it must redistribute incomes, putting more money in the purses and pockets of the lowest paid. It will require realignment of the tax and benefit systems to avoid new poverty traps and care in its introduction to ensure that, for example, low paid women's earnings are not eroded by increased childcare costs;
2   The work of the low paid is, in general, substantially undervalued. Low pay is largely a problem of women's pay, particularly in such occupations as cleaning, catering and caring. Unrecognised skills are paid well below their marginal value. The minimum wage is a logical development of equal pay legislation (indeed it was considered originally as an alternative to such legislation). It is important that the new procedures for a minimum wage should be consistent with, and reinforce the connection with equal pay;
3   Minimum wage legislation should underpin collective bargaining. To be effective, a framework of minimum rights needs to be integrated into broader bargaining agendas aimed at encouraging innovation and investment.

The evidence brought together wide-ranging statistical support for a minimum wage of £4.42 an hour. Because many of the workers the minimum wage was designed to protect – agency staff, temporary workers, casual workers, home workers – had uncertain employment status. UNISON's submission argued for a new, broader definition of 'worker'; for a definition of pay (based on article 119 of the European Treaty) based on earnings but excluding overtime; and for tough enforcement procedures. UNISON was the last organisation to give oral evidence to the Commission in February 1998. George Bain summarised its position: it was first of all concerned not just with providing a floor, but a living wage, and the formula was as much a campaigning tool as a scientific figure; that if you pursued a formulaic approach it could provide figures in the pay range of £3.70 to £4.42; but while the union would not reject the arithmetic or logic behind the lower figure, it would argue it was inadequate for a decent standard of living.

The minimum wage law came into effect on 1 April 1999. The legislation provides a clear and durable framework for implementation. The definition of who is covered extends to all but the genuinely self-employed, cutting through legal difficulties that have bedevilled earlier discussion. There will be no regional or sectoral variations, but a lower rate for 18–20-year-olds. The union argued for a multiple, interlocking enforcement strategy, and this is to a large extent reflected in the legislation. It should provide the basis for an effective minimum wage law.

UNISON's bargaining agenda

Because of the negotiating autonomy of UNISON's service groups a coherent bargaining strategy over the minimum wage took time to emerge. In practice it has developed primarily at two levels: first within national sectoral agreements; and secondly, through local bargaining, where minimum wage levels have been secured in line with the union's pay target. An early research paper produced in May 1995 argued that while the concentration on the level of a minimum wage and the legislation necessary for its implementation was entirely understandable, it neglected the impact it would have on bargaining structures especially within the public services.

As with all external shocks to the bargaining system, it could provide opportunities to negotiate changes, perhaps especially to the advantage of women workers who were disproportionately represented on the lowest grades. In many cases deleting a few points at the bottom of the scale would be enough to ensure that the pay structures remained intact and that knock-on effects were minimal. In others, however, the structure would be so distorted by bringing all those currently paid below the minimum up to it, that it would give us the chance to argue for a new structure entirely. As the paper argued: 'we will be arguing to incorporate equal pay for work of equal value principles into the structure . . . if we can assume that a Labour Government will want to see an expansion in public provision we could look to a major exercise in job redesign, upskilling workers and multiskilling posts . . . in fact taking practical steps towards of our vision of "high wage, high skill economy"'. The paper went on to argue that if it was possible to redesign jobs so that workers who used to be paid below the National Minimum Wage could be more effective in the work they do, taking on greater responsibility and undertaking higher skilled work then the union could argue that pay per unit of output (the traditional productivity measure) had not increased in the public services, but that only output had increased. The paper concluded that discussions were needed on how the minimum wage target was negotiated in areas where we had bargaining rights. A National Minimum Wage would give us a great opportunity to renegotiate structures to ensure equal pay for women members. However, if we were to avoid large-scale redundancies we would have to look creatively at job redesign and skill enhancement to go hand in hand with substantial pay increases.

National pay agreements

The most significant breakthrough was in the single status agreement in local government in 1997 which provided a minimum wage of £4 an hour. With the reduction in normal weekly hours for manual workers that was also part of the agreement, but negotiated at local level, this established a minimum of £4.22. Because the agreement covered the whole pay range, it allowed the costs of increases in the lowest scales to be more equitably shared. Building on the equal value pay restructuring of the manual workers' agreement in 1987, it also provided a framework for equalising pay. In the health service also the union has argued for a new pay determination system. At its core would be a national pay framework agreement that provides an underpinning minimum wage level. The commitment is to eradicate low and unequal pay. However, although the union has consistently argued for a combination of flat rate and percentage pay increases, a significant problem of low pay remains.

In the higher education sector manual workers got higher increases than other workers in the two-year deal agreed for 1996 and 1997. As part of the 1997 agreement an independent pay review, carried out by Hay MSL, concluded that the great majority of higher education staff were paid substantially below comparable private and public sector market levels.

Local bargaining

Local negotiators, particularly within the health care sector, reached agreements establishing a minimum wage above the national level. Some 29 agreements have been reached with NHS Trusts. One interesting example is at the Royal Hull Hospital where minimum rates were increased from £3.51 to £4.20 in an agreement covering all ancillary staff. A staged 3.3 per cent increased this to £4.28 from 1 April 1997 and £4.34 from 1 December 1997. The new rate subsumed previous bonus, performance and proficiency allowances; but remained for unsocial, shift and overtime. The agreement also included a reduction in the working week from 39 to 38.5 hours. Resistance by supervisors, concerned that differentials were being eroded, was met through negotiations with the Trust that these would be reviewed in a future pay round. Difficulties experienced by the Trust because of its reputation as a 'bad' employer have been turned round and ancillary jobs are now sought after.

Such minimum rates have rarely been negotiated in isolation. They have usually been part of a wider strategy to improve work practices, restructure grading systems and increase productivity. Where there has been resistance it has been resolved through discussion. The experience seems to have been that it has improved morale and resulted in more efficient services.

Conclusion

The Low Pay Commission announced their recommendations in June 1998. Their report contained a valuable analysis of contemporary problems of low pay, at the conclusion of which they recommended a starting figure of £3.60 an hour from April 1999 rising to £3.70 from June 2000. In April 1999 the government implemented a minimum of £3.60 an hour for workers over the age of 21. The level is well below the target advocated by UNISON. But the union will use it as a foundation on which to build, arguing that the UNISON figure of £4.61 an hour represents the mark-up for being in a union. Achieving the union's target will require new strategies, no less innovative than before. However, it is at least arguable that without the doggedness and persistence of UNISON and the unions that formed it, there would have been no prospect, let alone the present reality, of a national minimum wage.

Appendix

The Development of UNISON's Campaign for a National Minimum Wage

1965   The NUPE Conference passes a resolution on wages which sets the pattern for the coming years: 'Recognising that any national incomes policy based on fixed percentage growth rate will increase the gap between the highest and the lowest paid workers, Conference urges the Executive Council to impress upon the TUC the need for a policy which will give priority to the needs of lower paid workers'.

1966   NUPE supports a resolution passed at the TUC which called for 'effective measures to assist lower paid workers'.

1967   The TUC passes a T&G-sponsored motion calling for a minimum wage target of £15 per week for 40 hours – the first TUC target. This target was to be achieved through collective bargaining.

1968   TUC passes a resolution moved by the General and Municipal Workers' Union: 'Congress calls upon the Government to investigate the possibility of buttressing the TUC's proposal for a national minimum by introducing legislation'.

1969   In response to pressure about low pay and unequal pay for women the Labour Government bring in Equal Pay legislation to be phased in between 1970–75. The TUC General Council agreed a strategy of action on low pay with a minimum basic rate target of £16.50 per week. This was a voluntary policy and any decision on 'statutory backing' was deferred to be reviewed after studying the experience.

1970   Six-week strike by local authority manual workers for TUC target of £16.50 p.w. Scamp report gave weekly rise of £2.50 – only 25p short of the target.

1971   Tory Government introduce Family Income Supplement as a 'solution' to the problem of inadequate incomes amongst wage earners. Widely criticised as a subsidy for low wages.

1973   NUPE resolution to Labour Party Conference calling for a programme to introduce a legally enforceable minimum wage. This was defeated by a 3:1 majority on the basis of non-interference by Government in free collective bargaining of wages.

1974   TUC sets minimum wage target of two thirds of male manual earnings – £30 p.w. Election of Labour Government. Local authority and NHS ancillary staff achieve basic weekly rate of £30. Halsbury award for nurses.

1978–79   NUPE policy to achieve minimum two thirds target of £60 following years of wages policies. 'Winter of Discontent'. Establishment of Clegg Commission which failed to deal adequately with low pay in the public services.

1983   NUPE motion on minimum wage to Scottish TUC defeated. TUC discussion paper on how to tackle low pay and consideration of statutory national minimum wage. NUPE resolution passed at 1983 Congress states:

> Congress resolves to continue the discussion among affiliated unions on the introduction of a Statutory National Minimum Wage. To assist the debate the General Council should:
>
> i   provide a paper summarising the arguments on both sides put forward by affiliated unions;
> ii explore further whether a statutory minimum wage would assist to bridge the gap between male and female earnings: The experience of other countries: the relationship with collective bargaining machinery: and the method by which the trade union movement would be involved in negotiation on the level of the minimum wage and;
> iii prepare detailed targets, towards which unions can be encouraged to bargain until legislation exists.

The 1983 Labour Party Conference also passed a NUPE resolution which included a commitment to a statutory National Minimum Wage, with a minimum wage target set at not less than two-thirds of average earnings; while passed, the resolution did not get the two-thirds majority needed to entrench it as policy.

1984   Special TUC Conference on low pay policy – reaffirmed commitment to two-thirds target and for this to be a greater focus for co-ordinated campaigning in the 1984–85 pay round. Further discussion within the movement about role of a statutory National Minimum Wage. TUC publish *Low Pay – Objectives and Guidelines for 1984/85 Pay Round*.

1985   Labour Party Conference, NUPE led composite calling for consultation on implementation of minimum wage (as agreed in 1983) alongside strategies to end poverty pay based on strong union organisation, underpinned by legal rights, wins overwhelming support.

1986   TUC supports National Minimum Wage, by large majority although opposed by TGWU, and the Electrical, Electronic, Telecommunications and Plumbing Union (EETPU).

1987   Labour Party policy working group proposes formula for calculation of half male median earnings. Adopted by Labour Party NEC.

1990   Labour Party working group on legislative framework for National Minimum Wage set up on NUPE's initiative.

1992   General Election: Labour Party policy for national minimum wage of £3.40 an hour, based on formula for half male median earnings.

1993   UNISON formed.

1994   Commission on Social Justice advocates minimum wage at £3.50 an hour (based on 1993 data).

1995   Labour Party rejects approach based on formula, commits itself to setting up Low Pay Commission, if elected to Government.

1996   Key debate at UNISON Conference

  i   reaffirming union policy for minimum wage at half male median earnings (£4.26) uprated over time to two-thirds average earnings;
  ii   instructing the union to submit motion to TUC and instructing the delegation not to compromise on the union's demands;
  iii rejecting an amendment requiring other pay elements to be secondary to the central objective as 'vital in convincing our lowest paid, part time, women manual workers that their interests are also the interests of our better paid members'.

  High profile debate at TUC. Congress adopts £4.26 target from UNISON/National Union of Mineworkers (NUM) composite; £4 target, and TUC statement supporting half male median earnings figure, but noting this provides figures in a range £3.80–£4.26. Single status agreement in local government, providing £4 an hour minimum.

1997   Labour elected, sets up Low Pay Commission of nine under Professor George Bain. Rita Donaghy from UNISON NEC member of Commission. UNISON submits evidence. Negotiations in health on national framework for pay bargaining with underpinning low pay minimum. Local negotiations on £4/£4.42 minimum.

1998   Minimum Wage Bill. Low Pay Commission report.

12 UNISON and low pay policy

A comment on Morris

Carole Thornley

Peter Morris's chapter offers a fascinating insight into the long and arduous struggle to put low pay firmly in the public mind and on the legislative agenda, and highlights the pivotal role played by UNISON and former constituent unions in doing this. In some important respects, the chapter allows us both a brief respite in which to celebrate UNISON's achievements and provides some important pointers for the future direction of policy.

The context of low pay

It would be difficult to overstate the task facing UNISON at its formation. The issue of 'low pay' hits upon all the sensitivities so well laid bare in Phelps Brown's seminal work on pay inequalities. Where pay is so deeply interlinked with status, then the perceived legitimacy of the existing pay and status structure remains the first hurdle to be jumped by anyone interested in social reform (and the ideological and material obstruction to change by employers and owners of capital constitutes a second, and even greater, hurdle). Writing in 1977, Phelps Brown thought that there had been a general reduction in the 'fatalism' and 'deference' that had bolstered the existing social structure: this territory had been traversed (Phelps Brown, 1977: 8–9). However, the last two decades and the impact of 'Thatcherism' and 'Reaganism' have seen a vigorous renewal of blinkered economic tenets and a sustained ideological and material challenge to social equality.

At an ideological level, a misuse of the so-called 'marginal productivity' theory implied that workers are paid, or should be paid, what they are personally 'worth'. Thus low-paid workers could be characterised as 'feckless' and 'lazy', unwilling to invest in their own education and skills or to take on responsibility, 'greedy' beyond their own economic contribution, and 'ignorant' of the 'trickle-down' effects that would be produced by a 'free-market' economy in which risk-takers and entrepreneurs were rewarded. At a material level, this rhetorical onslaught was accompanied by a wide-ranging series of legislative and policy changes designed to weaken trade unions, move forward deregulation and decentralisation of the labour market, and increase rewards for 'entrepreneurs'.

The material outcomes were a reversal in factor share trends, and a massive increase in inequality and low pay. After decades of a proportionate rise in employment income and a decline in private corporate profit and rent, these trends reversed, giving rise to greater income inequality.[1] This redistribution was dramatic. Income inequalities reduced in the 1960s and 1970s. However, in the last two decades income inequalities increased to a level which is 'much more unequal than since before 1949 (and almost back to the 1938 level estimated by the Royal Commission on the Distribution of Income and Wealth)'. Internationally, 'the UK was exceptional in the pace and extent of the increase in inequality' (Joseph Rowntree Foundation, 1995a: 14–15). Over the period 1979–92 'the poorest 20–30 per cent of the population failed to benefit from economic growth, in contrast to the rest of the post-war period' (ibid.: 6).

These changes have also been reflected in trends in distribution of wealth, where as the poor have got poorer, the rich have been benefiting. The distribution of wealth remains even more unequal than the distribution of incomes, and the 'richest 10 per cent of wealth-holders had nearly 50 per cent of individual wealth in 1992' (ibid.: 29–31) , with the top 50 per cent actually increasing their share (Griffiths and Wall, 1997: 594). The Joseph Rowntree Foundation Inquiry into Income and Wealth points out that until the 1980s wealth inequalities narrowed rapidly, but have now levelled out (1995a: 29–31).

Changes in the distribution of earnings for those in work have also been dramatic and have been a major contributor and corollary to the above changes in income and wealth distribution.[2] The gap between the high-paid and low-paid widened rapidly from the late 1970s, with the male earnings distribution 'now wider than at any time in the century for which we have records' (Joseph Rowntree Foundation, 1995b: 42). The Low Pay Unit calculated that, on the Council of Europe decency threshold measure of low pay, the low paid increased from 7.8 million in 1979 (38 per cent of the workforce) to 10.4 million in 1996 (48 per cent of the workforce), 6.6 million of whom were women and 4.8 million part-time workers (Low Pay Unit, 1996: 8–10). Compared with median earning levels for their gender, 'men and women in low paid occupations had by 1996 lost, on average, around 20 percentage points since 1975' (Sachdev and Wilkinson, 1998: 19). The pace and extent of widening of the earnings distribution in the UK is again 'exceptional' by international standards (Joseph Rowntree Foundation, 1995a: 19–20). On a comparison of nine European countries, the UK had the fourth largest proportion of full-time workers earning less than 50 per cent of the median wage and the highest proportion of workers earning less than 80 per cent of the median wage (Griffiths and Wall, 1997: 599).

The results of these changes, and of associated changes in the tax and benefits system, have been unprecedented growth in poverty – both in-work (Low Pay Commission, 1998: 31) and out-of-work. While measures of poverty will always remain contentious, most give an unambiguous picture of the direction of change. The number of people receiving Income Support has increased from 3.0 million in 1978 to 5.8 million in 1995; 24 per cent of the total population were dependent on these benefits by 1995. The number of people living in households whose income is below 50 per cent of average UK income rose from 5 million in 1979 to

14.1 million in 1992/3; on this measure, poverty increased from 9 per cent of the population to 25 per cent in this period. Taking the Child Poverty Action Group's definition of the 'margins of poverty', some 33 per cent of the UK population were living in poverty by the late 1980s. Once again, there is little to reassure on international grounds, where 'the UK's relative poverty position in comparison with other EU countries continues to be problematic' (Griffiths and Wall, 1997: 596–600).

Contrary to a popular misconception, the largest single group amongst the poor is those *with* an income from employment (Low Pay Unit, 1995: 6–9) and the role of earnings is here evidently critical. The ideological and material stance of Thatcherism meant that the creation of a new tranche of low-paid workers and people in poverty could be ignored, or characterised as 'inevitable' and as making 'good economic sense' over the longer term because it reflected market realities and attracted inward investment.

What constitutes 'good economic sense' has, of course, been much disputed in recent years. Paradoxically, the growth in inequality may have obscured or exacerbated underlying problems in trends towards manufacturing decline. As Glyn notes, 'much of the apparent prosperity of the 1980s came from redistribution away from those made unemployed and from workers towards shareholders, rather than from increased production' (Glyn, 1992: 87). The Joseph Rowntree Foundation also notes that 'increasing inequality can damage the economy . . . the experience in Britain since the trend towards greater equality of incomes was reversed in the late 1970s has not been a faster rate of growth than in previous periods when the gap between rich and poor was smaller' (Joseph Rowntree Foundation, 1995a: 9). Moreover, many also doubt that the UK can – or should – compete internationally on the basis of a low-wage, low-productivity economy (Desai, 1989: 304; Nolan, 1989), because over most of this period inward investment flows did not compensate for outward investment (Coates, 1994: 164–7). However, the moral force of Thatcherism has been both pervasive and pernicious; with rhetoric reminiscent of the worst of the Victorian era, the low-paid and poor could be castigated as culpable for their own position, and 'ignorant of economic realities' if they protested.

A case for celebration

In this context, the creation of UNISON could hardly have been more timely, or more challenging. It is a huge credit to the union, and to the individuals who constitute it, that the importance of the urgent need to address low pay and poverty has been put at the heart of UNISON's policies from the outset, and vigorously pursued since – in part culminating in the historic achievement of a statutory National Minimum Wage.

One of the great strengths of the merger was that it created a union which not only had every reason to tackle low pay as a priority, but also had the potential power to do so. Workers across the public sector could for the first time be united in a single representative organisation. The numerical strength of membership lay with workers who in their own service would have a direct interest in confronting the issue of low pay.

Taking the NHS as an example, it is clear that low pay is a continuing fact of life for a large swathe of membership: more than half the administrative and clerical, and over two-thirds of ancillary workers fall below the Council of Europe decency threshold.[3] Moreover, despite repeated claims from ministers that nurses have benefited from their Review Body, recent evidence continues to show an underpaid and feminised workforce, the great majority of whom are still paid less than the national average and considerably less than male non-manual occupations (Thornley, 1996a). Many nurses have actually seen a deterioration in their relative pay positions, and low pay is a large and growing problem. One in three nurses is low paid on basic wages under Council of Europe definitions and the introduction of locally paid health care assistants in 1990 has created fresh problems of low pay (Thornley, 1997).

Across the public sector as a whole, as UNISON's highly-researched and excellent submission to the Low Pay Commission (UNISON, 1997: 2) points out, 43 per cent of UNISON's 1.3 million members earn less than £4.42 an hour (the then target minimum wage). Moreover, low pay (even at the conservative level of minimum wage debates) is concentrated among women, black workers, the young and disabled, with particular pertinence for part-time workers. This brings us clearly to a second major area for celebration, namely that, if low pay is at the heart of the new union, equality of treatment and opportunity is also fundamental.

Peter Morris's valuable contribution highlights one of the ways in which UNISON has succeeded in raising the level of sophistication of the 'low pay' debate, while at the same time addressing issues of equality. One of many great failings in orthodox labour market theorising is its wholly inadequate treatment of discrimination. Yet the evidence that low pay is deeply embedded in discriminatory labour market practice is overwhelming: as Rubery points out, 'when investigating the characteristics of low-paid workers, two features stand out above all others: the majority are women and most of these are part-timers' (Rubery, 1995: 547). A crucial part of our understanding of low pay is therefore concerned with exploring both the 'undervaluation of women's skills' – where, as Rodney Bickerstaffe has put it, 'skills like cleaning, cooking, sewing or caring, associated with women's work, have been consistently undervalued and accordingly badly paid' (Bickerstaffe, 1998: iv–v) – and employers' interests in perpetuating such misconceptions. We return to this point below.

UNISON has also led the way in challenging the Thatcherite consensus about the economic efficiency and social rationality of a low-pay economy. In its evidence to the Low Pay Commission UNISON argues that 'a minimum wage introduced with skill and care should not cost jobs and could create them. If it encourages efficiency, provides an incentive to training, reduces staff turnover, and improves the spending power of millions of households, it is likely to create jobs in the long term. It should be seen as a crucial part of a strategy to increase productivity for a high-skill, high-wage economy' (UNISON, 1997: 2). These are critical arguments, which were picked up in the First Report of the Low Pay Commission (1998: 119), along with UNISON's detailed comments on implementation.

A final point for celebration is that the union has always pursued a dual approach to the fight for better pay encompassing both legislative change (of which minimum wage legislation is one example) and direct organisation and collective bargaining. Peter Morris reminds us of this; it is this realistic and dynamic amalgamation of approaches that provides UNISON's real strength, and a key to understanding the potential scope for future policy and action.

Future prospects

The new National Minimum Wage came into force on 1 April 1999. The Low Pay Commission's final recommendation was for £3.60, rising to £3.70 in June 2000, with a Developmental Rate of £3.20 per hour for younger workers and those in training. The headline adult recommendation was accepted by the government, but an amendment was made for the case of 18–21-year-olds to just £3.00 (with £3.20 standing as an 'adult' development rate).

However, the key figure of £3.60 per hour (or around £7,000 per annum) has particular significance. While it represents an achievement for low-paid workers at the very bottom of the wage hierarchy (the Commission estimates that it will affect the bottom 9 per cent of employees), the particular level leaves a large amount of scope for further improvement. One of the fears about a minimum wage more generally is that it might provide an 'employers' maximum', which would 'justify' low pay levels rather than act as a 'minimum floor'. Clearly, £7,000 per annum is not a figure which will reassure workers or the general public that low pay has been eradicated, especially if some employers choose to pursue the 'maximum' principle. As the Commission itself notes, 'introducing a *minimum* for wages is not a pay policy, nor is it the "going rate" for pay . . . successful employers will continue to pay well above this floor' (Low Pay Commission, 1998: 5–7).

In this context, UNISON's dual-strand strategy becomes vitally important. At the level of minimum wage legislation, the union will no doubt be continuing its long-standing campaign for a higher level, with automatic indexation and uprating mechanisms. Here, UNISON can build on the Commission's own recommendations that continuing review and periodic uprating of the wage are necessary. There is also still a lot of work to be done to ensure the implementation and enforcement of a minimum wage, particularly as the Commission's recommendations have already been weakened. At the same time, UNISON will no doubt be building on the position noted by Peter Morris; advertising the 'mark up for being in a union', and for the collective bargaining benefits which unionisation confers. Here, UNISON can build on an outstanding reputation, both for national-level activity and negotiations, and for local bargaining expertise.

This has had, and continues to have, particular relevance for the public sector and the National Health Service in particular. The deliberations of the Low Pay

Commission have almost certainly understated the scale of low pay problems in the public sector; this is quite apart from their finding that the continuation of collective bargaining for most public sector employees has probably secured higher rates at the lowest point of the wage distribution (Low Pay Commission, 1998: 123) – an accolade for UNISON. Nor is it solely because of the very modest level of the national minimum wage itself, which focuses only on the most-exploited workers in the bottom decile of the wage hierarchy (had it been introduced nearer the figure recommended by UNISON, large numbers of public sector workers would have been covered). It is also a result of the growing inadequacy of wage statistics, with accurate data increasingly unavailable across large parts of the public sector.

The Commission itself has noted problems with wage estimates for the public sector. This problem is seen to be particularly severe in the NHS, even though this is where the 'largest impact' is likely to be: 'calculating this effect is extremely difficult, since the NHS Management Executive stopped collecting detailed pay data some years ago' (ibid.: 124–5). These problems were recently acknowledged by Frank Dobson, Health Secretary: 'the statistics in the Department of Health are appalling. . . . What would the impact of the national minimum wage be? No one could give me a figure. We've got to sort this out' (Dobson, 1998: 14–15).

The issue of the unavailability of crucial wage data is inextricably linked to movements towards a fragmentation of public sector pay systems. As elsewhere, the Conservative government pursued policies in the NHS designed to reduce trade unions' influence, re-establish 'managerial prerogative', and restrain pay. One vital strand of this policy was to adopt an increasingly vigorous pursuit of decentralised pay determination mechanisms (local pay). To the extent that local pay has taken root, it has complicated the collection of pay data and obscured what is really happening. Once again, the last two decades have been challenging but have equally left a legacy which leaves much to build on.

At both national and local levels, UNISON has joined with other trade unions and representative organisations in contesting this fragmentation, providing evidence on the links between local pay and low pay. As the largest union in the NHS, it led a remarkable combined opposition to 'local pay' and pay individual-isation, which (in the case of nurses) brought about a historic U-turn immediately before the General Election (Thornley, 1998). At the same time, it has been vigorous in its pursuit of favourable bargaining outcomes where local pay negotiations have taken place – or are continuing to do so. Finally, it has played a key role in collecting and collating data for use at national and local levels.

A good example of this activity has been the work conducted on the rise of a new, locally-paid, employment category – that of health care assistants (HCAs). National research carried out in 1996 and 1997 (Thornley, 1996b; Thornley, 1997; UNISON Health Group, 1997) provides conclusive evidence that official statistics severely underestimate both the numbers of HCAs employed, and the work actually performed. Detailed evidence on pay has been produced for the first time, and this demonstrates that pay rates are unambiguously very poor and undercut Whitley rates. Evidence has also been compiled to show that this is leading to a situation of deteriorating industrial relations and staff morale, with grave implications for recruitment and retention and for the efficiency and effectiveness of healthcare provision.

This work also enables UNISON to build on its role in combating the 'undervaluation of women's skills'. The research shows that contrary to Department of Health claims, HCAs are widely engaged in carrying out nursing tasks and duties to the extent of being used regularly to substitute for better-paid categories of staff in the wards and in the community. The official denial of the work which workers actually do – 'task invisibility' – provides an example of the double jeopardy faced by this feminised workforce: undervaluation of caring skills *per se*, and a refusal to acknowledge the caring and 'technical' work which is in fact conducted. The lack of public recognition for tasks actually performed, the training accumulated, and (importantly) the skills acquired through long years of on-the-job experience, mean that pay and career prospects are very poor.

This kind of work is used at national level to highlight concerns through the media, to provide evidence to the Review Body, and to build on broader low pay concerns. At the local level, it provides bargaining arguments with supporting evidence. More work is no doubt planned to highlight the endemic problem of low pay and exploitation in the NHS, and to campaign and bargain for improved pay outcomes and recognition for workers. The paradoxical legacy of the last two decades is this: as pay determination mechanisms have become fragmented, decentralised, and brought to a state of national confusion, public sector union negotiators have gained experience and adeptness in recruiting and representing public sector workers. The experiences of the last 20 years have been salutary ones, arousing strong feelings, not least about the extent to which attacks on the public sector wage bill also mean attacks on the quality and quantity of public services provided (Thornley, 1997).

UNISON is now the largest union in the country, and the effects of its efforts in combating low pay are felt beyond the public sector. It is a role which places the union in the privileged position of safeguarding the most vulnerable. In the present cold climate of an ongoing pay squeeze in the NHS and public sector, compounded by proposals for yet more changes to the pay determination system, the dual track approach of combining political lobbying and effective collective bargaining will be the key to future successes. When UNISON campaigns against low pay for public service workers, it raises low pay as a significant issue for *all* workers. When it militates for minimum wage legislation and the best possible level, it militates for all workers. When it strengthens collective bargaining processes and outcomes for public service workers, it sets an example for all sectors and workers. In arguing for a 'decent' wage, it argues too for a 'decent' society. This must surely be the real spirit of a new Millennium.

Notes

1   See figures in Atkinson (1983) where the difficulties of making these calculations and interpreting them are also discussed; for most recent figures, see Griffiths and Wall

(1997), where the recent rise in income from self-employment is argued to be an important factor in the increase of inequality.

2   As income from employment provides over 62 per cent of all income received.

3   Calculated from New Earnings Survey data 1995.

References

Atkinson, A. B. (1983) *The Economics of Inequality*, Oxford: Clarendon Press.

Atkinson, A. B. (1996) 'Income Distribution in Europe and the United States', *Oxford Review of Economic Policy*, 12: 1.

Bickerstaffe, R. (1998), 'Foreword', in Sachdev, S. and Wilkinson, F. (eds) *Low Pay, The Working of the Labour Market and the Role of a Minimum Wage*, London: The Institute of Employment Rights.

Coates, D. (1994) *The Question of UK Decline: The Economy, State and Society*, London: Harvester Wheatsheaf.

Desai, M. (1989) 'Is Thatcherism the cure for the British disease?' in Green, F. (ed.) *The Restructuring of the UK Economy*, London: Harvester Wheatsheaf.

Dobson, F. (1998) Interview in *Nursing Times*, 1(94): 26 (July).

Glyn, A. (1992) 'The "productivity miracle", profits and investment' in Michie, J. (ed.) *The Economic Legacy 1979–1992*, London: Academic Press.

Griffiths, A. and Wall, S. (1997) *Applied Economics*, London: Longman.

Joseph Rowntree Foundation (1995a) *Inquiry into Income and Wealth*, Volume 1, York: Joseph Rowntree Foundation.

Joseph Rowntree Foundation (1995b) *Inquiry into Income and Wealth*, Volume 2, York: Joseph Rowntree Foundation.

Low Pay Commission (1998) *The National Minimum Wage: First Report of the Low Pay Commission,* Cm 3976, London: HMSO.

Low Pay Unit (1995) *New Review of the Low Pay Unit*, 33: (May/June).

Low Pay Unit (1996), 'Coming apart at the seams', *New Review of the Low Pay Unit*, 42: (Nov/Dec).

Nolan, P. (1989), 'Walking on water? performance and industrial relations under Thatcher', *Industrial Relations Journal*, 20: 2.

Phelps Brown, H. (1977) *The Inequality of Pay*, Oxford: Oxford University Press.

Rubery, J. (1995) 'The low paid and the unorganized', in Edwards, P. (ed.) *Industrial Relations: Theory and Practice in Britain*, Oxford: Blackwell.

Sachdev, S. and Wilkinson, F. (1998) *Low Pay, the Working of the Labour Market and the Role of a Minimum Wage*, London: The Institute of Employment Rights.

Thornley, C. (1996a) *Dispelling the Myth: Nursing Pay Trends 1979–1996*, London: UNISON.

Thornley, C. (1996b) *Poor Prospects: The Realities of Local Pay Determination in the NHS*, London: UNISON.

Thornley, C. (1997) *The Invisible Workers: An Investigation into the Pay and Employment of Health Care Assistants in the NHS*, London: UNISON.

Thornley, C. (1998) 'Contesting local pay: the decentralisation of collective bargaining in the NHS', *British Journal of Industrial Relations*, 36: 3.

UNISON (1997) *Submission to the Low Pay Commission* (2 October), London: UNISON.

UNISON Health Group (1997) *Negotiating Pay and Conditions for Health Care Assistants*, London: UNISON.

13 UNISON's approach to lifelong learning

Anne Munro and Helen Rainbird

Besides being an act of knowing, education is also a political act.

(Paulo Freire)

Introduction

In *UNISON's Aims and Values* the role of the union's education service is defined as having the objective of 'encouraging members to take part in education and training, and giving representatives the opportunity to achieve the highest quality of education and training for their union duties and in their own lives'. The Department of Education and Training thus had a key role to play in the creation of the new union. In a context where the member is seen as being at the centre of the union's activities and concerns, the provision of activist training and staff training and development in particular, has been central to the objective of achieving proportionality and fair representation.

Whilst many trade unions provide training for activists and officers, as far as education, vocational and professional training are concerned they see their primary responsibility as representing members' interests on external bodies. UNISON is unusual in being a significant provider of learning opportunities to members as well as to activists and this extends not just to training which is directly work-related but to learning opportunities for personal development. This partly reflects historical developments within NALGO which started to provide vocational courses for members seeking promotion through the NALGO Correspondence Institute in 1920 and in NUPE which, since the late 1980s, introduced programmes of membership development aimed at its predominantly manual membership. The bringing together of COHSE, NUPE and NALGO through the merger process created a unique situation in which the union was able to offer a breadth of educational provision to members ranging from unskilled manual workers through to professionals in health care and local government. This was provided alongside more traditional forms of union 'role' education aimed at activists, which drew on the strengths of the different union traditions.

This concept of trade union education goes beyond definitions of lifelong learning which stress the individual's responsibility for developing skills, knowledge and understanding. It brings together learning for personal and professional development, on the one hand, with learning which contributes to democratic participation and representation in the union. It does this through a framework which is 'underpinned by a clear set of principles and objectives, flexible methods of access, a coherent approach to accreditation, a broad range of provision and is firmly grounded in partnership' (UNISON, undated: 2). This approach has given UNISON an authoritative voice on the subject of lifelong learning within the trade union movement and in the broader public policy arena on the basis of its own practice.

The formation of UNISON in 1993 brought together three unions with different cultures and traditions, which were reflected in the organisation of their education departments; in the resources and personnel which were allocated to them; and in the focus of provision in relation to activists, officers and members. The merger created new challenges for organisational development and renewal in which the education and training department was to play a significant role. It also created opportunities for the organisation to learn from the different experiences of its constituents and for the cross fertilisation of ideas from the different functions within the department. In addition, it brought together three approaches to public policy intervention in the broader field of education and training.[1] In this chapter, we analyse the consequences of the merger process for the organisation of the education and training function itself and for the specific groups of membership, activist and staff. We consider key developments in provision, in internal policy, in the development of partnerships with providers and employers, and in public policy interventions. An argument is developed that there are some unique aspects to UNISON's approach, particularly to membership education, which both contribute to members' development as employees and can encourage membership participation in trade union activities. Finally, we set an assessment of the achievements over this period against the challenges for the future identified by staff in the department.

The consequences of the merger for the education and training function

Three distinctive education departments from the partner unions made up the new department of education and training. The NALGO department was by far the largest: out of forty-four staff in the department the majority were engaged in providing vocational and professional education, ranging from BTEC qualifications to professional qualifications. This involved the commissioning of distance learning materials, administering the receipt of scripts for marking and sending them on to tutors. The majority of staff were involved on the administrative side of this work. In addition, there were three staff in activist training and a further two in staff development. Both COHSE and NUPE set up trade union education departments in the 1970s in common with many other unions. These departments provided national programmes of education and developed educational materials for use in regional programmes provided for branch activists. In contrast to NALGO, both the COHSE and NUPE departments were relatively small. COHSE had three staff who concentrated on activist education. NUPE had six staff and the major focus was on activist training and membership development for non-traditional learners. Its educational programme had developed out of the need to prepare shop stewards for negotiations with local authorities on bonus schemes in the early 1970s. Initially organised through regional structures, a national programme was in place at the end of the decade. In NUPE trade union education was seen as a political tool: it was not restricted to workplace issues and shop stewards had an educational function. In COHSE education played a central role in union campaigns in defense of the National Health Service and in the organisational development of the union, as well as providing activists with the knowledge and skills they needed to cope with the many changes in the NHS industrial relations during this period.

When UNISON was created in 1993, it had a combined Education and Training Department at head office with fifty-three staff, which had been reduced to forty after 5 years. The challenge presented by the merger was to successfully accommodate staff and heads of department from the three constituent unions and to reconcile the different traditions, while reflecting the principles enshrined in UNISON's aims and values which put the member at the centre of the union's activities and concerns. The three departments were organised into four units: education for activists and organisers; general membership education in the form of the Open College; staff training and development; and a policy and resources unit which contributes to policy-making process and cross-departmental initiatives.[2]

Membership education – UNISON Open College

UNISON inherited strengths in education and training, which went far beyond traditional trade union activist education. In particular, the continuing vocational training and lifelong learning needs of members in the new organisation required a reassessment of the range of educational opportunities available and certain vocational courses were identified as inappropriate to the overall profile of provision. For some courses, direct provision was replaced by access to externally provided courses at discounted fees, (for example, personnel management courses are now provided by the Manchester College of Art and Technology). Both vocational courses and membership development were situated within the four phase structure of the Open College. This meant that low paid members whose educational ambitions had previously been circumscribed by the kinds of jobs they did, now had access not only to programmes such as NUPE's 'Return to Learn' but also to progression routes into higher level qualifications.

Because of its centrality to the department as a whole, it is useful to outline the structure of the Open College. It was launched in 1994 and has become a key feature of UNISON education and training. It is based on providing every UNISON member with the opportunity to enter at any appropriate level, to have access to flexible learning, which recognises experiential learning, and enables accreditation at every level. The idea is to foster a passport approach to education and training, with recognition of learning as a lifetime activity. The Open College has not been designed as a linear educational programme in which students start at the beginning and work their way through, but rather a series of learning opportunities into which all members can dip at appropriate points in their personal development. It is divided into four phases with provision at phases 1–3 accredited through the National Open College Federation, which means credits can be accumulated that are recognised by for access purposes by colleges and employers. The courses at these levels were established specifically for UNISON members, with no fees being charged. Phase 1 is concerned with the development of basic learning skills, such as literacy and numeracy. Phase 2 introduces a number of courses for members who wish to return to education or to make a 'fresh start' into education. Within this section of the Open College, two particular programmes have risen in prominence, the Return to Learn (R2L) and Women, Work and Society programmes. Women, Work and Society is unique in being the sole women-only educational provision offered through the Open College, and it is aimed at members with relatively low levels of participation in the union. One aspect of Phase 3 is concerned with enabling individuals to create their own portfolios of evidence of prior learning with UNISON support. A range of other courses has been developed and UNISON has established its own Access course at this stage. At Phase 4, members and non-members can study professional vocational courses. Fees are charged for these courses, although UNISON members are entitled to a lower fee. Also because of the job-related benefits of the professional courses, it is expected that most employers will accept responsibility for financing these courses.

In the different parts of the Open College, UNISON works with a number of different providers, and is continually developing links. UNISON has a national agreement with the Workers' Educational Association (WEA), the main provider for the R2L programme, and partnerships have been established with other educational institutions. The Open College allows the union to deliver courses leading to vocational qualifications in a range of occupational areas, such as community care, housing and social administration. Examples of these include the BTEC Higher National Diploma in Housing Studies, the Diploma in Consumer Affairs and courses in Post-Registration Education and Practice (PREP) for nurses. Nurses are now required by the United Kingdom Central Council to undertake 5 days of professional updating within any 3-year registration period. UNISON is able to offer professional support equivalent to that offered by the Royal College of Nursing in the form of twenty distance learning modules which meet the UK Central Council for Nursing, Midwifery and Health Visiting (UKCC) requirements.

UNISON has developed links with some educational institutions, in particular Sheffield Hallam University and Northern College to develop open learning routes into university degrees. With Sheffield Hallam this has been in the context of their Health Care Practice courses. The programme is designed to allow students to achieve credits through the accreditation of informal learning on-the-job alongside courses which can lead to the achievement of a diploma or a degree.

UNISON education and training department is recognised as an associate college of Sheffield Hallam University.

Whilst some courses are provided directly others are outsourced, with UNISON acting as an 'enabling authority' and dealing annually with the contracts with each institution. Increasingly, strategic partnerships are being developed with universities for the provision of degree level courses for example at Ulster, Southampton and the Open University. In this way a wide range of opportunities are opened up for working class members who may enter the Open College initially through R2L, women's education, or trade union studies. Central to these developments are also partnerships with employers, who may pay fees and/or provide paid time off for study. R2L can be customised with a vocational component but these Phase 2 courses can equally lead on to higher level vocational courses, for example, those leading to nursing qualifications, which can allow working class members to move into professional roles as well as undergraduate level courses.

The R2L programme has increasingly become regarded as the 'jewel in the crown' of the Open College, as it has developed it has been seen as epitomising the UNISON philosophy to education and training generally, therefore it is useful to consider its history in a little more depth. The R2L programme was initiated by NUPE in association with the WEA in the West Midlands in 1989, and delivered by WEA tutors. It was aimed at members who had been disadvantaged in the formal educational system and was designed around a combination of distance learning and small study groups. After the formation of UNISON, the geographical scope of the programme was extended and by 1998, 6,000 students had completed the R2L course. The programme was regarded as a significant success, not only was it reaching members who usually had little access to educational opportunities, the low-paid, part-time, low-skilled, manual workers, but it was having a dramatic impact on the people who took part in the programme. The achievements of the students who have studied under the programme have been documented in Helen Kennedy's report *Return to Learn: UNISON's Fresh Approach to Trade Union Education* (1995). This survey of former students found that many reported becoming more confident, frequently continuing in education or developing in their job. Twenty-three per cent reported that they had become involved or more involved in the union, of these 25 per cent had taken positions within the branch and 9 per cent had taken positions beyond the branch (Kennedy, 1995: 23). For many taking part in R2L is a life-changing experience. In this context, the Open College facilitates access to learning for non-traditional learners, and has been instrumental in developing partnerships with both providers and employers. The recent and significant development of partnership arrangements with employers are discussed later.

Activist training

When thinking about education within a trade union, it is perhaps activist training which first comes to mind. For historic and cultural reasons, activists' education did not have the same high profile in each of the partner unions. Despite the progress that has been made since the merger and the high value that is placed on it, there is a perception that activists' education has had a lower profile than some other services in the union. The Activists' Unit provides a range of national residential courses for all activists including a growing number of courses designed to develop the skills and confidence of national committee members, strengthening the union's democracy at national level. The unit is also a key contributor to the development of UNISON*direct*, a new 'call system' for members, and the design of the UNISON intranet which provides on-line training and education around the introduction of the new membership system. The Unit provides published course books and tutor's notes for the training of the thousands of activists attending regional and branch-based courses every year.

Since the merger, many of the Regional Education Officers (REOs) have had to face change to the nature of their jobs. The formation of UNISON resulted in an examination of the balance between various aspects of education and training at head office, but also some redefinition of the work of the REOs, many of whom come from a NALGO background. In relation to activist training, these REOs saw their role as supporting general courses for branch activists, shop stewards courses, health and safety courses, branch officers courses etc. There has been a shift of emphasis towards service group and workplace issues. At a national level this has meant developing relationships with personnel in the different service groups and developing training materials specifically for the for activists in the service areas. The aim is to give a personal contact for each group, which has been established for local government, the health service, gas and electricity. UNISON also has four self-organised groups representing women, black, disabled and gay and lesbian members. They all have their own structures and their education requirements are built into national and regional activist programmes. In order to ensure that their training needs in relation to representation and collective bargaining are effectively met, the aim is to provide the self-organised groups with a contact in the activist training unit.

The role of the REOs has changed in other ways since the creation of UNISON: decentralised collective bargaining has increased their workload, whilst the objective of achieving proportional representation has also generated work for them. As a consequence, there is a developing need to involve regional officers more in the training and development of their branch activists, with regional education officers coordinating and leading this effort by organising programmes and tutors, limiting the time they spend in delivering training themselves to concentrate on new and innovative projects. An example of the latter is the REOs' assistance to shop stewards in drawing up of Branch Development Plans which include an education plan. This process is contributing to the organisational development of the union by enabling branches to take on more tasks themselves. It is also resulting in increased demand for training courses. In some ways the activist section has been a victim of its own success, having raised its profile with membership, this has generated an increased demand for training which it is difficult to meet. One response has been to develop a system of courses whereby different levels of training are delivered at the relevant level of the union. For example, there is a high demand for courses on the law. Basic courses can be delivered at branch level; intermediate courses at regional level; advanced courses at national level. This development requires large numbers of tutors and increasingly lay tutors are being trained for this role. This training can be accredited, through the national Open College Network (OCN) and CATS schemes.

Some staff training is provided through the activist unit, whilst staff development is mainly provided through the staff unit. Full-time officers often need similar training to activists on industrial relations issues and negotiating skills. When a request is received for courses in areas of identified weakness, the activist section organises staff training seminars. For example, seminars have been run for regional officers on the development of employer partnerships. This area of work has been very successful in meeting certain training needs but also providing an important arena for communication between staff from different service groups, and between those who are nationally and regionally based.

Two key areas have been identified as central to the future development of the activist section. Firstly, there are a number of initiatives linked to the women's development project. A mixture of programmes is being designed, including some women only courses tackling assertiveness and skills training. Alongside these, programmes are being established which address issues of specific relevance to women, such as maternity rights, which are open to men and women. A second area of growth relates to the Innovators of Technology projects and the design of CD-ROMs in areas such as health and safety and the global economy.

Staff and management training and development

The staff training and development section is responsible for the training and management development activities. Prior to the merger, staff development in NALGO was located within the education department, but in NUPE and COHSE there was a split between general staff/management development which was a personnel department responsibility and the training of officers and activists which was the responsibility of the education departments. UNISON retained both sets of activities in the Education and Training Department, largely following the NALGO model. Nevertheless, there is close liaison with the union's organisational development and personnel functions and work is often organised through project teams and steering groups incorporating these interests. There is also a staff training and development planning group, comprising representatives of the three departments and the Assistant General Secretaries (AGSs) to whom each of these report.

Whilst the work of the activist unit and membership development within the Open College have contributed to the objectives of proportional and fair representation amongst the membership, the staff and management training and development section is responsible for achieving this with respect to UNISON's own staff. This role has been defined in two ways: the first is through encouraging women employees particularly in secretarial and administrative grades to gain work experience outside their current core jobs through the 'Spring-Board' project. The second has been to encourage more women to become officers and to progress into more senior positions. As only forty of the current 180 regional officers are women, a trainee regional officer scheme has been set up. This required examining their traditional career paths, which usually originate in experience as lay negotiators. Although the National Executive Committee has targets for achieving proportionality in this area, there is no clear mechanism for achieving this. This is partly because there are relatively few openings for new regional officers, but it is also due to the fact that positive discrimination is illegal and the decisions of appointment panels must be seen to be fair. The report *Women, Work and UNISON* (UNISON, 1998) presents a range of recommendations in relation to improving opportunities for women staff in all areas of UNISON.

Finally, this internal training and development function has a substantial budget of its own and a network of thirteen regional staff development co-ordinators. It is engaged in a number of initiatives, for example, the Management Charter Initiative, and is making a commitment to Investors in People on a region by region basis. As part of the latter a UNISON-wide programme of development reviewing was initiated, to ensure that all staff will have had a development review with their manager by the end of April 1998.

There are questions about the extent to which unions can or should utilise managerialism to the achievement of a participative and democratic form of unionism. Dempsey, in this volume, describes how UNISON made use of external management development programmes during the merger as a part of a move toward the adoption of a wide range of managerial techniques. He describes the traditional discomfort which unions have had with this approach. The shift of the staff training and development function from Education and Training to Organisation and Development could be interpreted as a consolidation of these developments.

Achievements since the creation of UNISON

There are six main areas of achievement since the merger: those relating to activist education; to staff training and development; the creation of an innovative approach to membership development through the framework of UNISON Open College; the development of partnerships with employers on the provision of learning and development opportunities for employees; and particularly since the election of the Labour government in May 1997, the union's inputs into public policy on education and training. In addition, the department has developed international links which have supported the organisational development of trade unions in Russia, the Palestinian Authority and South Africa.

As far as activist training is concerned, the main achievements have been in creating a partnership between the activist education structures at national and regional level and in devolving responsibility for the identification of activists' training needs to the branch level, through the branch development plan. This has resulted in a greater emphasis on the use of lay tutors in the provision of activist training, which has been accompanied by the development of the lay tutor training scheme and mechanisms for accrediting prior learning. In addition, there have been some notable successes in the development of multi-media learning methods, in particular, the use of video, CD-ROMs and on-line services.

The union's own staff and management training and development function has made important steps in introducing development reviewing for all staff as a means of identifying future learning needs, alongside the introduction of initiatives to encourage women to progress into more senior positions within the union.

UNISON Open College has been significant in establishing a range of learning opportunities for members building on the experiences of NUPE's approach to membership development and NALGO's provision of vocational and professional education as a service to members. This is not just a framework for providing a series of courses, but rather a process for recognising informal learning, for accrediting episodic learning and for providing progression into access courses and into vocational courses. This process is particularly significant for unskilled manual workers who are non-traditional learners and generally have low levels of participation in work-related training and in adult education. We have already discussed how participants in the Return to Learn programme described it as transforming their lives, in giving them confidence in their own abilities and encouraging participation in education, in the workplace and in the union. New developments are now being established, linking the generic aspects of R2L into occupational progression routes for care workers, nursery nurses, learning and healthcare assistants. From 1999 there is now a progression route through a part-time diploma in social work. In this way, unskilled manual workers will be able to significantly enhance their salaries by achieving a professional qualification. In other words, the union is contributing to the establishment of an occupational progression route within employment which has political implications for the way in which workplace interventions are approached. As indicated above the Return to Learn programme constitutes a potential vehicle for recruitment as well as contributing to members' propensity to be active in the union. This suggests that membership education, while being an individual service, has implications for collective organisation. Williams (1997) has argued that individualism and collectivism should not be regarded as dichotomous and Smith (1995) has indicated that addressing individual interests may not necessarily inhibit collectivism. The significance of the R2L is that it illustrates a situation where individual services can serve to reinforce collectivity. In this way the programme highlights the contribution of membership education to the development of participative trade unionism.

Another significant achievement has been in establishing partnerships with employers for the provision of learning and development opportunities, initially on a pragmatic basis. In 1995, a communications course was provided for a north London authority on a partnership basis, at Phase 1 of the Open College, delivered by Workbase. Following this, a number of partnership arrangements were set up to provide the R2L course, starting in health trusts and universities, followed by local authorities (see Munro *et al.*, 1997). Under these arrangements the student has the equivalent of 10 days paid release from work and the employer pays a per capita fee for tuition. UNISON's role has been in facilitating contacts between the employer and the WEA as the education provider, and in subsidising development and training costs and course materials. Partnership courses are not limited to UNISON members and are increasingly being seen as contributing to changing the public face of trade unions. The union is defining a new terrain of activity, outside the normal structures of industrial relations which is characterised by a joint problem-solving approach. Rather than education and training being an additional demand on the bargaining agenda, this is seen as being part of a 'new learning agenda' in which the union provides solutions rather than simply makes demands. There are now more than one hundred partnership arrangements with employers in the public sector and with a number of subcontractors working for the public sector. Amongst employers a more positive approach to the union has been observed and this is beginning to have an impact on employment issues. For example, UNISON agreed to provide R2L to two housing associations where the union had been derecognised, on condition of re-recognition. In addition, the piloting of 'best value' contracts in local government may create a situation in which more reputable contractors will want to be seen as part of the local government establishment through observing 'good employment practices'. In this respect, membership education and partnership arrangements can be seen as defining a new terrain of union–employer relations which affects the way employers relate to UNISON and may eventually contribute to defining the basis for training agreements and committees at establishment level. It has been suggested that the partnership approach can serve to inhibit workplace union organisation (Kelly, 1996). However, the UNISON–employer partnerships on workplace education are distinct from the general purpose workplace partnership agreements in which unions make significant compromises with employers. As indicated above, where employers are keen to develop a partnership with the union in the provision of educational opportunities, R2L may be used as a lever to extend recognition and provide a route for extending union involvement.

In addition, UNISON has made a significant contribution to public policy on lifelong learning, particularly since the election of the Labour Government in 1997, which has undoubtedly reflected its achievements in education and training. UNISON's influence has been evident in a number of spheres: the Director of Education and Training chaired the task group on workplace learning which reported to the National Advisory Group for Continuing Education and Lifelong Learning and has been on the steering group for the Health Department for the Scottish Office. UNISON has been involved in several University for Industry projects, is represented on the executive of the National Institute for Adult and Continuing Education and on national training organisations. Its influence on the boards and governing bodies of educational institutions has been consolidated. It has contributed responses to the Dearing and Kennedy reports.

The final area of achievement has been in the growth of international links and support for the development of union organisational capacity. With financial support from the Department for International Development, UNISON has been involved in working with the Palestinian General Federation of Trade Unions in developing lay tutor training programmes. It has offered similar types of support to the Russian Public Services International and the health union in South Africa.

Conclusion: challenges for education and training in UNISON

Since 1998 UNISON has been implementing fundamental changes in the organisation and delivery of education and training, based on the findings of a functional review of a range of options in relation to their location in the organisational structure of UNISON. A central intention has been to develop synergies, for example, between activist staff and management training and development, and between activist education and the work of the UNISON Open College.

The organisation needs to address a number of major issues. The first of these concerns the distinctive role of the union as a provider of educational and training opportunities and the extent to which learning opportunities can constitute a tool of union organisation. There is clearly a debate about the extent to which a union, which is not primarily an education provider should be engaged in the direct provision of learning opportunities outside those provided for activists and the extent to which it should be merely a facilitator or an enabler, brokering contracts with other providers. Within this, there are questions concerning the extent to which this service is provided solely for members, or is also available to non-members (though at a higher fee) in the 'open' NALGO tradition. In fact, UNISON discontinued the direct provision of personnel management courses, following an analysis of its take-up by members and non-members, when the latter were found to be the primary users of them. This raises more interesting questions about the political and strategic role of unions in relation to education in general and towards lifelong learning in particular. It raises questions about the distinctiveness of having a collective framework within which provision is negotiated and its linkages into the world of work, work-based provision and occupational progression routes.

Second, there are questions concerning the way in which the provision of learning opportunities can be seen as a tool for organisational renewal. There is evidence that all three types of provision: activist education; staff and management training and development; and membership development can contribute in their own ways to building the union as an effective organisation, contributing to democratic participation and representation. The question is how can this strategic resource contribute to the on-going development of the union? There is already evidence that programmes such as Return to Learn and Women, Work and Society can contribute to organisational renewal through serving as a recruitment tool and through giving members the confidence to become more active in the union. These programmes have been of particular significance to manual workers who formed the traditional constituency of NUPE. The fact that provision for members at Phases 1 to 3 of the Open College structure has been free is an indication of the political significance attributed to provision for this section of the membership, particularly those who have been most adversely affected by the development of subcontracting relationships in the public sector. The more recent addition of occupational progression routes into nursing and social work from the generic Return to Learn programme can also been as part of a strategy with implications for equality of opportunity involving the allocation of resources for learning to the most disadvantaged groups of the membership. At the same time strategies towards lifelong learning are also significant to the more highly qualified and professional workers who constituted the NALGO membership and will be increasingly important to new generations of public-sector workers whose experience of education will differ from that of older generations. The union's approach to lifelong learning is not just a tool for the recruitment and retention of members but also a means of promoting activism.

A third major area that provides challenges for the future is the development of partnerships with employers on education and development. This raises questions in particular about how the union should approach a new arena for intervention in the workplace, in terms of the process of developing partnerships, the content of what is agreed, the opportunities they provide for creating a framework for enhancing members' terms and conditions of employment and for addressing workplace inequality. What are the linkages between the establishment of a joint problem-solving approach in one arena and other areas of negotiation, which may be more conflictual in nature? The development of partnerships with employers requires a consideration of the ways in which members, activists and officers can themselves take up issues relating to work-based learning and this, in turn, has consequences for the ways in which they can become a part of their own learning agenda.[3]

UNISON has succeeded in establishing a distinctive approach to lifelong learning, as a tool for building union organisation, as a service to members, as a subject on which partnerships with employers can be established and in its policy interventions. The extent to which education can be developed as a strategic resource and its interaction with the traditional bargaining agenda raise important questions which are of significance not just to UNISON but to the trade union movement as a whole.

Acknowledgements

We would like to thank the members of the UNISON Education and Training Department who have given their time for interviews and have commented on this chapter, in particular, Tony Chandler, Ted Dixon, Adrian Pulham, Jim Sutherland and Steve Williams. Any errors and omissions are our own responsibility. We are also grateful to Mike Terry for comments on an earlier version of this chapter.

Notes

1   This chapter draws on a series of interviews conducted with the staff of the Department of Education and Training in the spring of 1998 and an earlier research project which was conducted for UNISON in 1997 on four of the earliest partnerships with employers on the Return to Learn programme. The latter involved open-ended interviews with the relevant regional officer, branch representatives, senior managers, training managers, Workers' Educational Association tutors and course participants. It was published as Munro, Rainbird and Holly, *Partners in Workplace Learning. A Report on the Union/Employer Learning and Development Programme* (1997).

2   Since the retirement of Jim Sutherland, UNISON's Director of Education and Training, at the end of May 1998, the Department has been split. UNISON Open College, which includes Membership Development is now part of Membership Services. Union education, called Learning and Organising Services, has become part of the Regional Branch Development Group. Staff Training and Development is now part of Organisation and Staff Development.

3   The National Executive Council put a motion to the National Delegate Conference in June 1999, urging branches and branch education organisers to promote lifelong learning; to develop partnerships with employers around workplace and community learning; to establish lifelong learning advisers; to develop a team approach to education in the branch; and to build lifelong learning objectives into the Branch Development Plan.

References

Kelly, J. (1996) 'Union Militancy and Social Partnership', in P. Ackers *et al.* (eds) *The New Workplace and Trade Unionism*, London: Routledge.

Kennedy, H. (1995) *Return to Learn. UNISON's Fresh Approach to Trade Union Education*, London: UNISON.

Munro, A., Rainbird, H. and Holly, L. (1997) *Partners in Workplace Learning. A Report on the UNISON/Employer Learning and Development Programme*, London: UNISON.

Smith, P. (1995) 'Change in British trade unions since 1945', *Work, Employment and Society*, Notes and Issues: Debate, 9(1): 137–46.

UNISON (1998) *Women, Work and UNISON. First Report of the Women's Development Project*, London: UNISON.

UNISON (undated) *Employee Development in a Global Community*, London: UNISON.

Williams, S. (1997) 'The nature of some recent trade union modernisation policies in the UK', *British Journal of Industrial Relations*, 35(4): 495–514.

14 UNISON's approach to lifelong learning

A comment on Munro and Rainbird

Jim Sutherland

In my brief contribution I should like to focus, first, on the general philosophy and objectives underlying our approach; second, to briefly touch on the benefits of this approach to individual members and the organization; third, to explore some of the challenges for this approach and finally to say something about the future direction and structure of the Union's education service.

The philosophy

The Education and Training Department is not an educational institution chasing students for its own sake but a trade union education service geared to organisational as well as individual needs. The UNISON Open College – not a separate institution but a component of the Department – was created to bring together, in particular, the NUPE provision for non-traditional learners exemplified by the Return to Learn programme and the distance learning driven vocational provision offered by NALGO. The nature of our provision is determined by three particular considerations: the membership, the quality of public services and the wider issue of citizenship.

The membership

At one end of the membership spectrum is a significant cross-section of that part of the population who have suffered greatest disadvantage from the inadequacies of the compulsory education system. Most are women, the majority of whom work part-time. Many come from minority ethnic communities and significant numbers are employed in low-paid and low-status manual occupations. The very people who need access to high quality learning if the UK is to have an economy based on high value-added production and services. At the other end of the spectrum are many managers, technicians and others who are in the front line of economic and structural change and who require support in developing their capacity to respond to change.

Public services

Trade unions have traditionally been largely concerned with the interests of 'producers', their members, and only tangentially with the interests of consumers. Increasingly, particularly in the public services, it has been recognised that if the public do not value the services they receive, they will not value those who provide them. Conversely, however, employers cannot expect low status workers to concern themselves with quality unless they are provided with the necessary 'tools' and incentives. Learning opportunities are the tools and the incentives will come from the security and improvement in pay and working conditions deriving from public support for public services.

Citizenship

If trade unions are to be in the forefront of creating a thriving democracy with cultural wealth and economic health they have to contribute to enabling the whole population to become continuously engaged in learning. This involves not simply developing the skills and competence for task-specific, job-related purposes of a short or medium term nature, but developing learning which provides real choices in employment and lifestyle. In developing its approach to learning at, for or through the workplace UNISON has avoided placing all its emphasis on seeking greater access to learning opportunities from employers through the traditional collective bargaining process. Instead, we have adopted an approach that offers solutions rather than makes demands. A methodology that transcends the vagaries of day-to-day collective bargaining and allows learning development to by-pass the legitimate, if short-term, industrial relations conflicts between employers and unions. A trade union cannot, of course, substitute itself for government or employers in terms of the volume of provision required. Nevertheless, it can innovate, pump-prime, plug gaps and demonstrate what can be done.

Some objectives

Our provision is driven by the fundamental trade union objectives of recruitment, retention and service to members. Besides those objectives, however, there are some that are specific to the education service. First is the need to maintain the momentum of our influence on the wider lifelong learning agenda. This influence has been established through our success in offering new approaches to learning opportunities for non-traditional learners in particular. It led to my being asked to chair the Workplace Learning Task Group of the Secretary of State's National Advisory Group on Continuing Education & Lifelong Learning. The union has also won a number of European and UK awards for its provision. We want to continue to develop that influence and ensure, for example, that the government adopts the recommendations of the Task Group Report. We also believe that the four-phase Open College model is one that could be adopted by the University for Industry (UFI).

UNISON will seek to continue its engagement in wider projects. For example, we are currently involved in a number of UFI-based projects, running a Leonardo project on taking our four-phase model into Europe, working with the Open University on widening access and improving accreditation, continuing to develop our wide range of partnerships with employers and learning providers, and seeking to ensure innovative developments through the new Trade Union Learning Development Fund. A major objective is to continue to develop the concept of 'social partnership' through new bargaining approaches to learning. Our approach has not been simply to make demands on employers through traditional collective bargaining structures but to develop the capacity to offer employers solutions to their employee development needs. This does not take learning outside bargaining *per se* as much negotiation takes place on the curriculum offer, resources and access. However, it does ensure that discussions and negotiations on learning are not tied to either day to day industrial relations problems or annual wage rounds and it has successfully avoided 'trade-offs' between wage increases and learning opportunities. For example, more than one hundred employers are in partnership with us on 'Return to Learn' where members – not activists – get the equivalent of 10 days' paid release and the payment of the £150 tutorial fee paid by the employer. Trade unions frequently cannot get that sort of treatment for their shop stewards.

Some benefits

The benefits accruing from UNISON's approach can usefully be outlined in two categories. Firstly, benefits to the organisation. It is becoming apparent that the Return to Learn (R2L) project is producing a new kind of activist. Some 25 per cent of those who participate in R2L become active. At present around 2,000 members are involved in R2L each year and 80 per cent are women. This means that around 400 new women become active in a variety of ways each year. They bring with them into their activism a commitment to and loyalty towards the union because it gave them 'something for themselves'. This contrasts quite markedly with those activists who appear to believe that activism is synonymous with criticising the organisation and its leadership. These new activists also bring with them newly developed learning skills which enable them to respond effectively to their new responsibilities and the various technical and communication issues that confronted them.

The benefits to individual members have been well documented in the research reports to which Anne Munro and Helen Rainbird refer. In brief, these are the acquisition of confidence, marketable skills and the capacity to make real choices on employment opportunities and life style.

Some challenges

The challenges to the union in the field of education and training are manifold. So far as the education service is concerned some of the key challenges can be identified under the headings of internal and external challenges. The immediate internal challenges are: first, to ensure synergy across activist, member and staff provision without losing the capacity to respond to the specific needs of each constituency; second, to develop our approach to membership learning generally, and to vocationally orientated provision specifically, on the R2L model. That is to operate as a strategic centre based on a consultancy/interventionist, brokering model, assisting branches and regions in establishing partnerships with learning providers and employers and so avoid the administrative costs of 'delivering' distance learning directly to members.

Some of the external challenges have been outlined in the section on objectives, above, but others need attention. For example, we need to challenge the distinction that often exists between so called vocational training, non-vocational learning and employee development. I have yet to encounter high-quality, so-called non-vocational learning that has no application within the workplace. We also have to ensure that the emphasis on 'competitiveness' does not narrow provision down to task-specific learning only and that new methods of funding learning do not lead to those who have always benefited from learning opportunities capturing the new opportunities.

A further challenge is to develop arrangements with other trade unions in the public sector which open up our model to all employees. In order to safeguard the investment UNISON has made in developing its model, other unions might be encouraged to make their contribution through the development of additional programmes within the framework of the four phase model

Future structural developments

UNISON is undergoing a strategic and functional review with the objective of shifting the emphasis of the centre from an operational to a strategic role (see Dempsey's chapter in this volume). The education service has a major role to play in any future organisational changes. Members, activists and staff have to be involved in, and convinced of the necessity for, changes to be made. They have to be enabled to develop the skills for involvement in ongoing change processes and to respond to those changes in a positive way as policy makers, employees and recipients of services In considering longer-term and more wide-ranging change, consideration has to be given to the nature of the organisation. While the methodology for the functional review exercise and many other practices can be borrowed from more conventional employing organisations in the public and private sectors, careful consideration has to be given to the voluntary nature of a trade union. For example, while employed staff are the single focus of human resource functions in commercial and industrial organisations, within a trade union 'human resources' include activists and members as well as staff.

It is suggested that consideration be given, in the longer term, to the creation of a function which might be named 'Organisation and Human Resource Development'. Such a function would provide the opportunity for achieving desired organisational development over time by bringing together those functions and activities which can influence the perceptions, attitudes and actions of staff, activists and members at every level within the union. In essence, this would mean – in time – bringing together education and training, organisation development and the present responsibilities of the personnel function and the administrative function for staff at national and regional levels.

As the first stage in this process it could be suggested that a merger take place between education and training and organisation development to create a department of education and development. It is self evident that there is a potential synergy in the work of the education and training department and the directorate of organisation development. For example, the continuing improvement in the efficiency, effectiveness and responsiveness of the union can only be successfully achieved if the support of members, activists and staff is won. The education and training department is in the unique position of having the capacity and opportunity for reaching those groups and individuals, developing their capacities, knowledge and skills, influencing their perceptions, activities and performance.

The structure of such a department would have to be carefully considered in order to ensure that currently successful achievement in each of the present directorates was continued and new opportunities developed. The successes of R2L in developing individual commitment to, and support for, the union demonstrates what might be achieved with an integrated, holistic approach to the union's 'human resources'.

15 Between elation and despair

UNISON and the new social policy agenda

Mick Carpenter

Introduction

One of the driving forces behind the creation of UNISON at the end of the 1980s was to create a union that in two ways could make a substantial difference to the social policy climate in Britain. First, by combining forces and expertise that were previously distributed among the three unions, and second, by making the renewal of the public services a central priority of the new union they wished to create. It had been increasingly recognised by the partner unions during the 1980s, that while the 'bloody-minded' image of public service unionism was a long way from the reality, there was a need to campaign in ways that cemented alliances between users and providers in the public services. This did not necessarily mean wholly abandoning 'traditional' trade union methods of industrial action. In fact the commencement of the tripartite discussions between COHSE, NALGO and NUPE coincided with a major strike of ambulance personnel which won widespread public support. Nevertheless, there was a perception that the way that 'bread and butter' campaigns had been fought in the past, notably during the so-called 'Winter of Discontent' 1978–9, had been capitalised upon by the Conservatives to undermine support for the trade union and labour movement. The impact of the Conservative radical third term upon public service unions should not be underestimated. Having imposed draconian legal restrictions on trade unions, the Conservatives had embarked upon a wholesale privatisation of public utilities, were targeting local government through the 'poll tax' and seeking to transform the heartland of the welfare state through the 1990 NHS and Community Care Act. These were the kinds of experiences that led the three unions to put aside old animosities to see if they could forge something that could start to reverse the tide.

This chapter therefore reviews the effects of UNISON's efforts on the social policy front since 1993, compared to those of its forerunners. This is such a short period that it will only be possible to provide a provisional assessment, with the aim of helping members, activists and officials to get to grip with the wide range of complex issues involved. What I do is to try to set these efforts within an analytical framework which focuses on the relationship of public service unions to the welfare state, before turning to analyse the challenges that New Labour presents for the union movement as far as social policy issues are concerned, and the ways that UNISON is seeking to deal with them.

Unions and social policy: before the welfare state

In developing this analysis, much of the academic literature of social policy and industrial relations is of little help. Industrial relations has finally caught up with the fact that public services are a major site of employment, but rarely gets to grips with policy issues, except as they impinge on employment relations. Social policy on the whole still focuses on legislative reform and questions of entitlement, and largely ignores the fact that the welfare state is a major site of employment within contemporary capitalism. Although some researchers are developing bridges between the two forms of analysis, this is still in its early days.

The place to start then is by some examination, however rudimentary, of the role of trade union and workers' movements in creating the modern welfare state. This is required because we need to be wary of constructing a simplistic myth that the trade union movement through its link with the Labour Party 'delivered' the welfare state as a result of sustained pressure mounted from the turn of the twentieth century. While this was *finally* the case in 1945–51, much of the impetus for reform and its administrative shape was the work of social liberalism, through the Liberal Government 1906–14, and subsequently influential figures such as Beveridge and Keynes. Though the Labour Party was on the whole 'statist' in orientation, this was not necessarily wholeheartedly the case with the union movement. This was because historically working people in Britain had every reason to be suspicious of the state as it had often acted in repressive ways through legal restraints on trade unions, restrictions on public meetings, breaking up of demonstrations (most notoriously, the 1819 Peterloo massacre) and limits on the freedom of the press. The early trade union movement therefore fought hard to establish the right to bargain freely and wage strikes independently of state interference, out of which the British tradition of 'voluntarism' emerged. Another defining experience of the state was the 1834 Poor Law, which associated the state in people's minds with the hated workhouse (Henriques, 1979; Davis, 1993).

This situation changed because of pressures from both above and below. As long as British capitalism was the leading force in the world, and could count on social peace from below, there was not much incentive for its ruling classes to change course from a broadly *laissez-faire* political economy. The fading of the Chartist challenge and the unparalleled capitalist expansion of the 20 years from 1850 when Britain became 'the workshop of the world', also opened up divisions among working class people by creating a male 'labour aristocracy' who gained most from rising prosperity through well-paid, secure jobs, and who became anxious to protect this by job controls against what Marx called the 'reserve army of labour' (Alford, 1996). Although living standards generally rose, through rising incomes and cheap food imports, those outside the élite groups, in agriculture and the less mechanized sectors of industry and the service sector, at most only saw modest improvements in their condition (Benson, 1989). It was this which gave the Victorian establishment the confidence to extend the franchise to male urban workers in 1869 in order to integrate 'respectable' elements of the working class into society.

The situation became more turbulent towards the end of the nineteenth century, with the end of the Victorian boom, the rise of economic and inter-imperialist tensions between Britain and Germany, economic restructuring involving the rise of mechanised industries, white collar, and state employment, and the rise of the 'new unionism' and socialist ideology. As far as the last is concerned, there was a symbiotic relationship between the rise of new unionism and socialist ideology at the end of the nineteenth century, both among those who formerly had not been organised and new occupational layers. The emphasis on militant struggle and conflict with the employers was a challenge to the emphasis that the labour aristocracy had placed on conserving funds at all costs. As Tom Mann and Ben Tillett put it in a penny pamphlet in 1891,

> . . . many of the older unions are very reluctant to engage in a labour struggle, no matter how great the necessity, because they are hemmed in by sick and funeral claims, so that to a large extent they have lost their true characteristic of being fighting organizations.
>
> (cited in Davis, 1993: 95)

There was thus a shift from exclusive unionism in which high subscriptions and friendly society benefits played a central role, to an open unionism in which mass strength at the workplace was emphasised, combined with a political struggle, which could be reformist or revolutionary, against industrial capitalism. Thus, the union movement became increasingly politicised in the years up to 1914, the main effect being a turn to reformism. Some of this was a response to employer strategies, who sought both to break the new unionism, but also where necessary to reinforce the power of union officials by ceding national systems of collective bargaining. A partial coming together of the old and new unionism was also made possible by the fact that, while craft workers' privileges were eroded by deskilling, some unskilled groups like dockers started to gain local exclusive job rights (Hobsbawm, 1968). The second important factor, which should not be underestimated, was the influence of Fabianism upon the British labour movement, in contrast to Marxism's influence on the development of continental labour movements. In contrast to Marxism's doctrine that the state was an expression of capitalist interests, Fabianism saw its framework, and the pro-fessionals and civil servants who worked for it, as a neutral force for social betterment (Sullivan, 1999).

The prime reason why the trade union movement decided to sponsor the emerging Labour Party in 1900 was the pragmatic concern that the legality of its basic activities were placed in doubt by the Taff Vale judgement of 1901. As Minkin points out British union pragmatism grew out of a profound ambivalence to 'politics' which on the right led to a grudging acceptance of the need for state action and on the left to syndicalism. This shaped the dualistic notion of a labour movement with two sets of functions and centres of power (Minkin, 1992: 7). Despite this bifurcation, what emerged by 1918 when the modern constitution devised by the Webbs (the leading Fabians) was adopted, was a highly unified and strongly reformist labour movement. There was never in Britain any serious contest between revolutionary and reformist wings of the labour movement, despite the rise of Communist Party in the interwar period, and no religious versus secular divide that occurred in continental countries where Catholicism was a significant political force (Sassoon, 1997).

In these early days, public sector unions hardly existed, and cannot be counted a significant influence on social policy. They did, however, gain a foothold by the wave of activity at the end of the nineteenth century onwards that both brought new layers of workers into the movement, while at the same time expanding the employment base of state workers, like local authority gas workers, who were one of the key groups of new unionists. Significant numbers of public service workers subsequently became organised in the chief successors of the new unionism, the TGWU and the National Union of General and Municipal Workers (NUGMW). The notion of a distinct public service unionism cut across these traditions, opposing the poles of both craft and general unionism. NUPE, though founded in 1928, dates back to the London Vestry Employees' Labour Union in 1890 (Dix and Williams, 1987: 39). It was the only truly 'public service' union among the three founders of UNISON, though its base was primarily manual workers. COHSE, formed in 1946, with roots further back in asylum workers, aspired to industrial unionism in health but until the 1970s was primarily a male psychiatric nurses' union (Carpenter, 1988). NALGO emulated the wave of early twentieth century clerical and 'supervisory' unionism. It stayed aloof from the TUC as well as the Labour Party, and had strong friendly society and educational functions which made it a hybrid between a union, professional association and friendly society. What added to this byzantine complexity was the fact that groups like doctors and general nurses subscribed to 'non-political' and non-TUC organisations like the British Medical Association (BMA) and RCN. This complexity, which seriously weakened the public services political and industrial voice, is summarised in the following diagram:

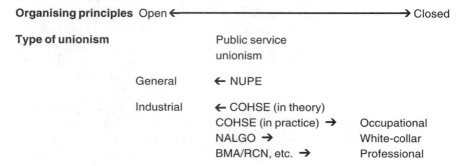

Organising principles Open ⟵————————————————————⟶ Closed

Type of unionism   Public service
                                            unionism

                        General   ⟵ NUPE

                        Industrial   ⟵ COHSE (in theory)
                                     COHSE (in practice) ⟶   Occupational
                                     NALGO ⟶   White-collar
                                     BMA/RCN, etc. ⟶   Professional

The implications of this are that UNISON is closer to the model represented by NUPE than the two partner unionism in terms of its organising principle and type of unionism, if not necessarily its structure.

None of the specifically public sector unions had much influence on emerging social policies at the beginning of the twentieth century, though the uneasy parliamentary alliance between the Liberal and Labour Parties undoubtedly did. The key Liberal reforms of 1906–11, school meals and medical inspection, old age pensions and National Health and Unemployment Insurance were the product of this political situation in which Liberals were always looking over their shoulder at the rising Labour opposition, desperately (and vainly as it happens) seeking to retain a base of working class support. As Whiteside (1987) has shown, the TUC, however, was often ambivalent about these measures. Even new unions like the Workers' Union (the TGWU's forerunner) was seeking to emulate the craft unions and provide cash benefits to unemployed members – to develop what in modern parlance would be called 'stakeholder welfare'. The TUC accepted the 1911 Act because it enabled unions to become official agents for provision of benefits under both health and unemployment insurance. However, they resented the centralisation of regulations and the fact that unemployment benefits were not payable when unemployment was due to an industrial dispute. After 1918, the union movement was initially cagey about the extension of unemployment insurance and often sought exemptions for particular industries. However, as the bargaining situation and funding base of unions worsened in the high unemployment of the interwar period, the union movement did increasingly look towards a universal state-funded scheme, though one they insisted should be contributory and administered by themselves (Whiteside, 1987).

While the trade union movement only moved in a faltering way towards universalism and statism, Fabian socialists were its enthusiastic advocates, as embodied in the proposals of the renowned Minority Report of the Royal Commission on the Poor Laws, which advocated the wholesale scrapping of the Poor Law and its replacement by a universally available 'national minimum' and national health service. By the 1930s a *de facto* national system of unemployment benefits had been established, not directly by labour movement strength, but through the piecemeal response of governments anxious to control costs by curtailing the ability of local Labour councils to respond to pressure from the unemployed to set generous dole rates. Whiteside (1998) has shown also that the insolvency of the health insurance scheme led to creeping centralised control of the panel system. Hospital services, however, remained divided between local authorities and voluntary hospitals. The Labour Party from the 1930s onwards adopted the policy of a National Medical Service. However this was mainly prompted by the Socialist Medical Association (SMA). The TUC however largely sought reform of the health insurance system and cooperated with the BMA rather than the SMA towards this end (Walters, 1980).

To summarise: a conservative and weakened trade union movement was increasingly statist by the 1930s, especially as the significance of friendly society activities declined. It was union opposition to the cuts in unemployment benefit which helped to bring down the 1930 Labour government of Ramsay McDonald. Following it the TUC established a Social Insurance and Social Welfare Department which monitored developments and developed pragmatic plans. It was its pressure to deal with anomalies in the insurance system that could be said to have created the Beveridge Committee when World War II began (Minkin, 1992: 43). However Beveridge's proposals in his Report in 1942 were far more visionary and uncompromisingly statist than anything the TUC had proposed.

The trade union movement and the heyday of the welfare state

The trade union movement were therefore supporting players in the creation of the welfare state rather than its chief architects (Addison, 1975). Beveridge and Keynes were social liberals, and there was no alternative socialist plan emanating from the TUC or Labour Party for post-war reconstruction. That is not to dispute the importance of working class mobilisation, including the union movement, in bringing about the welfare state. The labour movement campaigned for the full implementation of Beveridge, which helped to bring Labour to power on a landslide in the 1945 election. The war greatly enhanced the power of the state as a regulatory force fostering a collectivist 'equality of sacrifice' ethos, and created tight labour markets favourable to labour, both of which were conducive to the post-war development of a welfare state.

The war and the post-war welfare reforms were a significant boost to public service unions. National rates of pay were initially a by-product of wartime labour controls, as was collective bargaining in local government, which did not come in the health service until 1948. The repeal of the punitive 1927 Trades Disputes Act enhanced labour within a 'voluntarist' framework, but not until the 1970s did workers gain *positive* rights to organise in the workplace. Another problem was the divisions between TUC unions, and between them and professional associations like the BMA and RCN, whose right to sit at the bargaining table had in fact been underwritten by the Labour government. It was not surprising therefore that local government introduced dual bargaining machinery for manual and white collar workers, especially since the trade union movement was similarly divided. The government's approach to the health service, while insistent on the principle of universal access to treatment, was to compromise with the medical profession and give them the professionally dominant structure they wanted, free from local democratic 'interference'. In the wider political environment, the voice of public service unionism, such as it existed, was still largely subsumed within the two large general unions, the TGWU and the NUGMW. The welfare reforms and continuing price controls had helped to create a climate in which these big battalions were able to deliver TUC support for wage restraint, despite growing rank-and-file discontent (Whiteside, 1996).

The years following the defeat of Labour in 1951 to the coming to power of Margaret Thatcher in 1979 were ones in which public service workers increasingly found an independent voice, in which each of the partner unions played a key role, not least through a spectacular growth in membership, riding on the crest of the expansion of the health and welfare workforce. NALGO also became increasingly 'unionate', joining the TUC in 1964. It was a period during which trade unionism in general, and public service unionism in particular, became an increasingly dynamic force. There were a number of reasons for this. The first was the radical challenge to authority from below that emerged in the 1960s, that manifested itself in a number of ways within and outside the trade union movement. A new generation of trade unionists were not prepared to simply go along with the edicts from above, and now took full employment, high living standards and the welfare state for granted and wanted to see them substantially improved. The demands of new voices, notably of women and black people, also started to be articulated through union channels.

The wider economic circumstances also favoured union activism. When the Conservatives returned to power in 1951, they removed the wartime controls on the economy that had been maintained by Labour, seeking to govern primarily through full employment alone. This generated demand for labour through strengthened workplace unionism, leading to the phenomenon of 'wage drift'. This was all occurring at a time of growing concern at the performance of the British economy. Although Macmillan's claim that 'you've never had it so good' in the 1959 election was generally valid, the wider backdrop was one of relative decline: economic growth rates during the boom were higher in every other industrialised country and Britain's share of manufacturing exports had dropped dramatically (Alford, 1996: 205). The years from 1960 can therefore be seen as attempts to deal with this situation (the Heath government 1970–4 excepted) within a corporatist framework embracing union leaders, which finally collapsed in 1979 over linked issues of welfare state expenditure and public sector pay.

There is no space to provide a full review of these developments but Macmillan did two things which worked against each other. He imposed a public sector 'pay pause' at the same time as seeking to establish tripartite discussions between the TUC, the Government and the Confederation of British Industry (CBI) through the creation of the National Economic Development Council. The Labour Government of 1964–70 sought a more thorough social democratic solution by combining prices and wages control with national planning. However, it was blown off course by its failed attempt to introduce legislation curtailing unofficial strikes, and by the sterling crisis of 1967. The Heath government departed from corporatism by imposing a restrictive Industrial Relations Act, at the same as imposing a pay policy which was famously demolished by the miners' strike of 1974. None of these policies was either economically or politically successful. They did not reverse Britain's relative economic decline, or significantly raise levels of productivity. They also discriminated unfairly against public sector workers, whose pay was determined centrally.

This underlying trend, combined with the huge surge in inflation due to the oil crisis, did not provide a fortuitous set of circumstances for an incoming government, and in retrospect it is perhaps remarkable that Labour managed to hold things together for so long after 1974, given its precarious parliamentary position. The 'Social Contract' was initially an ambitious attempt to revive corporatism by repealing the Industrial Relations Act, granting unions positive rights, and expanding the social wage by raising pensions and controlling prices. There was a longer term goal of both addressing the distribution of wealth and income, and tackling Britain's productivity problem (Whiteside 1996). Legend has it that the shift to monetarism occurred in 1976 due to International Monetary Fund (IMF) imposed public expenditure cuts in return for a loan , but Timmins (1996: 325) points out that the break with Keynsianism occurred a year earlier when the government cut spending in the midst of a recession. The combination of public expenditure cuts and the reimposition of wage controls, in the context of rapidly expanding trade union strength, eventually overwhelmed the attempts of union leaders to hold the line. The rest, after the watershed of the 1978–9 'Winter of Discontent' is, of course, history.

The militancy of the 1970s was primarily about pay. Essentially public service unions were rejecting the restraints which had been accepted as part of Whitleyism, because the government had reneged on its side of the bargain by making an example of them rather than acting as a 'model employer'. However, there was also a degree of political radicalisation by welfare state workers in the 1970s that particularly manifested itself in campaigns against the cuts, and even to hospital work-ins that were primarily aimed at preventing closures, but also 'prefigured' a more democratic welfare state. Some social workers started to see themselves as in alliance with poor clients against an oppressive state, particularly at a time when managerial hierarchies were rapidly expanding (Joyce *et al.*, 1988). The most pronounced example of politicisation was the campaign around NHS pay beds which escalated in 1974 from a refusal of NUPE ancillary workers in Charing Cross Hospital to service private patients. The government's decision to introduce legislation gradually phasing out pay beds (repealed by Thatcher in 1980) bought precious time for the private sector to develop alternative facilities outside the NHS (Timmins, 1996: 338). There were a variety of perspectives developing which sought to place these developments in an analytical framework. On the left an optimistic scenario was developed by O'Connor (1973) which perceived a growing 'fiscal crisis of the state' caused by the tendency for welfare expenditure on people's needs to exceed that required to secure the conditions of capitalist profitability. However, public sector unions would combine with users to prevent attempts to prune the welfare state back. A right wing version of this was the Bacon and Eltis (1978) thesis, popularised through *The Sunday Times*, that Britain's economic ills were primarily the result of public investment 'crowding out' private market activities. Though the latter has been effectively refuted (e.g. Beaumont, 1992: 18–19) it added academic legitimacy to first the ideological turn of the 1974–9 Labour government, and the more wholehearted shift to monetarism by Mrs Thatcher. As her first public spending White Paper put it boldly in 1979: 'Public expenditure is at the heart of Britain's present economic difficulties' (cited in Timmins, 1996: 371).

Surviving Thatcherism I: the welfare state itself

Unfortunately O'Connor failed to acknowledge the potential for antagonism between workers in private and public sectors, as users and producers of services, which Thatcherism was happy to exploit. The claims of a 'lost legitimacy' have been exaggerated by some on the left as an explanation for Thatcherism (see Hall and Jacques, 1989), as they underestimate the role of the electoral system in maintaining her government in power, and the weakening effects of mass unemployment and repressive union laws. Nevertheless, the left and the trade union movement could no longer take unconditional support for the welfare state and 'big government' for granted and therefore had to develop more sophisticated arguments and strategies. The contested nature of these changes is reflected by the fact that public service unionism and collective bargaining, and the welfare state itself, was still largely intact by the end of the Thatcher–Major period. These were real successes, in the circumstances.

It is the case that the state has been successfully 'rolled back' as far as the public utilities and transport are concerned, and this had been partially legitimised by creating shareholder constituencies of support. In the 'heartland' of the welfare state, however, in health, social security and social services the state's central role was maintained, with the important exception of state housing. Council house sales were the biggest single privatisation measure raising £28 billion over 13 years, more than the sale of gas, electricity and British Telecom combined (Timmins, 1996: 380). The state's role was also diminished in pensions where state pensions have been linked less generously to price levels rather than earnings, the state earnings related scheme (SERPS) cut back, and massive incentives given to people to take out personal pensions.

The reasons for this generally cautious approach to dismantling welfare are not hard to find: a political calculation after the reaction to the leaked 'Think Tank' Report on the welfare state of 1983 that it would be electorally unpopular, combined with a grudging acknowledgement that the welfare state is a force for social stability. Paradoxically the welfare state *facilitated* the neoliberal project, blunting opposition to the high unemployment associated with deindustrialisation. The Thatcher government's approach to state welfare was therefore incremental. Different strategies were adopted to those sectors of provision that were universal like the NHS, or primarily benefited the middle classes, such as student grants. Often the approach to universal provision, such as the basic pension and child benefit, was not directly to attack it but allow it to wither on the vine. A tougher approach was taken towards socially marginalised people living on benefit, based on theories of 'dependency culture', systematised as 'underclass theory' by Charles Murray (1990), who sought to demonstrate pseudo-scientifically that the benefits system was the major cause of long-term unemployment and family breakdown in the USA and Britain. This neoliberal reasoning was reflected in such measures as the Social Fund (loans rather than grants for those on income support), and the replacement of National Insurance by Job Seekers' Allowance for the unemployed.

One of the less noticed features of Conservative social policy however was the way in which in the field of community care state support actually expanded into new areas. Access to disability benefits was extended, partly as the unintentional result of a shift to a more discretionary system, accompanied by strong lobbying and effective use of system by disabled people themselves (Barnes, 1991). Thatcher also provided access to discretionary social security support for residential care, which spiralled to well over £1 billion a year by the late 1980s, with the intent of undermining local government and expanding private sector provision. However to bring this system under control and put it under some kind of rational basis, the government felt compelled to cash limit funds from 1993 and pass the buck to local authorities to administer (Carpenter, 1994).

Thus Conservative social policy cannot be solely characterised as 'cuts'. Nowhere is this more true than in the NHS which Thatcher felt moved to promise in 1982 that it would be 'safe with us'. Here again the reforms of the 1990s show the influence of US managerial methods of Alain Enthoven on the testing bed of a socialised system, which have subsequently been applied in other countries. The separation of providing and 'purchasing' had a twofold intention: to facilitate greater control and direction from above, and more dynamism and responsiveness at the base, but it was also linked to the longer term agenda of hiving-off the public sector to private providers. It cannot be denied that the Social Democratic welfare state was subject to certain rigidities, and was in need of reform, and that aspects of Thatcherism did, after a fashion, begin to address them. It is not necessary to romanticise or endorse the shift to 'new public management', consumerism, and greater pluralism in provision in the mixed economy of welfare, to admit that it was a response to pressing issues of account-ability to users, and concerns about the quality of public provision. Although it often had the wrong answers, mere opposition was not enough, especially since 'producer domination' of policy was seen as one reason for rigidities. This created dilemmas for the left and trade union movement that have still not been solved, although as we shall see public service unions like UNISON's predecessors had started to address them by the end of the 1980s.

Although services and forms and provision were largely maintained, the most lasting social legacy of the Thatcher period, however, was the growth of poverty and inequality, exacerbated by benefit cuts to the poor, tax cuts for the better off, and attacks on the bargaining strength of labour. Between 1979 to 1994–5 while average incomes rose by around 40 per cent, those of the richest tenth grew 65 per cent and those of the poorest tenth fell 8 per cent in real terms if housing costs are counted. In 1977 10 per cent of the population had incomes below the average, while by 1991–2 this had risen to 20 per cent (Hills, 1998: 5). This evidence contradicts neoliberal assumptions that allowing inequality to rise will provide 'trickle down' benefits to the poor.

Surviving Thatcherism II: the Labour movement and UNISON

Like the welfare state, both wings of the labour movement survived the tests of the Thatcher era. The Labour Party could have broken up under the challenge of the left and the defection of the right to form a new party, but held together in the barren opposition years, to win a landslide victory in 1997. The influence of the trade union movement has been curtailed by the end of corporatism, deindustrial- isation and legal restrictions, which led to a significant loss of membership. However, public sector trade unionism has remained relatively buoyant and its weight and influence has increased within the union movement. At the same time manual workers have declined significantly as a proportion of the public service workforce, mirroring broader trends (Bailey, 1996). This has weakened the traditional powerful manufacturing and general unions, and pushed UNISON to pole position within the union movement.

Clearly, both the Labour Party and the trade union movement have adapted in the intervening period, and survived at a price. The emergence of 'New Labour' has been paralleled by an organically linked growth of a 'new realism' among trade unions. The accomodation of New Labour to post-Keynsianism market 'realities' can, as we have seen, be traced to the Labour government of the 1974–9, and was particularly a feature of the premiership of James Callaghan. A further accelerated shift occurred after the loss of the 1987 general election, with the initiation of the 'Policy Review', strongly influenced by Tom Sawyer, then a senior official in NUPE, and part of a growth of 'new realism' in the trade union movement (Minkin, 1992: 467). There was in particular a softening of the line on repealing Tory anti-union legislation during 1989 – the period when the UNISON merger negotiations started – by Tony Blair as opposition employ- ment spokesperson. Alongside this policy shift was a wider structural shift towards the increased dominance of the Parliamentary wing of the Party (Minkin, 1992: 472). The emergence of New Labour was thus an evolutionary process which was undoubtedly accelerated further by another defeat of Labour in 1992, and the electorate's apparent rejection of John Smith's mildly redistributive shadow budget.

This time social policy figured prominently in the equation, with Smith's sponsorship of a semi-independent Commission for Social Justice (1994). This was partly funded by UNISON with Margaret Wheeler, its Director of Organi- sation Development, as one of the Commission's members. The Report set a new agenda for social policy which shifted priorities away from a consumptionist ethic, with the prime emphasis given to expanding wealth and re-channelling welfare towards social investment. Underpinning it is a 'Post-Fordist' argument that with technological change, globalisation, and cultural change, a return to Keynsian demand-management is not feasible or desirable. There is equal disdain for 'deregulators' (market liberals) and 'levellers' (who are presumably 'old Labour'). There is much on providing support for families while recognising diversity, reinvigorating communities, and the need to provide flexible public services which enhance personal autonomy. A premium is placed on 'making work pay' and a 'preventive' approach to poverty shifting welfare from a 'safety net in times of trouble to a springboard for economic opportunity' (Commission for Social Justice, 1994: 1). Many of the Blair government's social policy themes and approaches are a further development of the Commission's approach, particularly its emphasis on 'welfare to work' and partnership with communities.

However, albeit in a rather muted way, the Commission did place some emphasis upon the redistribution from rich to poor, and advocated a family policy linked to feminist principles. This is perhaps why one of the signatories, Professor Ruth Lister (1998) has become a notable critic of the Blair government's social policy, suggesting that the commitment to end poverty and tackle inequality has been abandoned in favour an attempt to combat 'social exclusion'. Her criticisms might thus echo 'realists' in the trade union movement who would broadly support, or at least be prepared to go along with the main drift of New Labour social policy, while being critical of these features of it.

There had been significant differences in the way that different public service unions had responded to Thatcherism. NALGO shifted to the left. Though as a non-affiliated union its main efforts were focused on affecting TUC policy, and public opinion through billboard advertising campaigns, it did provide discreet financial support for the Labour front bench. As a white collar and professional union it actually grew during the 1980s. NUPE had spearheaded the militancy in the 1970s, but it became weakened in the 1980s as manual workers bore the brunt of privatisation policies and growing professionalisation of health and welfare. The leadership began to feel guilty for its role in the 'Winter of Discontent', pinning its hopes on the return of a Labour government, now convinced of the need to turn towards the centre if Labour was to be electable. This helps to explain why the Policy Review, referred to above, was initiated from within NUPE. COHSE was in any case a traditionally cautious and conservative affiliated union. It had initially benefited from the wage militancy of nurses in the 1970s, but was overtaken by the Royal College of Nursing (RCN) in the 1980s in the reaction against it.

All three unions became increasingly sophisticated in dealing with the new policy climate of the 1980s. Since Thatcherism had capitalised, in part, on divisions of interest between users of public service workers and providers, it increasingly dawned on the latter that they could not take public support for granted. With the Conservatives politically entrenched, they had to find imaginative ways to draw on public support, including forging alliances with user groups, who in the conditions of the 1980s often had more clout than unions. One of the key vulnerabilities of the Conservatives was around 'quality'. While claiming to improve public services, their policies were shown to be primarily concerned with saving costs, particularly of labour, as privatisation and new managerialism drove wages and staffing levels down, and seeking to increase output. Unions also had some success in linking the quality issue to enhanced training and prospects for workers. While the shift from 'personnel' to 'human resources' was often linked to a more authoritarian management approach, its purported emphasis on 'total quality management' gave public service unions the possibility to raise issues of participation, skill enhancement and improved services for users.

Policy differences between unions sometimes reflected organisational interests. In the early 1980s, the Jay Report recommended a shift from institutional and medicalised services, which was predictably resisted by COHSE but embraced by NUPE, largely because of their different membership bases in health and local government. However, towards the end of the 1980s, a more principle-based user-centred approach emerged, with COHSE, for example, beginning to advocate a shift to community care in mental health, even though it threatened to erode their hospital membership base, and successfully joined with user groups to protest against proposals for compulsory treatment in the community (Carpenter, 1994). The need to show that it could claim the moral high ground was important in its struggle against its chief rival, the RCN. Many of the campaigns were rearguard actions, for example, those of NALGO and NUPE against privatisation of public utilities. However, the high state of readiness of public sector unions, their ability to mobilise the media and growing ability to link up with user groups, undoubtedly helped to protect the heartland of the welfare state in a hostile environment.

Joint working on anti-privatisation campaigns began to break down the often competitive relationships between the three unions, and therefore helped to bring about and accelerate the merger discussions between the three unions. The need to revitalise public services, and develop a new model of trade unionism linking the interests of workers and providers in a campaign for more responsive and democratically organised provision was a significant driving force. It is reflected in the high priority given to such issues in the UNISON rules *Aims and Objectives*. However this was in the late 1980s and early 1990s when the Tory government was on the defensive, unpopular because of the Poll Tax and the NHS reforms. Thatcher herself was deposed and Labour surged ahead in opinion polls. The attempt to construct UNISON occurred at a time of optimism when its architects looked forward to Labour achieving power in the 1992 election. Defeat in that election was a traumatic experience which pushed the three unions even closer together, but now in a more defensive frame of mind.

It is possible to see UNISON as a product and expression of a shift from what Heery (1996) characterises as the militantly workerist shopfloor 'new unionism' of the 1970s, to a softer focus, consumption-orientated 'new new unionism' of the late 1980s onwards, as initially pioneered by the GMB under John Edmonds' leadership. This new 'model' can be seen as reflecting the fact that union members are increasingly women, white collar 'professionals', interested in improving their skills and careers, and concerned about a wider range of issues than merely pay and conditions. It would, however, be mistaken to picture this shift as entirely a 'new realist' lurch to the right (as it was with the electricians union), for it also articulates a radical agenda of feminism, ecology, working with new social movements and user groups. The notion of creating a 'new union' by COHSE, NALGO and NUPE can be seen as an attempt to embrace these kinds of principles, for example, by their intention of creating a 'women friendly' union with proportionality in decision-making structures, and a decentralised power structure based on service groups and 'self-organised groups' of women, disabled members, and gays and lesbians. The attempt to be more responsive has thus been influenced by the perception that unions need to work harder to win the active support and involvement of members. They also needed to bridge traditional divides between public sector workers and the wider 'public', and relate to the fact that its members as citizens had interests as users in quality issues, thus articulating a more complex and diverse vision of union identities.

UNISON and social policy: dealing with New Labour

The concept that UNISON embodies a 'new new unionism' tailored to current circumstances does, however, need to be treated with a degree of caution, to avoid reifying union 'character'. The 'old' new unionism has not been entirely extinguished within UNISON, and the new forms are still emerging and express a variety of responses. It is not entirely a monolithic one-directional turn towards 'realism' which is consistent with 'New Labour'. 'Old style' trade unionism, with a central emphasis on wage militancy, conflictual relations with employers and anti-cuts campaigns, still represents a pole of opposition to this turn, and there are also competing radical and centrist versions of 'new style unionism'. The latter might broadly accept the need to 'modernize' British social, economic and political life, but they still differ markedly in approach. Although further research would be required to substantiate it fully, my perceptions, which arise from some involvement as a social policy advisor, are that there are three main emerging positions among activists and officials towards New Labour within UNISON:

Uncritical	Critical supporters	Oppositionists
←		→
Blairite modernisers	Radical modernisers	Traditional militants

There are of course right oppositionists in UNISON (particularly but not exclusively inherited from old NALGO) but I have rightly or wrongly not counted them as a significant force. My prediction would be that they are most likely to ally themselves with Blairite modernizers. These clusters are found on a continuum rather than dividing members and activists inevitably into three 'camps'. While it is possible to find significant numbers of adherents of each of the three types, there are many who prevaricate, for example between Blairite and radical modernism, or between radical modernism and traditional militancy. Thus it is possible to subject New Labour to two types of left criticism, not only from an 'old Labour' perspective but also from the perspective that its modernising agenda does not go far enough: for example, on the constitutional front, that its reform of the House of the Lords and proposals to widen 'freedom of information' are too timid, and that it is exercising excessive caution on electoral reform.

My perception is that the officials tend to be pulled from the middle to the Blairite end of the continuum, which is reinforced by mechanisms of accountability within their ranks. Activists are more likely to be pulled from the middle towards the oppositional direction. The chief issue is the extent to which UNISON should support New Labour. In the run up to the 1997 election, the main expected role of public service unions was to do nothing that might undermine the electoral strategy of 'safety first'. Such a situation was not one in which unions were going to play a central role in developing a social policy agenda. As policy making became centralised under Tony Blair's leadership, the direct influence of unions declined. Even after the 1992 election defeat, policy making was relatively open, e.g. with Policy Forums organised by the Front Bench health team, and yearly Consultative Conferences in health and local government where genuine discussion and exchange took place. However, the Forums gradually fell into disuse and the Conferences increasingly became showcase occasions for the Labour leadership. In theory, UNISON could have responded by developing its own policies. However, the bringing together of three large unions with different traditions and structures was a highly complex affair, and absorbed much of the energies of activists and officials. Only now is the organisation becoming sufficiently settled for UNISON to devote significant efforts to developing strategic policies.

In developing its work on the social policy fronts, UNISON has to deal with its own internal organisational complexities, as the lines of responsibility are not clear. The Service Groups, the National Executive, Self-Organised Groups and Affiliated Political Fund, are all potential social policy actors. In theory, Service Groups are by rule predominantly concerned with pay, conditions and occupational matters, but in practice they have had a significant role in developing social policy responses relevant to their sectors. This is particularly the case with the Health Group which deals with issues that are often in the forefront of the political agenda. When the merger discussions were taking place, 'citizenship' issues were defined as the property of the union as a whole, where members have interests not just as producers but also as citizens. Of course this could include many issues relating to health and social services which are largely handled by the relevant service group. Policy issues are more likely to handled centrally as a 'citizenship' issue when they are clearly matters of concern to the whole union, in which case they are developed through the Policy and Development Committee of the NEC. Recent examples have been evidence to Commission for Social Justice in 1994, and a more extensive statement on 'Unequal Britain' in 1996 (UNISON, 1996). Policy on public utilities has also evolved, restating the goal of a return to public ownership but also seeking to identify ways in which the privatised utilities should operate in the public interest and in relation to their workers (UNISON, 1997). Welfare reform has been handled in a similar way, with a cautious consideration of whether a shift to 'stakeholder' mutuality floated by Frank Field's Green Paper on social security reform of 1998, might have benefits for unions and their members.

What is apparent is that a 'policy dualism' is emerging. Thus, the Public Finance Initiative (PFI) of public–private partnerships, particularly resorted to for building local hospitals, is opposed in principle, and calls are made to retain public ownership and find alternative means of funding capital projects. At the same time in practice considerable effort has been made at national and local levels to influence the terms of the PFI. In this situation 'realism' does not involve an ideological shift but a judgement about what can be achieved. That criticism can be forthright was demonstrated by the widely-publicised mauling that Alan Milburn (then a junior health minister) received over continuation of the PFI at UNISON's 1998 Health Group Conference. UNISON has played a key role within the labour movement in consistently opposing the PFI in principle as against the public interest. It successfully challenged a General Council statement at the 1998 TUC to ensure opposition in principle in to PFI. Opposition has also born fruit in local campaigns and in shifting the government's strategic approach. By 1999 the government had conceded that in *future deals* the requirement that hospital ancillary staff would be transferred from trusts would end, and there would also be an expectation that after the leasing period of 30 years or more, the hospital would normally revert to the public sector. It has been suggested that these concessions were necessary to head off a rebellion in the Labour Party's National Policy Forum. Research into emerging PFI projects is serving to confirm rather than allay UNISON's fears that profit rather than local needs determine plans, that they will involve considerable costs in terms of charges for many years, and are likely to involve a 'downsizing' of beds and reductions in medical and nursing personnel. This in turn is likely to involve intensified rationing of NHS services (Cohen, 1999; Gaffney *et al.*, 1999). It is also clear that with public finances in an increasingly healthy state, there is no justification for the assertion that public–private partnerships are the only alternative to restore the fabric of public services.

There has been a stronger focus emerging in UNISON on evaluating policies in the light of members' immediate interests, rather than focusing solely on points of political principle. However, it must be said that this is the subject of much soul searching and debate. An interesting case study was UNISON's evidence to the Royal Commission on Long Term Care, in particular the extent to which a proposed new social insurance scheme should provide free accommodation at point of use. First, different stances to New Labour were revealed. Among officials, the goal was to seek to frame a policy which would have influence in the current climate, without sacrificing 'union principles', whereas among activists defence of these principles ranked high as an objective in itself, even at the risk of advocating policies against the current grain by disregarding pressures on public spending. Second, it showed that UNISON was generally not well prepared, as it had no existing policy in this area, despite the fact that Labour had announced intention of setting up a Royal Commission before the 1997 election. Third, it illustrates how policy developments are overtaking UNISON's structures, which are primarily organised around existing institutional boundaries (i.e. Service Groups). The future care of older people, however, crosses the health and social divide, and is just one example of government policies which seek to achieve 'joined-up government'; e.g. between local government, health and other services, and between the state and the private voluntary sector, e.g. Health Action Zones, Education Action Zones, etc.

Therefore, work on a specific policy task – framing evidence to a Royal Commission – uncovered a major organisational issue which UNISON needs urgently to tackle if it is not to be merely reacting defensively to events. There is nothing particularly strange in any this, as organisations are initially slow to respond to turbulence in their external environments. The key is to recognise that what is now a breeze may become a gale. This creates many challenges for UNISON as an organisation which uniquely spans all public services and a myriad of occupations. Other organisations do not have the same problems. For example, the Royal College of Nursing is also an alliance of often fractious interests, but ultimately needs only to define and press the nursing interest. For example, its evidence to the 1998 Health Select Committee on relations between health and local government argued for a health take-over of community care, with nurses in the driving seat. UNISON therefore needs to feel its way forward more cautiously. Nevertheless it is possible to see the beginnings of a policy approach emerging: (1) a commitment to partnership and emphasis on enhancing skills and opportunities as well as pay; (2) an incremental rather than a 'big bang' approach to overcoming the health and social service divide and creating a 'seamless service' (UNISON, 1998); (3) a preparedness to consider more 'flexible' working so long as it contributes to improved services and has advantages for workers, especially since the majority of UNISON members are women; (4) changes in services and social provision are not a substitute for policies to address the structural causes of social inequalites; (5) both health and local government need to be organised on democratic lines.

Although I have suggested that there are differences between activists and officials about the extent to which the union should work 'with the grain' of the Labour government, these are currently a matter of emphasis, and should not be exaggerated. Up to the end of 1999, UNISON had unified around support for the Labour government, and the 'centre has held'. An NEC statement 'UNISON and the New Labour Government', subsequently adopted by Conference in 1997, welcomed some policies, drew attention to problems such as widening inequalities, and looked forward to a partnership role:

> There will be difficult areas, such as the Private Finance Initiative, where our members' interests conflict with the Government's priorities. . . . We will serve our members best if we work with the Government where we can; and where we cannot we argue for clear rational alternatives, justifying our claims by the public interest as well as our own.

Despite strains, there are strong pressures cementing the alliance with Labour at least for the duration of the first term. However disillusioned some officials, activists and members may now feel after the elation of May 1997, the spectre of the 'Winter of Discontent' still hangs over their heads, and the last thing they want to feel responsible for is the return of a Conservative government.

At central level, therefore, any unease has so far expressed itself in subterranean rumblings, and resort to informal channels of influence outside the spotlight of publicity, rather than the highly publicised 'beer and sandwiches at Number 10' of the past. However, more overt conflicts are starting to erupt at local level, as tight control of public spending, the plethora of organisational initiatives associated with the pursuit of the radical 'modernising' agenda, the shift from compulsory competitive tendering (CCT) to 'Best Value' in local government, and further privatisation, starts to be implemented by Labour councils. UNISON also largely inherited the NALGO system of branch autonomy and significant control over resources. Oppositional activists and networks associated with organisations like the Socialist Workers' Party are also stronger within branches than in the higher reaches of the union. This has been highlighted by the crisis in UNISON's largest branch, Birmingham Local Government, which had taken an oppositional stance to the Council, which was suspended by the NEC in 1999 on the grounds of it being run by a self-elected politically motivated clique, or because it stood up to a New Labour Council's attacks on jobs and services – depending on which version is accepted (see http://www.labournet.org.uk/ for fuller accounts). In another instance striking members in UNISON's Tameside Care Group in Lancashire, stood as candidates in local elections against the Labour Council, to the concern of the national leadership.

Thus, in principle, UNISON policy rejects PFI and criticises Best Value, demanding fully funded public services, but the organisation as a whole feels constrained from taking concerted opposition against them. This does not come entirely from tribal political loyalties but a perception shared most intensely by the officials but also many activists and members that there is a kind of informal contract between New Labour and the union movement. This involves implementation of the EU's Social Chapter, a statutory minimum wage, extension of employment and bargaining rights, and 'redistribution by stealth' to the working poor through Gordon Brown's budgets. However, the difficulty as far as the public sector is concerned is that there is no bright news on the horizon on the key issues of services or wages. The version of the 'third way' which the Government is pursuing is set firmly down a neoliberal path, rather than the revitalisation or modernisation of social democracy it is claimed to be (Blair, 1998; Giddens, 1998). Certainly, the Prime Minister and the government seem ideologically closer to business than the values embodied by the public sector as indicated by Tony Blair's 1999 asides attacking public sector workers' 'conservatism' in a speech to the Institute of Directors, which was read by some as a coded criticism of UNISON (Addelman, 1999).

Conclusion – still defending and improving the welfare state after all these years?

This review of the dilemmas and difficulties which UNISON has faced in dealing with New Labour in power should not detract attention from the fact that it remains the most innovative and dynamic union on the scene, and its future success is crucial to the continued recovery of the trade union movement and the British left. UNISON continues to promote the cause of a revitalised public sector and welfare state. Its campaigning activities have also yielded some important victories – notably in 1999 winning £67,000 compensation for

Beverley Lancaster, in a landmark case which paves the way towards full recognition of employer responsibility for occupational stress.

It is clear that an over-supportive relationship for New Labour by UNISON is neither desirable nor sustainable in terms of pressing members' interests and, paradoxically, keeping a Labour government on its toes. The government has shown on occasion that it is not always good at reading public opinion, over Railtrack, the London Underground and genetically modified foods. Opinion research shows considerable public support for maintaining and revitalising public services (Jowell *et al.*, 1998). Ironically, therefore, UNISON may best help a Labour government in future by following William Blake's advice that 'opposition is true friendship'. As John Monks (1999), General Secretary of the TUC, puts it:

> The ideological struggle today is over which form of capitalism we want – a capitalism that has to give due regard to a welfare state, social rights and a sense of community, or the American way, where these are not present.

Modernisation need not therefore necessarily equate with Americanisation, although this assumption does appear to be a strong influence upon the New Labour project. Without wishing to launch into an anti-American tirade, the USA can in many ways be regarded as a *backward* society, lacking a national health service, with a primitive and custodial criminal justice system which keeps the death penalty when most civilised countries have abandoned it. The American model also leads to a decay of civil society and polarised urban relationships, in which the decline of public services in cities is a pronounced feature. It is therefore the case that the defence and improvement of public services is crucial to the future of civilized society (Wallace and Wallace, 1997).

This is therefore a difficult but interesting environment for the union. Because UNISON does represent the whole span of public service provision, it is uniquely placed to make a 'legitimate' contribution to social policy debates, starting from the needs of users while at the same time seeking to obtain justice for the legitimate claims of workers. There is time to learn the lessons of the last few years, and now that UNISON has established itself as an organisation, it has an opportunity to define itself as in the vanguard of the campaign to renew Britain's public services. To do this it will need to look ahead and anticipate future shifts in policy. The fact that Labour now increasingly defines itself as 'relatively autonomous' from unions potentially gives UNISON a freer role to develop public policies and to campaign for them in the public domain. This can also free it to work more closely with other organisations in 'civil society' to develop further the 'worker–user' alliance in favour of renewed public provision and greater social equality. In doing so, it can take forward one of the central and most exciting ideas at the heart of the creation of UNISON, that it cannot just press the workers' interest as workers and their families and associates are citizens and actual or potential users too.

References

Addelman, M. (1999) 'Too close for comfort', *Red Pepper* (October).

Addison, P. (1975) *The Road to 1945*, London: Jonathan Cape.

Alford, B. W. E. (1996) *Britain in the World Economy Since 1880*, London: Longman.

Bacon, R., and Eltis, W. (1978) *Britain's Economic Problem: Too Few Producers*, London: Macmillan.

Bailey, R. (1996) 'Public sector industrial relations', in I. J. Beardwell (ed.) *Contemporary Industrial Relations: A Critical Analysis*, Oxford: Oxford University Press.

Barnes, C. (1991) *Disabled People in Britain and Discrimination: A Case for Anti-Discrimination Legislation*, London: Hurst.

Beaumont, P. (1992) *Public Sector Industrial Relations*, London: Routledge.

Benson, J. (1989) *The Working Class in Britain 1850–1939*, London: Longman.

Blair, T. (1998) *The Third Way: New Politics for the New Century*, London: Fabian Society.

Carpenter, M. (1988) *Working for Health: the History of COHSE*, London: Lawrence and Wishart.

Carpenter, M. (1994) *Normality is Hard Work: Trade Unions and the Politics of Community Care*, London: Lawrence and Wishart.

Cohen, N. (1999) 'How Britain mortgaged the future', *New Statesman*, 18 October.

Commission for Social Justice (1994) *Social Justice: Strategies for National Renewal*, London: Vintage.

Davis, M. (1993) *Comrade or Brother? The History of the British Labour Movement 1789–1951*, London: Pluto.

Dix, B. and Williams, S. (1987) *Serving the Public: Building the Union; the History of the National Union of Public Employees, Volume 1 The Forerunners, 1889–1928*, London: Lawrence and Wishart.

Gaffney, D., Pollock, A. M., Price, D. and Shaoul, J. (1999) 'The politics of the Private Finance Initiative and the new NHS', *British Medical Journal*, 319.

Giddens, A. (1998) *The Third Way: The Renewal of Social Democracy*, Cambridge: Polity.

Hall, S. and Jacques, M. (1989) *New Times: The Changing Face of Politics in the 1990s*, London: Lawrence and Wishart.

Henriques, U. (1979) *Before the Welfare State: Social Administration in Early Industrial Britain*, London: Longman.

Hills (1998) *Income and Wealth: The Latest Evidence*, York: Joseph Rowntree Foundation.

Hobsbawm, E. (1968) *Labouring Men*, London: Weidenfeld and Nicolson.

Heery, E. (1996) 'The new new unionism', in I. J. Beardwell (ed.) *Contemporary Industrial Relations: A Critical Analysis*, Oxford: Oxford University Press.

Joyce, P., Corrigan, P. and Hayes, M. (1988) *Striking Out: Trade Unionism in Social Work*, Basingstoke: Macmillan.

Jowell, R. *et al.* (1998) *British Social Attitudes: The 15th Report*, Aldershot: Ashgate.

Lister, R. (1998) 'From equality to social inclusion: New Labour and the welfare state', *Critical Social Policy*, 18.

Minkin, L. (1992) *The Contentious Alliance: Trade Unions and the Labour Party*, Edinburgh: Edinburgh University Press.

Monks, J. (1999) 'Union man', interview with John Monks, *New Times*, 7 (September).

Murray, C. (1990) *The Emerging British Underclass*, London: Institute of Economic Affairs.

O'Connor, J. (1973) *The Fiscal Crisis of the State*, New York: St. Martin's Press.

Sassoon, D. (1997) *One Hundred Years of Socialism: The West European Left in the 20th Century*, London: Fontana.

Sullivan, M. (1998) 'Democratic socialism and social policy', in R. M. Page and R. Silburn (eds) *British Social Welfare in the Twentieth Century*, Basingstoke: Macmillan.

Timmins, N. (1996) *The Five Giants: A Biography of the Welfare State*, London: Fontana.

UNISON (1996) *Unequal Britain: Agenda for Change*, NEC Report No 2.

UNISON (1997) *The Privatised Utilities*, NEC Report No 2.

UNISON (1998) *UNISON Response to Partnership in Action.*

Wallace, R. and Wallace, D. (1997) 'Socioeconomic determinants of health: community marginalization and the diffusion of disease and disorder in the United States', *British Medical Journal*, 314.

Walters, V. (1980) *Class Inequality and Health Care: The Origins and Impact of the National Health Service*, London: Croom Helm.

Whiteside, N. (1987) 'Social welfare and industrial relations', in C. J. Wrigley (ed.) *A History of British Industrial Relations, Volume 2: 1914–1939*, Brighton: Harvester.

Whiteside, N. (1996) 'Industrial relations and social welfare, 1945–79', in C. Wrigley (ed.) *A History of British Industrial Relations, 1939–1979*, Cheltenham: Edward Elgar.

Whiteside, N. (1998) 'Private provision and public welfare: health insurance before the wars', in D. Gladstone (ed.) *Before Beveridge: Welfare Before the Welfare State*, London: IEA.

16 UNISON and the quality of public service provision

Any lessons from the rest of Europe?

Michael Terry

Much of the writing about British public sector – and in particular public service – trade unions and trade unionism is informed by a general, but rarely defined, implication that they are (or at least were) 'different' from private sector unions. Often this 'difference' was indicated by structural differences; public sector unions were more centralised, and more industry- or occupation-specific than their private sector counterparts. Such features, deriving in part from employer preferences for centralised collective bargaining and for sectoral and occupational administrative distinctiveness, sometimes led analysts of trade unions to categorise public sector unions as excessively bureaucratic and hence, at least for those who automatically associated 'bureaucracy' with such things, as oligarchic, dominated by powerful national officers and hence again, 'right-wing' and collaborationist, since according to some influential analyses it was in the nature of union bureaucracies to be so. Certainly the Thatcher governments appeared to go along with much of this analysis, since they set about the radical dismembering of what Ken Clarke labelled the 'cosy, collusive arrangements' believed to exist between union leaders and senior public sector managers and through the privatisation, marketisation and decentralisation of the public sector, sought to force it into aping private sector disciplines. In so doing, according to some commentators, Conservative policies were having the effect of reducing, possibly eliminating the differences between public and private sector unions, making the former more similar to the latter (see Mailly *et al.*, 1989).

Such alleged convergence is most often associated with evidence of structural change in public sector trade unions and in particular that they are rapidly decentralising, devoting more resources to local activity based around branch or shop steward organisation; as levels of managerial decision taking are decentralised, so too with unions. Attention has been drawn to the growth in decentralised structures, based around local representative structures, operating with increasing independence from weakened central bodies (e.g. Fairbrother, 1996). However, there are two other dimensions of change implicitly associated with this same trend. The first concerns the *subject matter* of such decentralised bargaining which appears to be increasingly economistic in nature, preoccupied with the detailed negotiation of local pay and working conditions, the characteristic activities of private sector unions. Ferner, for example, argues that the overall commercialisation of the public sector is likely to lead to increasingly economistic demands by public sector unions since they are likely to demand that 'if parts of the public sector are being run like a business, then staff should receive the salaries and fringe benefits on offer in the private sector' (Ferner, 1994: 64). He suggests that this is significant also insofar as it indicates a weakening of the 'public service ethos' and 'in particular the value of intrinsic, non-monetary motives that have traditionally been important aspects of public sector behaviour', a point to which I shall return later. But the argument is more complex than this allows, since it can also be claimed that the effective provision of high-quality services to the public has in turn been closely related to the traditions of co-operation in industrial relations at all levels. As Ferner again suggests, there is a risk that 'the traditional sources of co-operative change in the British public sector [will be] seriously eroded if not permanently lost by the aggressive strain of commercialism that has been pursued' (ibid., 1994: 76). Service quality and the nature of industrial relations institutions and processes thus appear closely interrelated.

The second claimed change relates to the nature of the *bargaining power* resources that may be deployed by public sector unions operating in the new environment of decentralised, commercialised systems. The essentially *political* nature of union bargaining power associated with 'traditional' (i.e. pre-1979) public sector industrial relations (see, for example, Beaumont, 1992: 115–32; Batstone *et al.*, 1984: 124–30) may be displaced, at least in the rapidly-spreading income-generating areas of the public sector, by a bargaining power analogous to that found in the private sector insofar as collective action hits the employers' revenue rather than, as in the past, their political–electoral standing. This too may indicate a growing similarity to private sector unionism.

The argument so far suggests that whatever the historical differences between public and private sector trade unionism may have been, they are being rapidly eroded, perhaps irreversibly, in such a way as to suggest that there is now only one 'model' of British unionism – fragmented, decentralised, and preoccupied above all with influencing the detailed regulation of their members' employment through whatever channels may be open to them. If this is indeed the case it is arguable that it represents not merely a significant change in the nature of public sector unionism but a dilution, possibly even an abandonment, of long-held public sector union objectives and philosophies, and to that extent might be held to represent a defeat for public sector unions in general and, in this particular case, for UNISON.

To understand just how significant such a setback might be one need look no further than UNISON's *Aims and Objects* as set out at the start of the union's rulebook. The first section, headed 'At Work and in the Community' devotes roughly equal space and weight to the protection of employees'/members' interests *and to the protection and improvement of the services provided to the public* (emphasis added). In this clear commitment we can observe a fundamental difference between public and private sector unionism not so far mentioned but challenged by the alleged 'convergence' outlined above. By and large private sector trade unions do not enshrine in their rulebooks the object of pressing for better-made motor cars or tastier foods. Such unions (quite properly) see such matters as the preserve of employers and managers, to be discussed if appropriate with recognised trade unions, but not to be seen as part of the unions' 'mission'. Public sector, and in particular public service unions (but also including the public utilities) have often sought, although not always through conventional collective bargaining channels, a say in the nature and quality of services provided to the public, although this has rarely been given the same attention as, for example, bargaining over pay. Sometimes referred to as unions' 'public service ethos' this thrust of public service unionism has at its heart the collective representation of what Ferner, cited above, described as the intrinsic rewards of public sector employment; those associated with the provision of effective and good-quality social services. In pursuing such objects public service unions are thus acting as the proper representatives of their members' collective wishes.

For as long as this is the case, trade unions representing public service workers must remain in certain respects distinctive from those in the private sector, for their pursuit of such service-related objectives necessarily involves engagement with processes of governmental decision-making and with the exercise of political influence. While it may well be the case that the methods deployed and the levels at which influence is sought may change, public service trade unionism necessarily remains ineradicably enmeshed with political actors and processes for the achievement of its fundamental purposes. To that extent public service unions will retain distinctive elements that will differentiate them from the private; any convergence will necessarily only be partial.

The significance of UNISON's engagement with political structures is examined with regard to government policy on low pay in the chapters by Morris and Thornley and on collective bargaining more generally by Thornley and her colleagues. But, as indicated above, a characteristic objective also traditionally pursued through such engagement has been the nature and quality of service provision. This important dimension of union activity is explored in regard to macro-level social policy by Carpenter. My preoccupation here is to investigate the potential for the pursuit of this objective through local, decentralised, union action.

Public service trade unionism and the pursuit of service quality

Notwithstanding all that has been said above concerning public service trade unions' stated objective of improving the quality of public service provision, it must be conceded that there has long been in practice a significant gap between this formal interest on the one hand and their ability to formulate and pursue effective policies for their achievement on the other. It is difficult to identify with confidence significant active union influence at work in the development and delivery of, for example, local government and health services in the period between 1945 and the election of the first Thatcher government. There are several possible reasons for this, including the absence of appropriate machinery through which union contributions to such policy development could have been made, and the long-standing hostility of British managers and employers, in the public as well as the private sector, to the idea that union discretion and influence should be allowed to spread beyond the carefully delimited handling of their members' terms and conditions of employment. The consequences of this in-activity were twofold: first that union responses to, and hence potential influence over, proposed changes to systems of service delivery were often negative, hostile to, or at least cautious about, change; and second, that service-related issues often were transformed into employment-related issues (job security, earnings guaran-tees, etc.) since this was the conventional means of getting them into recognised collective bargaining procedures.[1] Even in those cases where unions supported and helped develop changes in the delivery of public services it may be argued that they were motivated as much by a union organisational logic as by support for the reforms as such.[2]

Such a reactive, organisationally often conservative approach, almost inevit-ably led to tensions between the unions and those interested in change and improvement. In particular it led to problems in the construction of potentially progressive alliances between the producers (employees) and the users of public services (the public), since organisations representing the latter all too often saw unions as obstacles to beneficial change rather than potential co-champions. Ironically it was the public service cuts of the late 1970s and then, more dramatically, the Thatcher governments' assault on public service provisions that started to change this. As Fryer notes (1989: 49), the focus of disputes started to shift into significant areas of public policy such as 'private medicine and pay beds, hospital closures, public expenditure, public ownership, fuel and social policy'. More significant perhaps, even than the shift into new areas of concern was a gradual coming-together of ideas and then organisations between those who provided services and those who used them, most especially as campaigns to protect the social services meshed with those to protect jobs and, later, to keep public services in the public sector, a demand linked to union concerns to protect members' terms and conditions of employment threatened by privatisation (see Carpenter, 1996: 128–9). One important consequence of the privatisation drives of the 1980s was to create common ground between producers and users.

Even these alliances, however, were forged in a shared determination to *resist* unpopular change. In this context the unions' traditional armoury of collective demonstrations, backed up on occasion by strikes and other forms of collective action, were appropriate, since the objective was to draw public and press atten-tion to attacks on public services and in consequence to challenge the govern-ment's purpose. Such action was often successful in rallying public support, less so in deflecting the government. However, as Carpenter makes clear, out of these experiences, themselves rooted in a longer tradition of union support for public service, emerged what he calls a 'new public service unionism' (Carpenter, 1996: 129).

The new public service unionism has . . . achieved more than the necessary exposure of the negative features of Conservative policies and a check upon government power. Unions like UNISON have also recognised the need to respond to the government's restructuring of the welfare state by addressing the oppressive and sometimes abusive features of health and welfare services in the past and constructing alternative visions of how public services could be organised in the future.

(Carpenter, 1996: 129)

Such ambitious claims are echoed in Martin's recent assertion that public service unions, rather than managers and politicians are now the 'leading advocates' of changes in service provision, and that their proposed reforms are rooted in their own agenda of reconciling their members' interests with those of users (Martin, 1997: 16–18). It is clear that unions such as UNISON wish and intend to pursue such objectives (see Carpenter, 1994 for a good example of how UNISON is trying to continue the traditions of its predecessor unions in the area of community care), rather than to narrow their activities down to negotiating terms and conditions of employment.

However, the tactic most frequently associated with British public sector unions in this regard has been the organisation of public protest against service quality deterioration. In particular in the 1980s unions succeeded in developing broad coalitions with groups of concerned citizens to protest against cuts. In these cases the interests of employees and users of services were united in *defensive* coalitions designed to block proposed change. Here, by contrast, I am concerned with the potential ability of unions (on their own or in collaboration with others) to *initiate* change in pursuit of improved service quality, or at least to be able to develop their own agenda in response to managerial proposals, and most especially to do so at the point of service delivery, through local, decentralised, initiative. This means, among other things, examining the process unions have traditionally deployed to advance their members' interests, namely acting as their agent in collective bargaining with employers.[3] To examine whether such relationships between unions and employers could be used by unions as a vehicle for the improvement of service quality it is useful to summarise what is known about relevant recent such union activities, both in the UK and in other continental European countries where challenging new ideas are taking shape.

Evidence from northern European experience

The citing of examples of 'best practice' from countries with dissimilar structures and histories as a background to evaluating UK experience is problematic, and any inferences should be treated with caution. In part this is because they may well represent exceptional cases in their own countries but more especially because of the exceptionalism of UK public sector experience over the last two decades. Thus, while Ferner notes a widespread European tendency towards the emergence of a generalised commercialism within public service delivery and a consequent restructuring of public service provision, he stresses that the UK is at one extreme of the European spectrum, where the Thatcherite programme 'represents . . . an ideologically-propelled political project of hacking the state down to size, and with it the allegedly over-powerful public sector trade unions' (Ferner, 1994: 65). In other European countries, by contrast 'modernisation of the state has been pragmatic, gradualist, accomplished with labour rather than against it, often going hand-in-hand with the consolidation of pluralist industrial relations institutions within the state'. To this might be added that, at least in respect of the permanence and status of those 'industrial relations instiutions' marked differences could be noted between the UK and mainland northern European countries, even before 1979.

Despite these reservations concerning the appropriateness of comparisons, it is useful to search European experience for examples of initiatives that may be relevant to UNISON for the future. The starting point is Martin's recent summary overview of trade union engagement in reforms in local government in various European countries. His argument, based on case studies of four local authorities in northern European countries (Tilburg in the Netherlands, Hagen in Germany, Frederiksborg in Denmark and Malung in Sweden) is that even within the context of declining resources and job losses, unions have shown their ability to influence in important ways the reorganisation of work and the delivery of services. Indeed, he makes a stronger claim, namely that 'the key ingredient of efficiency and quality improvement is the genuine empowerment of front-line public service employees' (Martin, 1997: 16), a process which he implies requires the effective involvement of trade unions through appropriate consultation machinery. Hegewisch and Larsen (1994: 2) confirm that a central theme in mainland European approaches to reforming public service provision was collaboration with trade unions; the UK was the major exception in their European survey.

The most radical example of such developments appears to be the Swedish (see also Higgins, 1996: 166; Andersen *et al.*, 1997). In that country the public service union SKAF (*Kommunal*) developed a model for the reform of service provision through direct employee engagement in the analysis of their work, allocating responsibility, and looking at training, assessment and reward systems. Martin notes that

> under the [SKAF] approach, when a decision has been taken to set up a project in a workplace, all the employees are informed and then divided into groups of between 8 and 12 people, each with an appointed leader. Then the groups spend as long as 10 months analysing their organisation, identifying its strengths and weaknesses and finding ways to build on the former and eradicate the latter.
>
> (Martin, 1997: 27)

So successful has the project been that the union has established its own consultancy firm, linked to its training programmes and has succeeded in extending the initiative to 60 municipalities. Higgins claims also that the initiative successfully incorporated a significant equalisation of treatment and working conditions of men and women, as part of *Kommunal*'s wider initiatives in this area. He argues that the approach involved 'an ongoing, interactive process between the worker collective, responsible organs of local government . . . and the local community' (Higgins, 1996: 183). In short, it provides an example of the integrative potential of the concept of quality linking service producers' and users' interests through initiatives that address both service quality and the quality of working life.

A number of comments are worth making about this initiative. First, that the union committed 20 million kronor to developing the project, a financial commitment beyond the reach of any UK trade union. Second that any decentralisation over decision-making has taken place 'within the limits of the framework agreements concluded at centralised level . . . the threat of fragmentation . . . is limited by the need to act within the constraints of the centrally-determined framework' (Andersen *et al.*, 1997: 52). Third, related to this, that the union structures in countries such as Sweden are such that 'union workplace representatives – in contrast to British shop stewards – are wholly integrated into the national unions and their branches' (Kjellberg, 1998: 77). Finally, the union's involvement and approach are firmly located within an acceptance of the need significantly to cut costs, and their success in doing this is almost certainly the main reason for the widespread adoption by employers of the approach.

The other examples cited by Martin, though in different ways less radical and all-encompassing in their approach, provide useful insights into recent developments. At Tilburg in Germany the decentralisation of decision-making has been used to enhance employee influence over and involvement in work processes but has led to mutual recrimination between employers and unions that each was acting in too bureaucratic and centralised a manner. In Hagen, also in Germany, the ÖTV public service union, together with the Hans Böckler Foundation organised an 'action research' programme to show how their policies could be applied in practice. The outcome was a 'one-stop shop', open 45 hours a week, providing citizens with a 10-minute response to queries. For employees the major innovation was their own direct involvement in the organisation of their working time and patterns within the framework set by the collective agreement. In Frederiksborg the FOA union appointed national consultants to work alongside local hospital management and local employee representatives to redesign ancillary services such as cleaning and portering into new flexible work teams (Martin, 1997: 25) which have had the (intended) consequence of raising the status of women employees and, at the same time, intruding painfully into the cosy work and pay regimes previously enjoyed by the male porters.

These examples provide further evidence of the importance of the characteristic features of labour relations and union organisation summarised for the case of Malung in Sweden: the investment of union time and money; the integrated nature of national–local union relationships; and, although not described in detail, the circumscribing institutional framework of (national) collective agreements setting limits on local adaptation along with the legal rights to consultation and information enjoyed by employees or unions. To this list we can add the positive relationship between successful decentralisation and the presence of a strong system of co-determination (Hegewisch and Larsen, 1994: 4–5). While these examples come from different countries it has been argued that the similarities of labour market regime for the public sector in most Northern European countries outweigh any minor differences (Andersen *et al.*, 1997: 57) and that such initiatives can be treated as a similar phenomenon. The contrast with the deregulated UK environment is clear.

But one intriguing and important finding that emerges from both the Malung and the Frederiksborg examples, and which may provide opportunities also in the UK, is the radicalising potential of *gender* issues both with regard to work reorganisation and to union structure and representation in sectors and unions numerically dominated by women but with persistent patterns of segregation and disadvantage.[4]

The UK

As noted above, Ferner draws a sharp distinction between the experience of the UK and of other European countries with regard to the restructuring of public services and in particular of their labour relations. Andersen *et al.* follow this by arguing that the UK experience is not really comparable to that of any other European country.[5] The scale and speed of the changes are part of this, but the UK differs also by virtue of the overt political hostility towards public services as such, and towards the collective institutions that regulated employment relations within them. One further consequence was reduction in the priority often attached by local management to collective bargaining, consultation and other relationships with unions as useful tools in change management. The engagement of unions in responding to Compulsory Competitive Tendering (CCT) in local government and the NHS, vital though it was, effectively tied the unions into 'conservative' forms of concession bargaining, with the preservation of jobs and protection against deterioration in members' conditions of employment inevitably and understandably given highest priority. Opportunities for innovative developments exploring novel approaches to improved quality provision through new forms of co-operation and involvement were simply not on the agenda. Martin, contrasting the northern European examples cited earlier with the case of Lewisham, describes the latter as characterised by job loss, CCT, and flatter managerial structures, overall leading to a situation in which all were working harder for marginal pay improvements, with consequent declines in employee morale and goodwill. However, he asserts that by comparison with the northern European examples the key issue is not enhanced workload but lack of employee involvement such that 'the reorganised workload in the German and Danish cases may be greater than in Lewisham but the employees appear happier [in the former] because they are more in control of their time' (Martin, 1997: 30). This assertion is confirmed by Martinez Lucio and MacKenzie (1999: 156) who argue that the new management practices associated with the quality agenda have 'contributed to changes in the basic trust relations that have historically underpinned relations between employees, union and management'. In particular, they argue that employee autonomy in work and control over work have been reduced as quality management techniques have enhanced managerial control of the labour process (Martinez Lucio and MacKenzie, 1999: 160). It appears from these studies that mistrust and conflict – latent or overt – remain characteristic features of the UK situation, exacerbated by the emphasis on quality, despite the formal commitment of all to its improvement.

Part of the reason for the widespread low trust lies in the nature of the processes used during the 1980s and 1990s allegedly to drive up service quality in the UK. CCT and its related processes effectively equated quality to the users of services with cheapness, and hence with deteriorating conditions of employment and intensification of work. Kirkpatrick and Martinez Lucio (1995: 25–6) argue that the Conservative governments of the 1980s used the notion of quality both as a lever to force fundamental reform in the organisation and management of the public sector and to use it as a means of getting more for less. Principled union opposition, however difficult to maintain in practice, was a logical response and one which in addition was capable of mobilising significant public support in defence of public services and against privatisation. However, while successful as a mobilising and publicity vehicle, the national campaigns against privatisation had at best only limited local impact. As Foster and Scott (1998: 11) note, 'below national level these [campaigns] . . . were embraced by relatively fewer members than officials anticipated. . . . The serious impact of CCT on members' economic position deterred their active participation in politically-orientated initiatives'. The national campaigns therefore, while successful in their own terms, appear to have been at best only a secondary stimulus for local organisation and activity. In addition, and of greater significance for this article, they do not obviously lend themselves to the development and pursuit of a more *proactive* union approach towards the improvement of service quality and of members' employment conditions.

However, it is possible that more recent developments provide at least the beginning of such an opportunity. It has become clear that 'marketisation', CCT, and the other initiatives of the Thatcher era no longer enjoy the political and managerial support of the past. However, in the UK as well as in other European countries the importance of the quality of public service provision is a recurring theme, and to that end local authorities and others have become increasingly preoccupied with the principles of total quality management (TQM) and similar concepts imported perhaps in imitation of the private sector.[6] Among private sector unions there is increasing interest in the opportunities these new techniques may provide for enhanced employee and union influence over work organisation and performance, although this is hedged about with problems and uncertainties (see Fisher, 1995).

In principle, such initiatives as TQM and BS5750 should provide an opportunity for unions such as UNISON, with its strong commitment to service quality improvement, to develop its own quality-related agenda for local debate. The union's guidelines on TQM (Poynter, 1997) hint at the possible benefits of staff involvement for improving 'morale and job satisfaction', but generally the tone is studiously neutral, and the advice to branches on responding to such initiatives in general is cautious and defensive. This is entirely understandable, since there is no doubt that such initiatives can pose significant threats to workplace union organisation (although this is often more implicit than explicit) and conceal significant increases in workload and/or deterioration in conditions of employment. But equally the question must be raised as to whether managerial and government preoccupation with quality, at present represented in TQM initiatives, provides an opportunity for a proactive union engagement, seeking improvement for members and service users alike.

A study by Fitzgerald *et al.* (1996) of a UNISON local authority branch response to TQM introduction provides some interesting clues. They note a 'general welcome' from shop stewards for such ideas, in particular because the local authority concerned had involved the local branch in quality-related discussions. Roper's fieldwork confirms that UNISON members shared the view that 'quality management is an issue that management and staff can come together on' (Roper, 1999: 4). Despite this, Fitzgerald and his colleagues note both that there was no evidence of a coherent union policy on quality, and that the issue had not been properly discussed at the branch. No policy had been developed and no real moves were being made towards trying to thrash one out. Indeed, it appeared that such union involvement as did take place was largely at the instigation of management, and that the patchy nature of such engagement reflected managerial variation in how they chose to implement quality-related initiatives. It is worth noting that this case study was done in 'a sympathetic Labour-controlled council which shared the union's antipathy to privatisation and decentralisation' (Fitzgerald *et al.*, 1996: 127), operating a 'well-organised industrial relations framework', and involving an effective and self-confident branch of UNISON, arguably the most auspicious environment then and now available in the UK for the promotion of positive, proactive, union policies. But even there the union response was uncertain and muted. Roper found much the same: a quality agenda dominated by managerial preoccupation, an uncertain and suspicious response from UNISON branches, and a suspicion that one consequence of quality initiatives was a weakening of unions' representative capacity, by shifting their preoccupation from members' needs to managerial policy (Roper, 1999: 4).

Roper concludes with a comment that should be taken up as a challenge by unions, managers and governments concerned with public service quality.

> Quality management, in a public service context, could be considered an ideal vehicle for social partnership: unions, managers, political representatives and user groups could all be identified as being stakeholders, able to define the nature and application of quality.
>
> (Roper, 1999: 5)

The evidence of this happening in practice, in the light of case studies such as those reported above, is limited. The most obvious reason for this is the domination of the quality agenda by a political interpretation that defines quality exclusively in terms of presumed user ('customer') needs whose enforced implementation in a context of financial stringency, almost always leads to a deterioration in employment and working conditions. Quality for consumers has meant its opposite to public service employees. This generally gloomy picture notwithstanding, other developments may indicate the gradual emergence of a differently-focused quality agenda. By far the most optimistic-sounding reports involving UNISON in quality-related developments come out of NHS initiatives sponsored by the King's Fund and UNISON to investigate the contribution of staff and their organisations to the modernising of the health service and associated changes in service delivery (see IRS, 1997: 4 for a summary). Described as a 'genuine and open partnership between management and staff' these seek, among other things, to structure relationships between local management, staff, and union representatives in such a way as to separate the 'confrontational' issues such as pay and conditions, from allegedly more consensual ones such as reskilling and multiskilling in order to allow these 'to be discussed more creatively and successfully'. This has significant echoes of the northern European examples outlined above, in that it involves both collaboration with external experts and a separation of the 'conflictual' distributional negotiations over pay from the (allegedly) more consensual processes relating to work and its organisation. It will be of the greatest interest to see how this develops, since earlier examples suggest that such initiatives are rarely sustained in the context of British industrial relations. One possible set of reasons for this directly relevant to the challenges facing UNISON will be explored below.

The limitations of branch-based organisation in dealing with the quality agenda

Fitzgerald and his colleagues focus on the branch as the necessary and logical organisational unit for the effective articulation of issues relating to quality, although in effect they blame the national leadership for 'failing to develop a co-ordinated national, regional and local response that deals with restructuring as a whole rather than as a series of disconnected threats' (Fitzgerald *et al.*, 1996: 126). Later on they add that local union representatives will be unlikely to give a high priority to issues of quality at times when 'CCT, local bargaining, defending jobs and organising unified branches are all more immediately pressing issues' (ibid., 1996: 127). On this slightly contradictory view, branches are encountering problems both as a consequence of a failure of national leadership and because they and their members do not attach as much importance to them as to other, more 'immediate' issues.

In this section I want to suggest that there may be more fundamental issues confronting union branches and shop steward organisation than lack of leadership in tackling issues of public service quality; in particular that they may require both a more complex articulation of the relationships between branch and other levels of union organisation, and a degree of local union stability and security greater than presently available in the UK. At the same time it must be acknowledged that the primary responsibility for the content and context of management-union relationships in the 1980s and 1990s has been that of management and this is not being discounted. However, for the present it is issues of union organisation and policy that are of particular interest.

At the time of the creation of UNISON there was an explicit commitment to the development of shop steward-based form of branch organisation, within a general framework of large, well-resourced branches capable of providing professional expertise and service to members. In the context of the logic of devolution and decentralisation within public services, as well as the expanding role of stewards within the three partner unions over the previous 20 years or so, this was a sensible and coherent strategy. At the same time the union argued the need for an expanded form of 'partnership' between branches and regional and national officials, although the nature and content of this partnership were never fully developed, at least partly because this was an issue on which the unions differed (see Terry, 1996).

I have argued elsewhere that despite their self-evident strengths, in particular the democractic mandate derived from their closeness to members, shop stewards and their organisations also have limitations that need to be recognised. Two in particular are of concern here. First it can be argued that this very closeness results in a prioritising of immediate concerns relating to pay and conditions that preoccupy all employees on a day-to-day basis ('economism') at the expense of longer-term, more strategic issues (for a fuller discussion see Terry, 1994). One plausible interpretation is that branch organisation acting in isolation may experience problems in translating members' interests in issues relating to quality into worked-through and plausible policies, since by their nature they require both expertise and a long-term planning horizon, neither needed to anything like the same extent in the handling of pay and conditions. The emphasis placed in the northern European experiences above on training, expertise, time and, above all, the integration of local structures (union and management) into wider structures and policies indicates qualities that are all generally lacking in the UK.[7] In the UK, local emphasis on distributive, 'zero-sum' issues tends in turn to be reflected in bargaining and systems of union-management relationships that focus on the resolution of disagreement and potential conflict rather than on facilitating consensus.

This leads to the second point, the organisational vulnerability of workplace organisation in a system that provides no legal rights, and consequently makes local unions, in public as well as private sectors, dependent on management both for their continuing recognition and for the provision of information. This makes for a form of unionism, especially in times of general weakness, that in times of challenge is conservative ('defence of the status quo') and risk-averse in its dealings with managers and employers. New ideas, or radical challenges to a managerially defined quality agenda constitute risks that could lead to marginalisation or, at worst, union derecognition. In such circumstances the best guarantee of union stability might appear to be a degree of quiescence. One consequence is that, in comparison with their counterpart organisations in Scandinavia and Germany in particular, UK shop steward-based organisations tend to be reactive and defensive rather than proactive and innovative, and this is often as true of local government as it appears to be of private manufacturing industry (Terry, 1995).

The challenges for UNISON

Since the central purpose of this chapter is to argue the need for public service unions to develop and advance a quality-related agenda, both to articulate membership interests and to create a platform for alliances designed to influence local and national political agenda, it is necessary to address these apparent organisational shortcomings and possible alternatives. Important though resources, financial and other, clearly are in this respect, they are not the most pressing problems unions should be addressing (not least because few trade unions today, including UNISON, are wealthy organisations). Rather, unions should be considering, as suggested above, the reasons for the limited repertoire available to decentralised union structures, and, related to this, to the discretion that employers and managers have over the status, role and hence the responses and activities of trade unions. Union branches operating under the perceived threat of marginalisation or derecognition are unlikely to develop imaginative and challenging strategies. Martinez Lucio and MacKenzie (1999: 168–9) argue that some activists have already used 'the language of performance measurement . . . in quite innovative ways'. In the main this has been deployed in the context of forging defensive alliances with user and citizen groups; the challenge is to move into a more proactive engagement within the same alliances.

In considering the first of these we run up against an issue which – in UNISON as in many other British unions – is one of internal union politics and ideology as much as of material resources, namely the relationships of authority and discretion between local (branch) and other organisational levels of the union. While the concept of 'partnership' between branches and other organisational levels was endorsed as part of the UNISON merger agreement, for ex-NALGO activists in particular the relationship remained couched in terms of 'boundaries' or autonomous spheres of influence, retaining as far as possible the traditions of 'branch autonomy' (see Terry, 1996) rather than as an active integration. The celebration of the autonomy of branch or shop steward organisations from the 'bureaucracy' as the rest of the union is often unhelpfully labelled, is a characteristic and understandable feature of many British trade unions, but an increasing number of studies suggest that such autonomous activity is insufficient to deal with the new problems. In particular, the resources, expertise and capacity for long-term strategic thinking necessary for the development of an employee-centred position on issues such as quality of work and quality of service are rarely available to branch-level organisations, even those as well-resourced as UNISON's. In addition they are, inevitably, continually subject to membership pressures to prioritise more immediate, economistic, issues. Such information as we have suggests that should UNISON wish to pick up issues relating to the quality of services in ways comparable to those developed in other countries of northern Europe, it can only do so through developing greater strategic and organisational interaction between the branch and the wider union.

Second, the examples suggest that UNISON, and indeed all unions, might need to work at a political level for the establishment of a legal framework that provides greater security for workplace-based union structures and their activists. The recently introduced legal right to union recognition, which UNISON supports, although arguing it should be stronger, provides one such element. But what of the prospect of a so-called 'Works Council Directive' aimed at providing employee rights to information and consultation and enshrined in law? UNISON is opposed to this, seeing it as a threat to the 'single channel' of trade union representation. But in the present political and managerial climate is such opposition appropriate? With appropriate organisation UNISON should be the most powerful staff actor on such bodies, which might provide, as they appear to do in other European countries, opportunities for engagement with quality issues without being dependent upon management for information, often after plans have been developed. Such protections and rights could facilitate an environment within which branch members can develop responses to and independent proposals for, quality-related issues. Even though this might be helpful, however, the northern European examples suggest that it may not be sufficient, since all those suggested a degree of strategic integration in the design and implementation between members and branch activists on the one hand and national bodies and resources on the other. Here, the argument is that such an integration is necessary at least in the specific context of developing union responses directed at service quality improvement, at least if that is going to be built around more imaginative ways of working than out of work intensification and stress.[8]

Even if conditions such as these might be satisfied, what might provide the dynamic within UNISON to more from reactive to proactive intervention around the quality agenda? One agenda item of central importance to UNISON is the importance of gendered issues within both the union and the workplace. As several of the examples cited make clear (see in particular the Swedish case in Higgins, 1996) there are important and intimate reciprocal relationship between union initiatives to restructure work, and the representation of women's interests by unions. At least the rhetoric of developments such as TQM, containing ideas of devolved discretion, job rotation, enhanced skills, teamworking, and the breaking-down of established barriers and patterns, contains the possibility of improving the position of those traditionally in relatively disdvantageous, poorly paid, low-skilled, employment, often predominantly women. As such, as the German example shows, they may be resisted by men who find their previous relatively protected and privileged positions affected by teamworking and job rotation principles. It may be that the rhetoric of quality provides bargaining opportunities within the context of the development of equal opportunities policies that could be taken up by the committees within UNISON responsible for setting such agendas.

UNISON faces a significant challenge in its efforts to take up the quality agenda within public services, in particular at the point of delivery, and in doing so respond to the long-standing membership interest in enhancing the quality of service they provide and in improving the quality of their own working lives. To do so, as argued at the start, constitutes a continuing tradition within public service unionism that UNISON is committed to maintain. But it is equally a challenge for public service managers and the politicians, national and local, concerned with the quality of our public services. For no union initiative, however well-informed, can withstand managerial indifference or hostility, not least because quality is rarely an issue around which members are easily mobilised into strong action. If managers want, as they frequently claim, a modern trade union engaged with issues of quality, they have to provide an environment in which unions have the necessary resources and self-confidence.

Acknowledgement

I am grateful to Anne McBride for a number of useful suggestions that have been incorporated into this paper.

Notes

1   This process is, of course, not unique to the public sector. On the relatively rare occasions that private sector unions have tried to influence managerial decisions over such issues as the nature of work and, even more radically, the products their members make, they have been either ignored or rebutted.
2   Carpenter (1994: 41–2) argues that NUPE's support for the Jay proposals for helping people with learning difficulties owed as much to the organisational fillip it gave them *vis-à-vis* COHSE and the RCN as to their enthusiasm for the reforms.
3   More 'political' processes such as seeking to influence Labour Party policy, direct lobbying, etc., although clearly a part of any overall strategy, will not be examined here. For a discussion of relationships with the Labour Party and current government see the chapters by Sawyer and Carpenter in this volume.
4   Anne McBride's chapter in this volume illustrates the efforts made by UNISON to ensure effective participation by women in the government of UNISON, while making clear that this has not yet led to the effective representation of their *interests*.
5   They also argue that, for a variety of reasons, the UK experience is highly unlikely to be repeated in other European countries (Andersen *et al.*, 1997: 57).
6   The most recent of these is perhaps the 'best value' initiative which, it might be claimed, provides evidence of a specifically public service focus on quality rather than one 'imported' from the private sector.
7   Kelly and Heery (1994: 204) make a similar point in asserting that in confronting a new and radical agenda, unions require more, rather than less, centralisation.
8   This is not an uncontroversial claim. In particular Fairbrother (1996), in developing his recent arguments concerning the possibility of union renewal in the public service unions, argues in effect that a combination of the new managerialism and *enhanced* union branch autonomy (a reduction in the role of central/regional union structures) provide the necessary basis for renewed local activity. My argument is that, even if this were plausible with regard to issues such as pay and conditions, it would be insufficient for the development of strategies related to the nature, organisation and control of work – and hence service quality and delivery.

References

Andersen, S. K., Due, J. and Madsen, J. S. (1997) 'Multi-track approach to public-sector restructuring in Europe: impact on employment relations; role of trade unions', *Transfer*, 3(1): 34–61.

Batstone, E., Ferner, A. and Terry, M. (1984) *Consent and Efficiency: Labour Relations and Management Strategy in the State Enterprise*, Oxford: Blackwell.

Beaumont, P. (1992) *Public Sector Industrial Relations*, London: Routledge.

Carpenter, M. (1994) *Normality is Hard Work: Trade Unions and the Politics of Community Care*, London: Lawrence and Wishart.

Carpenter, M. (1996) 'Beyond "us and them": trade unions and equality in community care for users and workers', in P. Bywaters and E. McLeod (eds) *Working for Equality in Health*, London: Routledge.

Fairbrother, P. (1996) 'Workplace trade unionism in the state sector', in P. Ackers, C. Smith and P. Smith (eds) *The New Workplace and Trade Unionism*, London: Routledge.

Ferner, A. (1994) 'The state as employer', in R.Hyman and A. Ferner (eds) *New Frontiers In European Industrial Relations*, Oxford: Blackwell.

Fisher, J. (1995) 'The trade union response to HRM in the UK: the case of the TGWU', *Human Resource Management Journal*, 5(3): 7–23.

Fitzgerald, I., Rainnie, A. and Stirling, J. (1996) 'Coming to terms with quality: UNISON and the restructuring of local government', *Capital and Class*, 59: 103–134.

Foster, D. and Scott, P. (1998) 'Conceptualising union responses to contracting out municipal services 1979–97', *Industrial Relations Journal*, 29(2): 112–25.

Fryer, R. (1989) ' Public service trade unionism in the twentieth century', in R. Mailly, S. J. Dimmock and A. S. Sethi (eds) *Industrial Relations in the Public Services*, London: Routledge.

Hegewisch, A. and Larsen, H. H. (1994) 'European developments in public sector human resource management', *Cranfield School of Management Working Papers*, No. 10/94.

Higgins, W. (1996) 'The Swedish Municipal Workers' Union – a study in the political unionism', *Economic and Industrial Democracy*, 17: 167–97.

IRS (1997) 'Joint management-union initiative to take place in the NHS', *IRS Employment Trends*, 637 (August): 4.

Kelly, J. and Heery, E. (1994) *Working for the Union: British Trade Union Officers*, Cambridge: Cambridge University Press.

Kirkpatrick, I. and Martinez Lucio, M. (1995) 'The uses of "quality" in the British government's reform of the public sector', in I. Kirkpatrick and M. Martinez Lucio (eds) *The Politics of Quality in the Public Sector*, London: Routledge.

Kjellberg, A. (1998) 'Sweden: restoring the model?', in A. Ferner and R. Hyman (eds) *Changing Industrial Relations in Europe*, Oxford: Blackwell.

Mailly, R., Dimmock, S. J. and Sethi, A. S. (eds) (1989) *Industrial Relations in the Public Services*, London: Routledge.

Martin, B. (1997) 'Delivering the goods – trade unions and public sector reform', *Transfer*, 3(1): 14–33.

Martinez Lucio, M. and MacKenzie, R. (1999) 'Quality management: a new form of control?', in S. Corby and G. White (eds) *Employee Relations in the Public Services: Themes and Issues*, London: Routledge.

Poynter, M. (1997) *UNISON Guide to Human Resource Management*, London: UNISON. Online at HTTP: http://www.UNISON.org/polres/hrmguide.htm (14 April 1998).

Roper, I. (1999) '"Quality is something that unions and management can come together on": or is it? Trade union strategy and "partnership" in local government', paper presented to the British Universities' Industrial Relations Association Annual Conference, De Montfort University, 1–3 July.

Terry, M. (1994) 'Workplace unionism: redefining structures and objectives', in R. Hyman and A. Ferner (eds) *New Frontiers in European Industrial Relations*, Oxford: Blackwell.

Terry, M. (1995) 'Trade unions: shop stewards and the workplace', in P. K. Edwards (ed.) *Industrial Relations: Theory and Practice in Britain*, Oxford: Blackwell.

Terry, M. (1996) 'Negotiating the government of UNISON: union democracy in theory and practice', *British Journal of Industrial Relations*, 34(1): 87–110.

17 Towards an organising model in UNISON?

A trade union membership strategy in transition

Jeremy Waddington and Allan Kerr

Between 1979 and 1998 trade union membership in Britain fell from 12.6 million to 7.1 million and employment density from 56 per cent to 30 per cent (Waddington, 1992; Bland, 1999). The extent and rate of this decline reawakened interest among trade unionists in the different approaches to the recruitment, retention and organisation of members. As the period of decline lengthened, emphasis among trade unionists shifted away from explanations based on movements in economic indicators, the terms of legislation and the activities of employers, which had dominated debates during the 1970s and 1980s. Instead, greater attention was directed towards the measures that trade unionists could implement to stem, if not reverse, the decline. The debate on the most appropriate approach to the recruitment and organisation of potential members centred on the relative merits and limitations of the servicing model and the organising model. This debate took a similar course to that in Australia and the United States, where long-term membership decline has also contributed to a loss of union influence (Gahan, 1997; Bronfenbrenner *et al.*, 1998).

This chapter addresses the terms of this debate by reference to the development of a membership strategy in UNISON. It shows that UNISON initially pursued elements of both the servicing and organising models in parallel. Survey evidence illustrated that UNISON members expressed interests consistent with the organising model and identified the issues on which members sought improvements if the organising model was to be implemented. Where local organisation failed, members cite this failure as a reason for leaving the union. Wide-ranging changes were thus introduced in order to move to a target-driven version of the organising model in which servicing provisions were directed to the support of organising.

The chapter serves two additional purposes. It demonstrates that there is a false dichotomy drawn between the servicing and organising models. In particular, it argues that a prerequisite for the successful introduction of the organising model is the development of greater articulation between the different levels of union activity.[1] Failure to achieve such articulation is likely either to result in the isolation of workplace organisation and difficulties in the aggregation of members' interests, or in the bureaucratisation of union activities. The chapter shows that services and support provided from outside the workplace are essential to maintain articulation and, hence, operate the organising model. It also reviews the practices associated with the particular form of articulation employed by UNISON in the development of its membership strategy.

This is also a chapter about post-merger adjustment and the role of research in this process. UNISON has moved from pre-merger intention to address actual practice in the recruitment, retention and organisation of members. This process has involved the union in an extensive programme of research intended initially to discover the situation in the localities and latterly to monitor the impact of reforms. The interplay between research and policy innovation illustrates further interconnections between the servicing and organising models, and the range of post-merger adjustments required to establish a single, unified organising culture within UNISON.

To these ends the chapter comprises four sections. The first section sketches the nature of the debate concerning the servicing model and organising model, and outlines the initial approach of UNISON towards the two models. The second section outlines the survey method used in the research. The third section presents the data. The final section reviews the reforms that have been embarked upon in the light of these data. It thus illustrates the relationship between research and the development of a membership strategy in a major union. The technical details associated with the distribution of the surveys are found in Appendix A.

Servicing, organising or a bit of both?

There are two broad approaches to the development of union activity, the servicing model and the organising model. Although these two approaches are often presented as polar opposites, they are not mutually exclusive and tend to be pursued as complementary features of a trade union membership strategy. The distinction between the two models is thus analytical rather than practical. In reviewing the two approaches, this section highlights the different relations between workplace and wider union activities in the two approaches and argues that these relations are key to the implementation of a successful membership strategy based on the organising model. This section also reviews the initial position adopted by UNISON towards recruitment, retention and organisation. Data presented in a subsequent section allow examination of this initial position by reference to the views of UNISON members.

The servicing and organising models

The servicing model relies on initiatives from within official trade union structures. Trade union officers, rather than lay representatives,[2] provide support to members who encounter problems. Support is thus provided externally to workplace organisation. As such, the servicing model places an enormous burden on those within official trade union structures to undertake these duties. The reliance on official union structures in the servicing model is also associated with the development of national unions into service organisations. Implicit in this is the development of a union bureaucracy engaged in formal committee work and the top-down formulation and implementation of policy. As disciplinary and grievance procedures become more formal and legal, there is also a tendency for union officials to assume responsibility for individual cases, particularly at stages where more legal procedures predominate (Hurd, 1998). These developments tend to further distance those operating within official structures from their counterparts in the localities.

A traditional feature of the servicing model is the provision of industrial benefits, membership services, professional services and education services. Such services require no union presence at the workplace and tend to be reliant on a customer or client relationship between member and union. Commentators have suggested that this approach be extended if British trade unions are to adapt to a 'new individualism' (Bassett and Cave, 1993; Cave, 1994). The introduction of packages of financial services by many British unions during the late 1980s and 1990s, certainly constituted a development of the servicing model (Kelly and Waddington, 1995).

Within the confines of the servicing model the role of the lay representative is relatively restricted. In practice, a lay representative need be nothing more than mail box or distribution point. Passing information 'up' to the local full-time officer or 'down' to the membership are the prime tasks, rather than engagement in local decision-making, policy formulation and campaigning activities. In addition, undertaking branch administration is necessary to maintain a core of branch functions. In these circumstances the relationship between the lay representative and the local full-time officer is relatively straightforward, as the lay representative is responsible for basic administration while the local full-time officer takes responsibility for other issues. Direct contact between lay representatives and local full-time officers on the one hand, and members on the other, need not be extensive in order to ensure the 'delivery' of the union service. Furthermore, membership participation is not a prerequisite for the delivery of the union service. In short, there is no requirement for an articulated relationship between members, lay representatives and local full-time officers.

The decentralisation of bargaining, the proliferation of small sites of employment and the relatively small number of full-time officers employed by British trade unions, have led many unions to accept that the servicing model in its 'ideal' form is no longer viable as a means of supporting members at their place of work. There are insufficient full-time trade union officers to cover the growth in the number of workplaces and bargaining units (IRS, 1993; Kelly and Heery, 1994). Furthermore, emphasis is placed on the servicing of existing members. In times of rapid structural change within the labour force, such an emphasis may result in the defence of existing members to the exclusion of attempts to extend unionisation into the growing areas of employment. This is likely to result in a mismatch between the composition of local full-time officers and potential members. The former are drawn from areas of union strength and are familiar with an agenda appropriate to it, whereas potential members are employed in different areas of the economy where different sets of interests may be prevalent.

In contrast to the servicing model, the organising model rests on the assumption that higher levels of membership participation in union affairs are required if membership decline is to be reversed. An organised union presence at the workplace, an appropriate number of lay representatives and institutions that encourage membership participation throughout all levels of the union are central to the model. A prime task of the wider union is thus to create the circumstances which raise levels of participation among members. In order to establish workplace organisation, support may be required from outside the workplace. Once workplace organisation is in place, however, advocates of the organising model assume that the provision of training and specialist advice are the principal forms of external support provided by the union. (Conrow, 1991; Fletcher and Hurd, 1998). The provision of communications concerning union affairs and 'best practice' is also key to the organising model. The object of such communications is to stimulate participation and to encourage cohesion between members in their disparate workplaces.

Recruitment is often viewed as an isolated activity within the servicing model, conducted primarily by full-time officers. Follow-up activities involving members and measures to promote membership participation tend to be downplayed. In contrast, recruitment, retention and organising are treated as an integrated process within the organising model. The articulation of the relationships between members, lay representatives and local full-time officers is thus key to the operation of the model on three counts. First, representation is not undertaken by either lay representatives or local full-time officers, but is undertaken in co-operation, the terms of the co-operation being dependent upon the level of expertise and training of the lay representatives. Second, as members generate issues and share decision-making and problem-solving responsibilities with lay representatives and local full-time officers, institutions are required to facilitate co-operation on these issues. Third, once an initial union presence has been secured, unionisation of the workplace is the responsibility of members and lay representatives. Liaison between members, lay representatives and local full-time officers to establish the training and support requirements is essential in order to complete these tasks. This is particularly significant with regard to the identification of those facilities that enable the mapping of the workplace in terms of workers' attitudes and the presence of non-members. Whereas the servicing model assumes an essentially administrative relationship between lay representatives and local full-time officers and the dependence of members on servicing from full-time officers, the organising model requires a participative relationship.

The initial position in UNISON

The constituent unions exhibited different pre-merger membership trends. Between 1979 and 1992 the membership of NALGO rose from 735,220 to 764,062 (+3.9 per cent), whereas the membership of COHSE declined from 212,930 to 195,519 (−8.2 per cent) and that of NUPE from 691,770 to 527,403 (−23.8 per cent) (Certification Office, 1981, 1994). NUPE's membership was particularly hard-hit by the impact of privatisation and, in local government, by Compulsory Competitive Tendering (CCT). Over the same period, union density in the two sectors where the majority of UNISON's membership is concentrated also declined; in health from 75.8 per cent to 60.0 per cent, in local government from 77.8 per cent to 61.0 per cent (Waddington, 1992; Bird *et al.*, 1993).[3] Pre-merger membership trends thus sensitised the constituent unions in different ways to the prioritisation of recruitment, retention and organisation, which compounded the differences in culture discussed elsewhere in this volume.[4]

From the outset UNISON adopted elements of both the organising and servicing models, although it should be acknowledged that no explicit reference was made to the two approaches at the time.[5] At Head Office a Services and Development Department took direct responsibility for co-ordinating activities concerning recruitment, retention and organisation. A National Recruitment Plan was developed by the Department in 1995, which comprised membership targets for each of the Regions of the union (UNISON, undated). In addition, the Membership Services Unit developed a package of individual services, marketed as being tailored to the specific needs of UNISON members. Two other departments also influenced the pattern of development towards organising and servicing. The Education and Training Department offered support to the organising model through the provision of specialist training for lay representatives. UNISON also maintained a Communications Department, which is responsible for promoting both the servicing and organising aspects of the union's activities.

At this juncture we outline the principal features of the two approaches as they were laid down in pre-merger plans and as they emerged during the immediate post-merger period, 1993–95. The discussion is necessarily stylised as we are primarily concerned with stated intentions rather than detailed practice. The end-point of 1995 is chosen because it was during this year that the first of the two surveys reported below was conducted and the National Recruitment Plan was announced. Elements of the servicing model were explicitly abandoned during the pre-merger period. In particular, a 'top down' approach was rejected as it prohibited 'membership motivation and commitment'. Instead, it was argued that a 'membership-centred trade unionism' be established for which the crucial tests of success were the creation of structures for participation at local level, including 'membership meetings, steward systems, local communications and the rest of the apparatus of workplace and local organisation' (COHSE, NALGO & NUPE, 1990: 16). No specific blueprint was offered for the form and activities of local organisation, on the understanding that differences between the constituent unions would be resolved in the localities.

The duties of lay representatives were extensive within the new union. In terms of contact with members, they were expected to be in continuous interaction in seeking resolution to members' problems, grievances and queries. It was anticipated that networks of lay representatives would be developed 'sufficiently large and widespread to ensure that members are aware of the presence of the union as a routine factor in their working lives' (COHSE, NALGO & NUPE, 1990: 19). The burden of work falling on lay representatives was also seen as likely to rise, as decentralisation and privatisation were further extended. To mitigate some of the effects of this increasing workload 'new systems of keeping members informed' were envisaged (COHSE, NALGO & NUPE, 1991: 30). This intention was subsequently strengthened when it became a *member's right* 'to receive information about the union and its work on a regular basis and in language and design that can easily be understood' (COHSE, NALGO & NUPE, 1992: 15). The initial intention was thus to meet two key requirements of the organising model; contact between members and lay representatives and the provision of appropriate information.

A raft of measures was also planned to encourage member participation in the new union. These addressed organisation by reference to employer and by reference to the individual characteristics or preferences of the member. The work group was assumed to be the basic unit of the new union (COHSE, NALGO & NUPE, 1991). Regular workgroup meetings, called by either a member or a steward, were the means of participation nearest to the member at his/her workplace. In ascending distance from the workplace were branch, Region, and Service Group meetings. A second strand of opportunity to participate in union activities was developed around the principle of fair representation, which allows proportionality in the composition of committees, conferences and delegations. In UNISON this principle applies throughout. In addition, self-organisation for 'disadvantaged groups' is promoted among women, black members, members with disabilities, and lesbians and gay men to operate at local, branch, regional and national levels. The constitution of the new union thus promoted participation in terms of employer and in terms of individual characteristics and preferences. Our data examine the situation of women within this constitutional framework.[6]

The formation of UNISON also marked a development of the different aspects of the servicing model. During the final year of their independence, the constituent unions of UNISON spent a total of £14,280,000 in benefits to members. On a per member basis, NALGO expenditure (£12.72 per year) was about twice that of COHSE (£6.63 per year) and NUPE (£6.20 per year) (Certification Office, 1994). By 1995 the total expenditure of UNISON on benefits to members had fallen to £9,232,000 (a decline of £5,048,000 or 35.4 per cent) and per capita expenditure had dropped to £6.81 per year, a sum compatible to the pre-merger expenditure levels of COHSE and NUPE. In overall terms, however, expenditure on membership benefits still comprised almost 10 per cent of total expenditure in 1995. Commitment to the provision of membership benefits was not seriously questioned during the merger process. A package of so-called 'rule book' benefits was retained throughout.[7]

Pre-merger discussions committed UNISON to a broader service portfolio.

> Provision of non-work related benefits and services reaches a huge number
> of members who do not normally draw on the traditional services unions

have to offer; reinforcing the benefits of union membership. The provision
of non-work related benefits should be a particular feature of the new union.
(COHSE, NALGO & NUPE, 1991: 13)

This position followed the recommendation of the Special Review Body (SRB) of
the TUC to offer packages of financial services (TUC, 1988). Both UNISON
and the SRB anticipated that packages of financial services would be attractive to
a range of members stretching from the low paid, often working part-time or in
insecure employment, through to relatively high paid professionals. The analysis
underpinning the recommendation referred to the need to adapt to individualism, which was perceived as influencing significant groups of potential members,
and as appealing to the potential member as a consumer.

The adoption of the SRB's recommendations represents an extension of the
servicing model in so far as the packages of financial services were negotiated
with finance companies, administered and distributed by Head Office. Members
were only required to buy into the services in order for them to be effective.
While some commentators tended towards exclusive reliance on the service
model (Bassett and Cave, 1993; Cave, 1994), UNISON envisaged that financial
services would complement other forms of union activity. In other words,
UNISON did not anticipate the abandonment of the organising model in favour
of a service-based approach, but viewed the two as complementary.[8]

During the period following the founding merger, UNISON adopted elements
of both the servicing and the organising approaches. Two elements informed the
servicing model adopted by UNISON. Firstly, the union extended the range of
individual services available to members through the provision of a range of
financial services, intended to supplement the traditional 'rule book' services. A
second aspect of the servicing approach was the continued provision of support
to members at their workplaces by full-time officers. A key contrast was thus the
provision of financial services with the provision of support to members at their
workplaces. The relative efficacy of these two approaches and the viability of the
initial position adopted by UNISON is examined below.

The composition of the surveys

The data presented in the next section draw on two surveys, labelled here as
Survey I and Survey II. Survey I was distributed to UNISON members during
1995, while Survey II was conducted in early 1996 and was directed to those that
had just left UNISON. The technical details associated with these surveys are
outlined in Appendix A.

Survey I asked respondents to rank their reasons for remaining in UNISON
from a pre-selected list containing ten options. On average, each respondent
ranked seven items from this list of ten as constituting their reasons for retention.
The category 'another reason' was included in this list, but received few ranking
points and is thus excluded from the data presented below. The tabulated
data are based on the reasons ranked at positions one or two. This procedure

highlights the principal reasons for membership retention and points to those issues which members prioritise. It is computed by taking the reasons ranked 1 and 2, and expressing the sum of these as a proportion of the total number of respondents. The sum of each column calculated in this manner in Table 17.1 thus equals almost 200 per cent, as most of the respondents ranked more than two issues as underpinning their union membership.

The reasons for retention are considered in two broad categories; collective reasons and individual reasons (see Kelly and Waddington, 1995). Drawing this distinction allows us to examine the different approaches to union organising. Five collective reasons underpin membership retention: 'support should a problem arise at work' (hereafter referred to as mutual support); 'most people at work are members' (peer group); 'I believe in trade unions and want to take part' (belief); 'improved pay and conditions' (pay and conditions); and 'UNISON's national campaigning' (campaigning). While all of these reasons contribute to the operation of the organising model, two are of particular salience to our concerns. The issue of belief is important as it is an indicator of the extent to which existing members are prepared to mobilise in organising activities. Similarly, mutual support is important as it lies at the heart of both the organising model and an aspect of the servicing approach. The key difference between the two approaches lies in the source of the support. Whereas the organising model assumes support from lay representatives, the servicing approach relies on full-time officers to provide the support.

Individual reasons and their specific UNISON variants include: 'membership benefits', such as death, accident and incapacity benefit; 'membership services', such as convalescent home facilities, specialist welfare benefit advice, and counselling on bereavement and debt; 'professional and education services', including indemnity insurance, return to learn and study skills training, and professional and technical qualifications; and financial services, comprising insurance for buildings, house contents and holidays, mortgage discounts, credit card facilities, car rescue services and shopping discounts. Individual reasons thus underpin aspects of the servicing model.

The distinction between collective and individual reasons is not clear-cut. For example, mutual support is individual in that it is usually a single member who is advised or represented by a workplace representative. Yet mutual support also has a collective element in so far as it is collective union organisation that enables workplace representatives to provide mutual support, often within a framework of collectively negotiated procedures. For the purposes of this chapter mutual support is regarded as collective, as it is only through collective representation that the member can be supported by a union at the workplace (see, for example, Sapper, 1991; Kerr, 1992; Waddington and Whitston, 1997). Survey I thus examines members' views towards the different features of the organising and servicing models using data disaggregated by sex, and relies on the distinction between collective and individual reasons in analysing union retention.

Following van de Vall (1970) three features of internal union organisation are used in Survey II to examine why people leave UNISON: structural motives, where membership is seen as expensive compared to the benefits secured therefrom; functional motives, such as the provision of inadequate support to members in the workplace; and policy motives, comprising objections to leadership, policy or principles of the union. While the distinction between these internal factors is important, it should be noted that van der Vall's research was conducted during the 1960s in Holland, when economic and political circumstances were different to those prevailing in the UK at the time of our research. In particular, we assume that union leaving is also influenced by high rates of job turnover and redundancy. In other words, we accept van der Vall's differentiation of the internal reasons for union leaving, but add to them external factors over which UNISON has very little direct influence. Included among the external reasons are retirement and redundancy. It is the impact of the internal reasons on union leaving with which we are centrally concerned, as these are the issues over which the union can exert marked influence and are key to the implementation of the organising model.

Presenting the data

The data presented below examine the initial position on retention and organisation established by UNISON in the period following the founding merger to 1995 in four stages. The first stage examines members' views towards individual member services. It thus assesses the efficacy of this particular aspect of the servicing model as a tool for membership retention. The second stage considers members' views of three features of workplace organisation, identified by UNISON as being integral to its form of the organising model; union communications, contact between union members and representatives, and access to union meetings. It identifies a number of shortfalls in UNISON's original approach that limited the extent to which the organising model can be adopted. The third stage shows why people leave UNISON. Finally, the fourth stage identifies those aspects of workplace organisation that prompted members to leave. In other words, the fourth stage isolates those areas that require reform if the organising model is to be implemented on a more widespread basis.

Why do members retain UNISON membership?

Table 17.1 shows the reasons for membership retention. Reference to the 'all' column illustrates that collective issues are central to membership retention in that they occupy the first four positions in the ranking. The supposed 'new individualism' does not thus appear to have influenced public sector trade unionists. As only 6.6 per cent of UNISON members report being 'very secure' at work, it seems more likely that uncertainty about their future is a more important factor in retention than a new individualism.[9] There are marked similarities between the results on retention shown in Table 17.1 and results on union joining in the public sector (Kerr, 1992) and more generally (Waddington and Whitston, 1997). A collective reason also occupies the sixth position in the

Table 17.1 Reasons for membership retention in UNISON

Reason for retaining membership	All (%)	Men (%)	Women (%)
Support should a problem arise at work	63.6	60.2 (1)	64.8 (1)
Most people at work are members	40.4	36.4 (3)	41.9 (2)
I believe in trade unions	36.7	42.8 (2)	34.5 (3)
Improved pay and conditions	33.5	34.5 (4)	33.4 (4)
Membership benefits	5.2	6.4 (5)	4.7 (5)
National campaigning	4.1	4.9 (6)	3.9 (6)
Financial services	3.3	4.2 (7)	2.9 (7=)
Professional services	2.9	3.0 (8)	2.9 (7=)
Membership services	1.8	1.9 (9)	1.7 (9)
	$N=997$	$N=264$	$N=724$

ranking. The failure of members to attach importance to campaigning indicates the centrality of workplace issues to most members' trade unionism. Members appear to link campaigns with national political activity rather than their day-to-day circumstances at work, although such campaigns are often directed towards improving the situation in workplaces.

The importance attached to mutual support as the prime reason underpinning retention certainly duplicates results on recruitment and confirms the centrality of local union organisation in retention and recruitment. This result neither confirms nor denies support for the servicing or organising models. Advocates of both approaches claim that mutual support is provided, the difference is by whom; in the servicing model it is by full-time officers, in the organising model it is by lay representatives.

The importance of membership retention is further illustrated by the appearance of peer group at the second position in the ranking. This result indicates that the presence of large numbers of trade unionists encourages retention. In other words, once a union presence is established, there is a degree to which it is self-sustaining. This result also suggests that if membership falls beneath a specific threshold, the impact of peer group may decline, thereby leading to further membership decline. A belief in trade unions also has a major impact on retention, almost 37 per cent of members cite it as one of their two principal reasons for remaining in UNISON. This clearly indicates that there is a reservoir of existing members on which UNISON could usefully draw in moving towards a more extensive variant of the organising model.

Improved pay and conditions appears at four in the ranking, somewhat lower than in other studies drawing on aggregate data (Dibden and Millward, 1991). This finding is consistent with recent evidence on union joining in the public sector, however, which indicates that pay and conditions tend to be downplayed and greater importance attached to mutual support (Waddington and Whitston, 1997). Analysis of this result by reference to the different earnings levels of the respondents did not alter the position of pay and conditions in the rank order. In other words, there is no direct relationship between the importance attached to improvements in pay and conditions and the earnings levels of UNISON members.

Individual reasons underpinning membership retention occupy positions five and seven to nine in the ranking, thus confirming their secondary importance compared to collective reasons. Membership benefits are rated marginally more important than financial services among the individual benefits. We thus reject the proposition that the aspect of the servicing model underpinned by financial services is central to a membership strategy. Even when financial services are 'tailored' to the specific needs of the membership, they remain peripheral. Members were also asked to specify which elements of the package of financial services were most appropriate. Like other unions, UNISON anticipated that a credit card would 'bind' the member to the union, and thus regarded it as a central element of the package. However, the provision of a credit card was the least popular element of the package. No fewer than 36 per cent of members regarded it as being 'not at all important'.

Very few differences emerge between men and women in their reasons for retention. Men assign a greater importance to belief than women, whereas women are more influenced by their peer group. These differences in emphasis produce the only variation between men and women in the rank order of the responses. These results are not simply a function of sex, but are also associated with occupation (see Waddington and Kerr, 1999a). This association is likely to be a function of gender segregation within the labour market.

What do members think of local union organisation?

This stage of the data presentation evaluates members' views of local union organisation; that is, it considers members' views of UNISON where it is most important to them, in the locality. Three features of local union organisation are identified, contact, meetings and communication. Clearly, there are many other features that could have been identified for the survey. However, these were selected, as they are central to the organising model initially adopted by UNISON. Members were asked to specify whether the different aspects of local organisation were 'already well organised', 'need some improvement' or 'need much improvement' at their place of work. Table 17.2 presents the results for all members and disaggregated by sex.

Reference to the 'all' column indicates that there is a widespread dissatisfaction with local union organisation. Only about a quarter of members view the different features of local unionism to be well organised. A range of 31 to 45 per cent of the membership express their dissatisfaction, in suggesting that much improvement is required. Dissatisfaction is particularly marked regarding contact, with lay representatives and with full-time officers, and the timing of union meetings.

The dissatisfaction expressed by members regarding the extent of contact with local union representatives rests uneasily with our earlier finding that activity in the locality is central for most union members. It is perhaps not surprising that

Table 17.2 What aspects of local union organisation could be improved?

Feature of local union organisation	Already well organised (%)			Needs some improvement (%)			Needs much improvement (%)		
	All	Men	Women	All	Men	Women	All	Men	Women
Provision of information on union affairs	27.5	27.1	27.2	41.7	41.3	42.1	30.8	31.6	30.6
Provision of information on pay and conditions	25.7	25.8	25.8	43.2	43.1	42.9	31.1	31.1	31.3
More contact with lay representatives	22.1	30.1	19.2	39.1	38.0	39.5	38.7	32.0	41.3
More contact with full-time officers	18.6	23.3	16.7	36.9	34.6	38.0	44.5	42.1	45.3
Union meetings at more convenient times	20.4	25.9	18.1	38.7	37.6	39.3	40.9	36.5	42.6
Union meetings at more appropriate locations	28.5	34.0	26.3	35.2	34.0	35.8	36.3	32.1	37.9

dissatisfaction is most marked in the case of contact with full-time officers. UNISON, in common with other UK unions, tends to employ few full-time officers compared to its European counterparts, with the consequence that full-time officers are responsible for large numbers of workplaces, from many of which they may be absent for long periods. The decentralisation of bargaining has also increased the workload of many full-time officers and thus restricted their opportunities for site visits (see Colling, 1995). Furthermore, as a consequence of post-merger reorganisation UNISON implemented a voluntary severance scheme to which a number of full-time officers subscribed. The resultant decline in the overall number of full-time officers may have accentuated membership dissatisfaction on this contact issue.

Members also desire greater contact with lay representatives. Several factors influence the shortfall in contact perceived by members. First, UNISON has experienced difficulties in recruiting lay representatives with the result that some localities are understaffed. Second, it is becoming increasingly difficult for lay representatives to obtain sufficient time off to maintain adequate levels of contact. Third, the number of workplaces and employers coming within the scope of branches has increased, thereby making direct contact more difficult to sustain. Fourth, the impact of bargaining decentralisation has led to more demanding workloads for lay representatives. Attempts to promote the visibility of local representatives have clearly some way to go before members appreciate their presence. There is also anecdotal evidence to suggest that work intensification may influence the activities of lay representatives. Work colleagues may resent the departure of a lay representative to undertake union duties, because a consequence is that the work that otherwise would have been undertaken by the lay representative is left to his or her colleagues. For the colleagues of the lay representative, already intense workloads may thus become further intensified.

The extent of satisfaction among women on contact with lay representatives and full-time officers is markedly lower than that among men. This result suggests either that women members prefer more contact with union representatives than their male counterparts, or that women are more likely to be ignored by male union representatives, or that the difficulties of contacting women working in part-time jobs have yet to be overcome. Whatever is the case, and it is likely to be a combination of these factors, this result suggests that more women representatives are required in order to support the majority female membership of UNISON. In addition, it indicates differences between men and women extend beyond the substantive bargaining agenda to embrace procedural aspects of workplace activity. It supports the argument that women full-time officers may 'make a difference', and suggests that more women lay representatives may promote greater satisfaction with contact to UNISON among women members. The most recent data available, for example, suggest that in 1990 only 39 per cent of NUPE stewards were women, 42 per cent in NALGO and 52 per cent in COHSE (COHSE, NALGO & NUPE, 1990:19).

The location and, in particular, the timing of union meetings are also poorly received by members. Only one in five members thought the timing of union

244 *Redefining public sector unionism*

meetings to be well organised. Fewer women than men find the location and timing to be already well organised and more women require much improvement in existing arrangements, confirming earlier findings on the barriers to the participation of women in union activities (Rees, 1992; Cunnison and Stageman, 1995). Some of this variation is explained in terms of child caring responsibilities. For example, only 18.7 per cent of men and 19.4 per cent of women who share their households with pre-school or school-aged children consider existing arrangements on the timing of union meetings to be well organised. However, compared to only 28.0 per cent of men, 41.0 per cent of women with child-care responsibilities think that much improvement is required on the timing of union meetings. In other words, women with responsibilities for children were more dissatisfied than their male counterparts with the timing of union meetings. Responsibilities for children do not explain all the variation between men and women, because there is no difference in the desire for improvement between women with no child-care responsibilities and those with such responsibilities (41.6 per cent compared to 41.0 per cent). Generating greater participation of members in terms of higher attendance at union meetings thus remains problematic for all members, but will be particularly difficult among women.

Why do members leave UNISON?

Survey II required respondents to specify first, why they had left UNISON in general terms and second, to state the particular reason that influenced their decision to leave. Table 17.3 presents the results in terms of four broad categories: job changes, UNISON's structure and organisation, UNISON's policy, and another reason. The first three options were closed categories, whereas if the respondent entered 'another reason' s/he was asked to specify the nature of this reason. About two-thirds of the members that left UNISON had done so because of changes in their job circumstances. During 1996, 158,250 members left UNISON. In terms of the number of leavers, the survey result suggests that 106,977 members per year leave UNISON as a result of job changes. The effect of job changes on union leaving has a similar influence on men and women.

Almost 26 per cent of leavers cite either difficulties with UNISON's structure and organisation or disagreement with UNISON's policy as their primary reason for leaving. Expressed in terms of the annual number of leavers in 1996, this

Table 17.3 Why did you leave UNISON?

Reason for leaving	All (%)	Men (%)	Women (%)
My job situation changed	67.6	66.5	67.8
UNISON's structure and organisation	18.2	19.1	17.9
UNISON's policy	7.7	9.7	6.9
Another reason	6.5	4.8	7.4
	$N=2642$	$N=796$	$N=1786$

means that 40,987 members left the union for reasons that the union can directly influence. Around 18 per cent of members who leave do so because of problems with structure and organisation. Men emphasise this reason more than women. Under 8 per cent of leavers cite their disagreement with UNISON's policy as being the prime reason for their departure. Men are more dissatisfied with policy than women. The greater emphasis placed on structure and organisation compared to policy confirms van de Vall's findings that structural and functional motives are more important than policy motives in promoting members to leave the union.

'Another reason' is cited by 6.5 per cent of UNISON leavers. Respondents providing this reason were asked to specify why it was most important. While no systematic analysis of these responses is presented here, it is clear that the overwhelming majority refer to specific incidents at the workplace where the then member thought that the response of UNISON in the form of either a local lay representative or full-time officer was inadequate. In other words, most of these responses also referred to functional shortcomings. If we assume that 80 per cent of those citing 'other reasons' left UNISON because of functional short-comings, a further 5.2 per cent (8,229 members) of the number of leavers may be attributed directly to UNISON failings in organisation and structure.

Shortcomings in UNISON structure, organisation and policy

Changes in job situation are issues that do not arise from UNISON's post-merger development. They are thus examined separately in Appendix B. We now analyse the shortcomings in UNISON structure, organisation and policy that were cited as a reason for leaving the union. Almost 26 per cent of the total number of members that left UNISON during 1996 did so as a result of dissatisfaction with some aspect of the union's structure, organisation or policy. Among the 684 respondents citing such dissatisfaction, only 23.7 per cent had subsequently joined another union. In other words, dissatisfaction with UNISON had acted as a deterrent for union membership *per se* for over 75 per cent of this cohort. Table 17.4 shows the results for ex-members dissatisfied with UNISON. The functional motives identified by van de Vall (1970: 180–208) are represented by help to members with problems; negotiation of pay and conditions; little information; and the absence of contact. These functional motives are central to the organising model. The expense of membership is the only structural motive. Policy motives include an unwillingness to participate in industrial action; disagreement with post-merger policies and principles; and the inability to influence decision-making after the merger. Respondents were required to specify how important each of these features was in their decision to leave. In addition, Table 17.4 reports an importance ratio, calculated by subtracting the sum of those reporting 'not very important' and 'not at all important' from the sum of those indicating 'very important' and 'fairly important'. A positive score for the importance ratio thus indicates a tendency for an issue to be the subject of widespread dis-satisfaction, whereas a negative score suggests that an issue is not a source of dissatisfaction, although it may be influential among particular groups.

Table 17.4 What aspects of UNISON's structure, organisation and policy prompted you to leave?

Aspect of UNISON organisation	Very important (%)	Fairly important (%)	Not very important (%)	Not at all important (%)	Importance ratio all (%)	Importance ratio men (%)	Importance ratio women (%)
Not enough help to members with problems	52.9	16.1	12.0	19.0	+38.0	+28.3	+42.0
Did not negotiate my pay and conditions	30.2	14.9	14.9	40.0	−9.8	−20.6	−4.7
Received little information from UNISON	37.9	19.9	16.0	26.2	+15.6	−0.4	+23.2
Representatives hardly ever contacted me	51.3	19.1	11.6	18.1	+40.7	+21.6	+49.8
Membership is too expensive	25.0	21.3	22.8	30.9	−7.4	−5.3	−7.6
I did not wish to participate in industrial action	20.7	13.7	17.3	48.3	−31.2	−42.8	−25.3
I disagreed with UNISON's post-merger policies and principles	27.5	16.2	19.8	36.5	−12.6	−10.0	−13.6
After the merger I was unable to influence decision-making	28.7	17.1	14.8	39.4	−8.4	−10.3	−8.6

Note: these data are based only on the respondents who stated that their reason for leaving UNISON was either difficulties with UNISON's structure and organisation or because they disagreed with UNISON's policy.

Three of the four functional issues received a positive importance ratio score and on two of them more than 50 per cent of all leavers thought them 'very important' in the decision to leave. In other words, there is widespread dissatisfaction with the functional performance of UNISON. It is perhaps no surprise that dissatisfaction was more limited regarding the negotiation of pay and conditions, given that union recognition and collective bargaining remains fairly secure in the public sector. However, even in these circumstances, over 30 per cent cite UNISON's failure to negotiate pay and conditions as a 'very important' influence on the decision to leave. This may reflect the difficulties UNISON has encountered in reaching satisfactory settlements in recent years.

The very high importance ratio scores for 'representatives hardly ever contacted me' and 'not enough help to members with problems' is of the utmost concern, particularly as UNISON is attempting to implement an organising strategy based on high levels of membership participation and involvement of lay representatives at workplace level. The results from the leavers indicate that if adequate support and/or contact is not available, members will simply leave. This is not an argument against recruitment and retention strategies based on membership participation and the involvement of lay representatives, but is to highlight the range of issues that need to be addressed in order for such strategies to yield results. Put in positive policy terms, these results suggest that UNISON could usefully devote more resources to broadening its base of lay representatives, increasing their visibility in the workplace, extending facility time, and ensuring that lay representatives receive sufficient training to provide the support required by members.

While comparison with van de Vall's study is not exact in so far as we only include a single structural motive in the analysis, it is clear that functional issues are of greater concern to members than the expense of membership. This reverses the priorities between functional and structural motives expressed by Dutch trade union leavers to van de Vall. The absence of widespread dissatisfaction towards the expense of membership is important in two key regards for UNISON. First, setting the level of membership contributions for UNISON involved reconciliation of the pre-merger levels of contribution levied by each of the three constituent unions, and paid by members with very different earnings. The low level of dissatisfaction indicates that this process of reconciling the different levels of membership contributions has been relatively successful. Second, it suggests that it may be possible to raise the level of membership contributions, which, in turn, may allow more resources to be allocated to pursuing an organising strategy. The extent of competition for membership in the public sector, however, is likely to act as a limit on this option.

The results on policy issues confirm van de Vall's findings in so far as the importance ratios attached to them are low, indicating that they tend to be less important in union leaving than functional issues. These results also confirm the centrality of workplace activity to trade unions. Members are far less likely to leave UNISON because of the policies adopted, than they are because of the inability of the union to deliver support to members at their place of work. 'I do not wish to participate in industrial action' received the lowest importance ratio and the highest proportion of respondents indicated that it was 'not at all important' in their decision to leave. In other words, the question of industrial action is not a central issue of principled dispute for UNISON. Post-merger adjustment is also fairly unproblematic, as indicated by negative importance ratio scores, suggesting that the policies pursued after the merger were not a major influence on leaving UNISON.

Table 17.4 also presents the importance ratio scores for men and women leavers. The general pattern of the functional issues constituting a greater stimulus to leaving than either the structural issue or the policy issues is replicated when the results are disaggregated by sex. There are, however, some important variations between the sexes, which we now address.

On most of the structural and policy issues differences between men and women are small. Although a substantial variation of 17 percentage points is recorded on industrial action, the scores for men and women are very negative, suggesting that a reluctance to take industrial action is not a major issue for both sexes in union leaving. However, there are substantial differences between men and women regarding the impact of the functional motives on leaving UNISON. Women are more likely than men to regard each of the functional issues as having promoted their departure. In other words, dissatisfaction with workplace organisation increases the rate of membership loss more among women than among men. As over 70 per cent of UNISON members are women, this is a central issue to address if retention rates are to be improved.

Differences between men and women of 13.7 and 28.2 percentage points in the importance ratio scores are recorded on the help provided to members and on contact with representatives. A number of factors may contribute to this difference. Firstly, women express a greater desire for support from a union in joining and in retaining their union membership (see Table 17.1). In other words, women may receive the same support from the union and contact with the union at the workplace as men, but leave because they require more. Alternatively, women may receive less support and contact than their male counterparts. Fewer women serving as representatives and the location of large numbers of women members in small, disparate workplaces may account for this. A further contributory factor is likely to be the gendered nature of local union activities and the tendency to exclude women from many local activities. The low numbers of women local full-time officers is already acknowledged to influence the quality of support received by women members at the workplace. These propositions cannot be directly addressed by means of our survey results. However, our findings do suggest that the constitutional reforms introduced to ensure fair representation have yet to yield results in terms of the equality of satisfaction with workplace organisation between men and women.

There is a difference between men and women of about 24 percentage points in the importance ratio scores on the provision of information by UNISON. This is difficult to explain, as much written information, whether despatched centrally or locally, is sent direct to home addresses. Table 17.2 suggests that there are no substantial differences between men and women in the information sought from, and provided by, UNISON. It seems likely that this difference is associated with the provision of information in the workplace; that is, through face-to-face contact rather than written communication. In other words, the information shortfall perceived by women may be connected to the insufficient help and contact provided by the union in the workplace.

Drawing together the threads

These results show that recent developments of the servicing model based on the provision of financial services are peripheral to UNISON members. It is support at the workplace that is central to most members' trade unionism. This result is ambiguous in terms of the organising and servicing models. The provision of such support is an objective of both models, the difference between the two resting on who provides the support: full-time officers in the servicing model, lay representatives in the organising model. Proponents of the organising model would also argue that members' desire for more contact with full-time officers is evidence that there are insufficient full-time officers to support members at their workplaces and, therefore, more members should be engaged in such activities. Advocates of the servicing model, however, could claim that the same result suggests that a greater full-time officer presence in the workplace would be well received by members. Whether such a policy is financially practical remains very much open to question. Similarly, advocates of the servicing model could claim that the shortfalls in contact between lay representatives and members, and the large number of members that cite the absence of such contact as a reason for leaving, indicate that the organising model is inadequate as a means of providing support to members. By contrast, proponents of the organising model might claim that these shortfalls are evidence that more resources should be deployed to address them and, hence, limit the annual haemorrhaging of membership.

The extent of dissatisfaction with aspects of workplace organisation is widespread. The results suggest that UNISON could reduce membership losses by about 40,000 members per year by improving aspects of workplace organisation. In particular, ensuring that members are adequately supported, that there is more contact between members and union representatives, and that the information provision is improved, is likely to reduce membership losses. This view of workplace organisation was particularly strongly held by women members, who were more likely to leave the union in the absence of these features than were their male counterparts. In other words, if aspects of the organising model identified by UNISON could be improved the annual number of members that left UNISON would fall.

The absence of the articulation of workplace organisation with activities at other levels of union organisation was highlighted by members. In particular, members expressed a sense of isolation as evidenced by inadequate communications and contact with union representatives. The 'members' right' to satisfactory communications, as envisaged in the pre-merger documents, was clearly not being met. Similarly, the networks of lay representatives, foreseen as the basis on which UNISON's organising model would stand, was also not yet in place.

Some of the barriers faced by UNISON in attempting to promote greater membership participation as a means to reduce membership losses are also identified. The impact of the decollectivisation of employment relations in the public sector raises major policy questions for UNISON to address if it is to promote greater membership participation. Decentralisation, reductions in facility time, and difficulties in recruiting lay representatives militate against the development of an organising model. A large number of members express a desire to take part in union activities, however, suggesting that there is a potential to develop the organising model. The question thus arises; how did UNISON develop its membership strategy in the light of these results? The next section addresses this question.

From pre-merger intention to policy in practice

Development of the membership strategy revolved around interplay between activities surrounding the National Recruitment Plan (NRP) and the process of Strategic Review. Although the provision of packages of financial services was not abandoned, more attention was directed to those aspects of servicing that might stimulate greater levels of member involvement and would provide support to the member in his or her workplace. In other words, UNISON is shifting towards a more overt form of the organising approach.

Three factors underpinned this shift. First, post-merger membership fell between 1993 and 1997.[10] This decline, acting in conjunction with the specific subscription bands and rates adopted at vesting day, resulted in financial deficits in 1994, 1995 and 1996 (Certification Office, 1994, 1995, 1996). These were accompanied by a 25 per cent reduction in staff through voluntary severance in 1994 and a further 80 job losses in 1998–9. Total employment of UNISON declined from 1,800 to 1,200. Second, the survey results highlighted the importance attached by members to the different elements of the organising model and identified limitations in the initial post-merger approach towards recruitment and retention adopted by UNISON. Third, the on-going process of post-merger adjustment necessitated a range of further reforms. In particular, the merging of branches, completed during 1997, was accompanied by an extensive review of their objectives, resources and functioning within the new union, intended to move towards integrating them within the organising approach.

Central to the pattern of reform is the extension of articulating mechanisms in the area of the membership strategy. In particular, activities at the level of the Region and in Service Groups were incorporated within the membership strategy, thus widening the scope of member involvement and moving towards more articulated relations in the field of recruitment, retention and organising. The setting of recruitment targets, accompanied by a centralised system of monitoring, consolidated elements of this articulation. The Strategic Review Steering Committee (SRSC) identified parameters for good branch practice and set in train a process whereby the performance of branches is monitored. In other words, associated with the NRP and the SRSC were similar practices, in so far as objectives set at the centre will be implemented in the localities and progress monitored at the centre. These issues are examined below by reference to the NRP and the process of the Strategic Review.

Establishing and operating the National Recruitment Plan

Throughout 1994 and 1995 analyses were conducted of the circumstances within which UNISON was operating. In particular, labour market projections, the practices of competitor unions and the political environment were examined to identify the UNISON's strengths and weaknesses (UNISON, 1995). The output of this examination was the subject of wide-ranging consultation throughout the union, which involved active lay representatives, Service Groups and the Regions. Although several of the initial proposals advanced in this consultation process were abandoned, the NRP was retained and formally launched in 1995. It comprised two key elements: the setting of membership targets and the implementation of an increasing range of mechanisms intended to facilitate the achievement of the targets (UNISON, 1995).

The initial presentation of the NRP set annual membership targets for the entire union and regionally disaggregated targets for the period until 2000 (UNISON, undated). These targets are monitored from Head Office via reports submitted by the Regional Secretaries to whom formal responsibility for attaining the targets was allocated. In practice, within each Region the Service Group structure is used to agree recruitment targets within the localities. The setting of national targets was thus transformed into branch level recruitment targets via the Service Groups. As we argue below, devolution of these targets confirmed the weaknesses in local organisation identified by the surveys. These are being addressed through the Strategic Review process.

Resources were re-deployed to facilitate the meeting of the national targets. For example, a full-time officer within each of UNISON's thirteen regions was appointed Regional Recruitment Co-ordinator and relieved of some duties of representation in order to fulfil this function. The brief of the Regional Recruitment Co-ordinators is the co-ordination of the recruitment and retention activities of lay representatives and full-time officers in the localities.

Two other shifts in responsibility were also introduced. The first of these concerns the role of the local full-time officer, many of whom were moved from servicing to organising activities. Local full-time officers were withdrawn from handling the initial stages of individual representation in the expectation that lay representatives will undertake these duties. Only if cases reach higher stages in the procedure are local full-time officers expected either to 'take' the case or to support the lay representative in its pursuit. Local full-time officers are expected instead to be engaged more heavily in the co-ordination of recruitment activities; the support of new members, where lay organisation is not yet established; and in encouraging members to become more active.

A consequence of the shift of full-time officers from servicing to organising is that a wider range of responsibility falls within the ambit of lay representatives. The survey data, however, made clear that lay representatives are already unable to maintain sufficient contact with members. In order to accommodate these additional responsibilities and address the existing shortfall in contact, an activist recruitment campaign was initiated with the slogan 'beeactive!'. The objective of the beeactive! campaign is to create more active members. An establishment is planned of one steward for every twenty-five members and one steward in every workplace. A central issue underlining the approach adopted for the beeactive! campaign is that members can undertake aspects of the lay representatives' function without taking on the complete range of duties. For example, members can become active in UNISON by: offering to help out in your branch office; volunteering to become a local mailing contact; offering to keep a notice board in your workplace up to date; becoming a local recruiter; becoming a health and safety representative; letting your branch know what you are interested in; and by becoming a steward or representative (*UNISON Magazine*, 1999). The extent of the commitment to the union can thus be defined by the member, rather than it being open-ended, as is often the case when becoming a lay representative.

It is acknowledged that any results from the beeactive! campaign are likely to be medium-term, yet there are current shortfalls in membership support that must be addressed. The concurrent development of UNISON*direct*, a freephone and e-mail help-line for members and stewards, with the beeactive! initiative is intended to address this shortfall. Members who require support arising from a problem at work, but do not have access to a lay representative at their workplace, can thus obtain advice via the help-line. After trials in East London, UNISON*direct* went national in January 2000. In other words, until the results of the beeactive! initiative become widespread, the union relies on a servicing approach to meet the requirements of members.

Additional resources were also deployed to meet the recruitment targets in the form of trainees from the Organising Academy, established by the TUC. UNISON has consistently supported the Organising Academy and sponsored two trainees in 1998; four in 1999, although two of these dropped out; and intends to sponsor six trainees in 2000. In addition, a UNISON proposal led to the extension of the training period available to trainees from one to two years. While the medium-term objective is to deploy trainees to duties concerned with the extension of recruitment, particularly among manual workers employed by sub-contractors, the current emphasis is on deepening recruitment at sites where there is already a union presence, that is, to support lay representatives in organising activities. A further indication of a longer-term commitment to this approach is an ongoing discussion concerning the creation of an Organising Officer grade as a first point of entry to the cadre of full-time officers. Only after several years as an Organising Officer, during which the individual in post would acquire organising skills, could an application be submitted to become a Regional Officer.[11] If this new grade is established, the entire future complement of UNISON full-time officers will have been engaged in organising activities for some part of their careers, hence, it is anticipated, encouraging a change towards an organising culture.

Servicing support for the goals of the NRP has also been extended to address the shortfalls identified from the surveys. For example, all organising staff will have completed the 'Winning the Organised Workplace' (WOW) course by the end of 2000. In addition, six WOW courses per Region will be run during 2000 for lay representatives. The WOW course was developed by the TUC as part of its New Unionism initiative, with the aim of establishing the basis for an organising culture.

In developing the NRP, UNISON shifted resources from servicing to organising. Where servicing provision was maintained it was directed towards sustaining the organising approach. Key to this process was the setting of recruitment targets and their monitoring from Head Office. This approach was also to inform the practices of the Strategic Review to which we now turn.

The process of Strategic Review

Activities concerning the NRP are supplemented by the process of the Strategic Review. The Strategic Review Steering Committee (SRSC) was established as a result of Motion 187 (as amended) passed at the National Delegate Conference 1995. From the outset it should be noted that the SRSC comprises a majority of senior lay representatives (initially eighteen lay representatives and six officers). Ownership of the Strategic Review process is thus seen to be in the hands of lay representatives. While the brief of the Strategic Review is broader than the concerns of this chapter, several of the initiatives taken within this process impinge upon the development of the membership strategy. Two features associated with the Strategic Review are key to our purposes; the definition of the problem that underpins its objectives, and the approach adopted to meet the terms of its brief.

Citing the survey evidence as its point of departure, the first report of the SRSC set out to bring support services closer to members (UNISON, 1996: 4–6). The stated objective of the Strategic Review was to decentralise the support provision, while also addressing the isolation or lack of articulation felt by many members. In particular, bargaining decentralisation, the withdrawal of some employers from national bargaining arrangements and restrictions on facility time were regarded as the primary external sources of the failure to articulate union activities. The SRSC proposed that expenditure on branches should rise from 23 per cent of total UNISON expenditure to 27 per cent between 1996 and 2002. During the same period expenditure on central administration and support was projected to fall from 14 per cent to 9 per cent of total expenditure (UNISON, 1997: 11). In addition, more sophisticated information technology is to be made available to branches, and communication systems developed to facilitate internal branch communication between lay representatives and members and communication between the branch and the wider union. It is also intended that articulation between the different levels of union activity be improved by developments in the self-organisation mechanisms.[12] To address the poor membership attendance at union meetings identified by the surveys, the merging of branches was accompanied by changes in the timing and location of many union meetings to accommodate the requirements of the combined memberships.

Key to current proposals from the SRSC are Branch Development Plans which are 'a way of identifying the challenges each branch faces and making sure that they have the resources to meet these challenges' (UNISON, 1997: 7). Fourteen 'core branch responsibilities' were identified and branches were required to undertake or specify a review of current practice; targets and dates set; training needs; other activities planned; and the regional support agreed, on each of these core branch responsibilities. Several of the core branch responsibilities were taken directly from the survey evidence and all are related to the issues identified therein. In practice, the identification of these responsibilities set the parameters within which branches were expected to function, central to which were the terms of the organising model.[13] Within each Region a Regional Branch Development Team was available to assist branches in drawing up their specific Branch Development Plan. A Code of Good Branch Conduct specified expectations regarding the procedures of branch operations. Moreover, a complete training package was developed around the parameters of the Branch Development Plans to apprise lay representatives of the issues involved and to consolidate agreed procedures within which they might be addressed. Additional resources were thus allocated to branches by means of the Strategic Review, but the objectives to which they could be deployed and the procedures that accompanied this deployment were specified by the SRSC.

A twin track process of monitoring was also implemented to oversee the implementation of the Branch Development Plans. The first strand relies on monitoring via the Regions and the Service Groups, and is based on 'model planning forms' prepared under the auspices of the SRSC. This strand requires lay representatives and full-time officers to operate a monitoring process of their own activities within a prepared framework. Reports from this element of the monitoring process are submitted to the SRSC. The second strand of the monitoring process directly engages members. Panel surveys, distributed annually to members over a 5-year period, are intended to ascertain how members perceive the core branch responsibilities and movements in their delivery within the localities. The panel survey thus allows members to voice their opinions on the effects of deploying additional resources. Results of the panel survey are also reported to the SRSC, thus enabling an assessment of member attitudes to the outcome of the Strategic Review process.[14] The decentralisation of resources to branches implemented by the SRSC is thus qualified in terms of the parameters of local activity, specified procedures of good branch practice and the monitoring of the results of deploying additional resources. These qualifications constitute mechanisms intended to encourage the articulation of activities within UNISON as a membership strategy evolves. Integral to the membership strategy are both recruitment targets and the processes whereby they might be achieved.

Conclusion

This chapter has traced the development of UNISON's membership strategy since the founding merger. From an initial position that saw the parallel pursuit of both the servicing and organising models, UNISON's policy was adjusted to emphasise the organising approach in the light of survey evidence. Resources were shifted to the localities, full-time officers' roles were amended and a wider range of responsibilities passed to the branches. These elements of the organising model were bolstered by measures adopted from the servicing approach, which were specifically designed to complement them. The provision of dedicated training programmes on Winning the Organised Workplace and branch development plans are cases in point.

The adoption of an organising approach has accompanied new forms of relationship between the centre and the localities. Key to this relationship is the central definition of recruitment targets, priorities for branch organisation and the implementation of monitoring procedures. Branches and workplace organisation are afforded operational latitude, but the purposes to which activities are directed are set nationally. The development of the membership strategy has thus fostered a new mechanism whereby trade union activities may be articulated. Of course, it should be noted that other articulating mechanisms have been adopted to facilitate local bargaining and the operation of Service Groups and self-organising groups. To highlight those mechanisms which apply to the membership strategy is not to argue that they are universally applied in UNISON, but is to suggest that they are a particular form of articulation adopted by the union for specific purposes.

This reference is also not to suggest that the approach is unproblematic. There is, for example, no consistent evidence that members are coming forward in sufficient numbers to make up the shortfall in lay representatives. There is also little reference made at present to the measures that might be applied should centrally determined targets not be met in the localities. Attempts by the National Executive Committee to amend the disciplinary rules of the union at the National Delegate Conferences in 1998 and 1999 were rejected. There have also been problems with the monitoring of recruitment targets. Inadequacies in the Union Membership System (UMS) precluded accuracy in calculating shifts in membership at the level of the Region. Only after 1998, when new software was specifically developed, are accurate data available on union joining. Vested interests are also well entrenched. Shortages of facility time are exacerbated, for example, when it is allocated according to seniority, as senior lay representatives tend to be the older, male representatives and not those most likely to recruit the large numbers of unorganised women and young workers in UNISON areas. It also remains an open question whether the existing deployment of additional resources to the localities will be sufficient to promote the organising model. The SRSC, for example, estimates that only 5p in the pound of total resources is spent on organising non-members in existing and new workplaces, 'while the lion's share is spent on servicing a slowly shrinking pool of members' (UNISON, 1999: 23).

This chapter commenced by acknowledging that the distinction between the servicing and organising models was analytical rather than practical. This chapter qualifies the distinction still further. For example, 'support if I have a problem at work' is the prime reason that underpins the unionism of most members. There is no evidence emerging from the surveys to suggest that members have a preference for support from full-time officers, as is the objective of the servicing model, or from lay representatives, as intended by the organising model. The issue for members is the provision of the support, not the status of the provider. Similarly, members want improvements in contact with both full-time officers and with lay representatives, rather than with one or other.

The position of women members is a theme resonant throughout the chapter. There are few differences between men and women in the reasons for membership retention. However, women are more likely to want improvements in contact with full-time officers and lay representatives and in the location and timing of union meetings. Furthermore, greater dissatisfaction with these issues among women accounts for many of them leaving the union. This again suggests that it is not the status of the provider of support that is at issue, but that the sex of the provider may be important. The features of the union's constitution that are specifically intended to address the concerns of women – self-organisation and fair representation – thus appear insufficient to remedy the shortfalls in workplace organisation identified by women.

The development of a membership strategy within UNISON has required a continual process of reform since the founding merger. A wide range of innovations have been introduced, not the least of which is the use of a series of surveys to monitor the impact of reform. In so far as the founding merger set in train the unification of the disparate structures and cultures of the constituent unions, the extent of movement towards a unified membership strategy has been widespread. Recent data suggest that there are month-on-month improvements in the number of new recruits in 1999 compared to 1998. Whether these improvements can be sustained and built upon is the key issue for the future.

Appendix A

Survey I comprised a sample of 5,000 drawn from UNISON's computerised Union Membership System (UMS). This represented a 1:240 distribution of the entire union's membership. Characteristics such as sex, hours worked, occupation and industry were not controlled in the sample. The questionnaires were distributed centrally by the union and were returned in pre-paid envelopes to the researchers. In total, 1,026 questionnaires were returned, constituting a return rate of 20.6 per cent. The sex breakdown of respondents almost exactly corresponded to the union's membership in that 73.3 per cent of respondents were women compared to 71.9 per cent of members, and 26.7 per cent were men compared to 28.1 per cent of members.

Survey II comprised a distribution of 10,000 questionnaires, despatched centrally by UNISON and returned in pre-paid envelopes to the researchers. At the time of the distribution this represented 6.3 per cent of the number of members that left UNISON during 1996 (158,250 members or 12.5 per cent of total membership). The sample comprised the last 10,000 names withdrawn from the UMS on the grounds of leaving the union. As no previous analysis of union leaving based on the UMS has been undertaken, it is not possible to state whether the sample is statistically representative of union leavers across a wider period than that from which the sample was collected. No attempt was thus made to select the sample on any basis other than that the person had terminated membership of UNISON. For the purposes of estimating the number of members that leave for different reasons, we assume that our sample is representative of all leavers. A total of 2,651 responses were received from union leavers, representing a return rate of 26.5 per cent. Of these returns, 69.2 per cent were from women and 30.8 per cent from men, which compare with the distribution by sex among the entire membership.

Appendix B: changes in job situation

Table 17.B presents the results from respondents who stated that a change in their job situation was the prime reason for leaving UNISON, disaggregated by the different ways in which job circumstances change. This Appendix thus focuses upon the 67.6 per cent of respondents that cite job situation as their prime reason for leaving. The questionnaire required each respondent to specify which change in job situation was most important in their decision to leave UNISON from a pre-prepared list. From the outset it is clear that the distinction drawn by Gallie (1996) between the employed and unemployed is important in any analysis of union leaving. Those remaining in employment, however, outnumber the unemployed among the leavers. Among those who left because of a change in job situation 30.3 per cent were employed – but had left due to de-recognition, promotion, change of job and UNISON not recognised, and now working for a private contractor – whereas 20.8 per cent were unemployed, having been made redundant. Eclipsing both the employed and the unemployed, however, were the retirees. This was the largest category among those whose job circumstances had changed. Almost half the members leaving because of a change in their job

Table 17.B What changes in job situation led to leaving UNISON?

Change to job	All (%)	Men (%)	Women (%)
Retired	48.9	47.2	48.7
Made redundant	20.8	24.7	19.2
De-recognition	1.6	1.9	1.5
Promotion	3.8	3.1	4.3
Changed job and UNISON not recognised	15.6	14.8	16.4
Private contractor	9.3	8.3	9.9
	$N = 1755$	$N = 517$	$N = 1201$

situation did so as a result of retirement. There is no appreciable difference between men and women concerning the impact of retirement.

UNISON can do very little to influence this component of membership turnover. Although the union organises retired members, they remain a small proportion of the total membership and comprise primarily ex-NALGO members committed to the traditions of some of the local government professions, rather than solely trade unionism. The rising average age of UNISON members and the large number of people entering retirement, however, indicates that the recruitment and retention of younger workers will have to be intensified if the targets of the National Recruitment Plan are to be met. Members of the National Retired Members' Forum are encouraged to participate in these recruitment and retention activities. However, as 'like best recruits like', it is unlikely that retired members will have a marked impact on the recruitment of young workers and, hence, meeting the targets of the National Recruitment Plan (Heery and Kelly, 1988).

A further 20.8 per cent of those who left UNISON as a result of a change in job situation did so because they were made redundant. This result confirms earlier research showing that unions in the UK are unable to retain the unemployed because union services and activity are directed almost exclusively towards the employed (Barker *et al.*, 1984; Lewis, 1989). Redundancy appears to be a more important influence on men leaving UNISON than it is for women. The key variable on this issue, however, is industry. Particular industries where the male membership is concentrated, such as the utilities, were prone to high levels of redundancy as a result of post-privatisation restructuring (Waddington and Kerr, 1999b).

De-recognition explains only 1.6 per cent of membership losses due to changes in job situation. Given that the overwhelming majority of UNISON members work in the public sector, where de-recognition is relatively rare, this marginal impact is anticipated.

Fewer than 4 per cent of members left because 'UNISON membership is a hindrance now that I have been promoted'. Women were more likely to cite this reason than men. Among the members that left UNISON following a promotion, only 28.8 per cent ($N = 71$) had joined another union. In other words, promotion in such circumstances appears as a barrier to union membership *per se* rather than just UNISON membership. However, the inability of UNISON to retain these members does raise policy issues concerning the vertical Service Group structure adopted by UNISON. In particular, this raises the question of whether there are interests, expressed particularly by members in white-collar staff occupations, which are not adequately accommodated within a vertical structure, which might be better expressed through an occupational or horizontal structure? While this question requires more detailed analysis than is possible here, it is noteworthy that white-collar staff are the least likely to regard many aspects of workplace union activity as being 'already well organised', suggesting widespread dissatisfaction among such occupations (Waddington and Kerr, 1999a: Table 17.4).

Almost 16 per cent of members whose job situation changed had left UNISON because it was not recognised by their new employer, thus indicating the importance of union recognition to membership retention. This corresponds to 16,458 (10.4 per cent) of UNISON's current annual membership losses. This result indicates the difficulties of developing a retention strategy when the coverage of collective bargaining and union recognition is low. Heightened competition between unions for members may exacerbate these difficulties as sixty-seven (23.6 per cent) of these people had joined another union. The aspect of the servicing model reliant on packages of financial services and discounts, is clearly proving insufficient to stop this outward flow of members. The range of financial services, introduced by UNISON as being 'tailored' for its members, simply do not prevent workers who move to jobs where the unions is not recognised from abandoning their UNISON membership. Spreading union membership by such means thus appears a forlorn hope.

Employment with a private contractor accounts for 9.3 per cent of those that leave UNISON because of a change in job situation. The influence of this factor is marked in health and, in particular, in local government, reflecting the continuing impact of CCT and the externalisation or outsourcing of functions. Only 7.6 per cent ($N = 172$) of those leaving UNISON because they work for a private contractor now belong to a trade union. In other words, UNISON, together with other unions organising in these areas, has yet to secure widespread recognition among the contracting companies.

Notes

1 For the purposes of this chapter, articulation refers to the institutions and activities that enable effective linkages to be maintained between the different levels of union structure. It is concerned with vertical integration. Articulated union structures and activities are thus differentiated from bureaucratic national control, in which the centre retains power over members, and from independent local unionism, characterised as displaying an exclusive or 'factory consciousness' (Beynon, 1973). Indeed, articulated union structures may combine both strong centre and local union activities. Analytically and practically the issue is to integrate activities at the centre and the localities with each other.

2 The term 'lay representative' is used throughout this chapter to refer to both shop stewards and branch officers (irrespective of the actual position held within the branch). The data on which the chapter is based draw on surveys of members. Many members do not make a distinction between shop stewards and branch officers. Use of the single term thus avoids error in recording the responses of members. This issue is compounded as many representatives hold both shop steward and branch officer positions, thus obscuring any distinction.

3 These density data refer to employment density; that is, union membership expressed as a proportion of employment.

4 See the chapters by Dempsey, Fryer and Wheeler in this volume for discussions of the different 'cultures' of the constituent unions.

5 The language of organising and servicing was not used at the time of the events discussed here. It is only since the establishment of the TUC's Organising Academy that the distinction between the two approaches has been formulated in the context of union activity in the UK.

6 The choice of women does not imply that they are more important than any other group identified by UNISON. The choice was, in part, determined by the size of the sample, which allows meaningful comparisons to be made on the basis of sex. In addition, to include data on other groups would lengthen this chapter beyond the boundaries of editorial acceptance.

7 These 'rule book' benefits included death benefit, fatal accident benefit, incapacity benefit and accident benefit. In addition, within the same category of benefits, a welfare provision was available in the forms of convalescent homes, debt counselling, provision of wheelchairs for members with mobility difficulties and payment to visit sick relatives. Members could also claim education and training grants. Free indemnity insurance of up to 1 million pounds was provided to a wide range of health professionals. These individual member services are traditional benefits, offered by a large number of unions in combinations and packages considered appropriate for each specific membership. In UNISON, for example, indemnity insurance was considered to be of particular benefit to ex-COHSE and some ex-NUPE members, whereas ex-NALGO members were more likely to take advantage of the education and training grants, a factor which largely accounted for the differences in the patterns of pre-merger expenditure on benefits.

8 UNISON pamphlets directly appealed to the consumer in claiming that that package of financial services negotiated by the union could save 'hundreds of pounds every year'. Motor insurance, personal loans and independent financial advice were offered to members in a package negotiated with Frizzell Life and Financial Planning Limited. A further deal with UIA (Insurance) Limited offered insurance on holidays, buildings, house contents and caravans, while a discounted mortgage was available to UNISON members through the Brittania Building Society. UNISON members were also invited to 'travel the world' by UNISON Travel, the union's 'very own travel agency'. Credit card facilities were set in place through arrangements negotiated with the Bank of Scotland. An agreement with Brittania Rescue also made available discounted car breakdown cover to UNISON members. An extensive package of financial services was thus established by UNISON as a development of the servicing approach.

9 Members were asked how far the statement 'my job is secure' applies to their current job. Only 6.6 per cent reported that they 'strongly agreed' with the statement, 31.1 per cent 'agreed', 44.1 per cent 'disagreed', and 18.1 per cent 'strongly disagreed'.

10 The Certification Officer reports a decline from 1,486,984 to 1,300,451 between 1993 and 1997. However, the figure for 1993 is questionable, as during the period immediately following the merger it was necessary to combine the membership records of three large unions. The extent of this task resulted in some unreliable statistics. The Certification Officer's data are thus likely to overstate the extent of the immediate post-merger decline.

11 The Regional Officer post is currently the basic grade for full-time officers in UNISON. The establishment of the grade of Organising Officer would thus extend the hierarchy of grades among full-time officers.

12 See the chapter by McBride in this volume on the particularities of the development of self-organisation among women members.

13 The fourteen core branch responsibilities are as follows: recruitment, retention and organisation of activists; representation of individual members over grievances, discipline and other matters; local negotiations on conditions, pay, contracting out of services and employment changes; ensuring health and safety of members; promotion of UNISON's aims and values; local campaigning and political activity; development of self organisation for specified groups of members; education and training of activists; fair representation and proportionality for all members; regular communication with members; enabling participation of members in all of the democratic processes of UNISON; administrative functions – membership records, accounts;

information flows to and from regional and national level; welfare responsibilities (UNISON, 1997: 29).

14 At the time of writing (October 1999) two panel surveys from the planned set of five have been conducted.

References

Barker, A., Lewis, P. and McCann, M. (1984) 'Trades unions and the organisation of the unemployed', *British Journal of Industrial Relations*, 22(3), 391–404.

Bassett, P. and Cave, A. (1993) *All for One: The Future of the Unions*, Fabian Society Pamphlet, No. 559, London: Fabian Society.

Beynon, H. (1973) *Working for Ford*, London: Penguin.

Bird, D., Beatson, M. and Butcher, S. (1993) 'Membership of trade unions', *Employment Gazette* (May), 189–96.

Bland, P. (1999) 'Trade union membership and recognition 1997–98: an analysis of data from the Certification Officer and the Labour Force Survey', *Labour Market Trends*, (July), 343–53.

Bronfenbrenner, K., Friedman, F., Hurd, R., Oswald, R. and Seeber, R. (eds) (1999) *Organizing to Win: New Research on Union Strategies*, London: ILR Press.

Cave, A. (1994) *Managing Change in the Workplace*, London: Kogan Page.

Certification Office (1981) *Annual Report of the Certification Officer*, London: Certification Office.

Certification Office (1994) *Annual Report of the Certification Officer*, London: Certification Office.

Certification Office (1995) *Annual Report of the Certification Officer*, London: Certification Office.

Certification Office (1996) *Annual Report of the Certification Officer*, London: Certification Office.

COHSE, NALGO & NUPE (1990) *New Union: Report of the COHSE, NALGO and NUPE National Executives to the 1990 Annual Conferences*, London: COHSE, NALGO and NUPE.

COHSE, NALGO & NUPE (1991) *A Framework for a New Union: Report of the COHSE, NALGO and NUPE National Executives to the 1991 Annual Conferences*, London: COHSE, NALGO and NUPE.

COHSE, NALGO & NUPE (1992) *New Union: the Final Report to the COHSE, NALGO and NUPE National Executives to the 1992 Annual Conferences*, London: COHSE, NALGO and NUPE.

Colling, T. (1995) 'Renewal or Rigor Mortis? Union Responses to Contracting Out in Local Government', *Industrial Relations Journal*, 26(2), 134–45.

Conrow, T. (1991) 'Contract servicing from an organizing model', *Labor Research Review*, 17: 45–59.

Cunnison, S. and Stageman, J. (1995) *Feminizing the Unions*, Aldershot: Avebury.

Dibden, J. and Millward, N. (1991) 'Trade union membership: development and prospects', *Policy Studies*, 12(4): 4–19.

Fletcher, B. and Hurd, R. (1998) 'Beyond the organizing model: the transformation process in local unions', in Bronfenbrenner, K., Friedman, S., Hurd, R., Oswald, R. and Seeber, R. (eds) *Organizing to Win: New Research on Union Strategies*, Ithaca: ILR Press.

Gahan, P. (1997) 'Strategic unionism in crisis? The ACTU Congress', *Journal of Industrial Relations*, 39(4): 533–56.

Gallie, D. (1996) 'Trade union allegiance and decline in British urban labour markets' in Gallie, D., Penn, R. and Rose, M. (eds) *Trade Unionism in Recession*, Oxford: Oxford University Press.

Heery, E. and Kelly, J. (1988) 'Do female representatives make a difference? Women full-time officials and trade union work', *Work, Employment and Society*, 2(4): 487–505.

Hurd, R. (1998) 'Contesting the dinosaur image: the labor movement's search for a future', *Labor Studies Journal*, 22: 4.

IRS (1993) 'The changing role of trade union officers 2: collective bargaining and working practices', *Employment Trends*, 527 (January): 3–11.

Kelly, J. and Heery, E. (1994) *Working for the Union*, Cambridge: Cambridge University Press.

Kelly, J. and Waddington, J. (1995) 'New prospects for British labour', *Organization*, 2(3–4): 415–26.

Kerr, A. (1992) 'Why public sector workers join unions? An attitude survey of workers in the health service and local government', *Employee Relations*, 14(2): 39–54.

Lewis, P. (1989) 'The unemployed and trade union membership', *Industrial Relations Journal*, 20(4): 271–9.

Rees, T. (1992) *Women and the Labour Market*, London: Routledge.

Sapper, A. (1991) 'Do members' services packages influence trade union recruitment?', *Industrial Relations Journal*, 22(2): 309–16.

TUC (1988) *Services for Union Members: Special Review Body Report on Services*, London: Trades Union Congress.

UNISON (undated) *Organising in UNISON, The UNISON National Recruitment Plan, 1995/96*, London: UNISON.

UNISON (1995) *The Recruitment Challenge: A UNISON Consultation Paper on Recruitment and Retention*, London: UNISON.

UNISON (1996) *Strategic Review: An Agenda for the Future*, London: UNISON.

UNISON (1997) *Strategic Review: Making Local Organisation our Priority*, London: UNISON.

UNISON (1999) *UNISON Annual Report, 1998/99*, London: UNISON.

UNISON Magazine (1999) 'Whatever your job and whoever you are, UNISON needs you to bee active' (September/October): 16–17.

van de Vall, M. (1970) *Labor Organizations*, Cambridge: Cambridge University Press.

Waddington, J. (1992) 'Trade union membership in Britain, 1980–1987: unemployment and restructuring', *British Journal of Industrial Relations*, 30(2): 287–324.

Waddington, J. and Kerr, A. (1999a) 'Membership retention in the public sector', *Industrial Relations Journal*, 29(2): 151–65.

Waddington, J. and Kerr, A. (1999b) 'Trying to stem the flow: union membership turnover in the public sector', *Industrial Relations Journal*, 29(3): 184–96.

Waddington, J. and Whitston, C. (1997) 'Why do people join unions in a period of membership decline?' *British Journal of Industrial Relations*, 35(4): 515–46.

18 Reflections on UNISON after 5 years

John Monks

I welcome this opportunity to contribute to this important debate on what is the most significant union merger in Britain probably since the creation of the Transport and General Workers' Union in the 1920s. The writing of this book, and the organisation of the conference on which it is based, both organised with the full involvement of UNISON's senior officers, all say much about the union's 'character'. In my opinion one of the most attractive features of UNISON has been its openness and willingness to subject itself to external as well as internal scrutiny; long may that continue.

As Bob Fryer's contribution makes clear, perhaps the first significant point about the creation of UNISON is the surprise that the merger took place at all. The fact that UNISON was created and was created with so little conflict or dissension is a tribute to those involved, including the academic advisers. Its creation provides lessons on the process of merger for all trade unions, and I am sure that others considering merger would be well advised to study the experience. Although many of the points of detail are UNISON-specific, the overriding lesson is that commitment and preparation, openness and determination are the key ingredients to a successful merger.

Normally my perspective reflects my position within the TUC, but here I would like to take a different starting-point and examine the momentum that led towards the creation of UNISON from the perspective of the potential members of this new union. What were their expectations and hopes?

First, it is clear that they wanted one public sector union to be created, catering for the needs of all who work in the public sector. Second, they wanted better services from their union, and third, and no less important they were concerned about union democracy and the governance of the union.

Since 1993 there have been considerable achievements in all these areas. The first two are perhaps easier to deal with. There have been tremendous strides made in achieving a UNISON culture that embraces the public service values and aspirations of all its members. At the same time UNISON provides high quality services, developing the earlier work done by the partner unions and especially NALGO over a long period of time. I have been particularly impressed by the 'Return to Learn' project (see Munro and Rainbird in this volume) and have looked with great interest at the emergence and operation of UNISON*direct*.

But my principal concern is with the third set of issues which perhaps reflect some of what Bob Fryer has called the 'unfinished business' and the way in which UNISON deals with the novel and important democratic challenges it faces. Indeed I would add to his list of such 'business' the following considerations. First, it should be stressed that the principle and practice of self-organisation and the ways in which UNISON utilises its position to press the case for disadvantaged groups have implications for the ways in which the TUC and other unions deal with these issues, which are assuming greater importance throughout the trade union movement. We are now all more relaxed about self-organisation, but we need to retain an awareness that a major union cannot be effective if it is perceived as a federation speaking with a number of different voices. It needs to retain a central identity.

The very size of UNISON – today one trade unionist in every five is a UNISON member – gives force to these points which would not apply equally to smaller unions. They can afford their idiosyncrasies. For example, it is common knowledge that there have been occasions in fairly recent history when NALGO and COHSE have stood out against the policy adopted by the Trades Union Congress on important issues that have an impact on trade unionism and on the interface between trade unionism and politics. Before the creation of UNISON this opposition was less dramatic and did not matter over much since it was clear that their positions would be minority ones. But now, if a position backed by UNISON goes down at Congress it marks one of those splits which have been so beloved of headline writers over the years. If it carries the day it becomes Congress policy. To put the matter simply and succinctly, *the luxury of opposition, of losing, is not one which is open to a union the size of UNISON.*

The fundamental issue which this raises and which has faced and continues to face UNISON is to reconcile these external responsibilities to the trade union movement as a whole with the concept of the *member-led* union and the inevitable internal focus which that creates. The only reconciliation can come through a mature leadership that recognises, and diffuses that recognition throughout UNISON, that being the biggest union in Congress inevitably imposes a leadership role which may on occasion constrain choice and policy.

This relates clearly to a further important aspect of the governance of the union. It is noticeable that UNISON's conference agenda consistently reflect the fact that there are sectarian groups who are making serious efforts to win the conference over to their point of view – a point of view which is well away from the political mainstream. The largest union in Congress needs a mature leadership. But of course leadership alone is not enough to create the strength of purpose that can unite all sections of such a vast union. Alongside mature leadership there is also a need for the union to be associated with and to pursue a particular 'cause' that touches all its members. The partner unions each had a cause with which it was clearly identified. NUPE in particular was associated with the cause of the low paid and the need for a National Minimum Wage. UNISON would be strengthened democratically and organisationally were it to find its own cause – a cause that could be achieved and one that would demonstrate the strength of the union.

Finally the union, like all other unions, needs to address the organising challenge. There is plenty of scope for recruiting, most notably in the local authorities especially in the south-east. Growth and increased membership density are necessary not just for their own sake, but as protection against any future employer offensive.

UNISON has come a long way in a short period of time. It is good to be reminded that its creation came about in the face of formidable obstacles. But there is still much to be done if it is to make the sort of impression which it is capable of doing.

Index